Entertainment Public Relations

This book is part of the Peter Lang Media and Communication list.
Every volume is peer reviewed and meets
the highest quality standards for content and production.

PETER LANG
New York • Bern • Frankfurt • Berlin
Brussels • Vienna • Oxford • Warsaw

Carol Ames

Entertainment Public Relations

Communicating with Audiences

PETER LANG
New York • Bern • Frankfurt • Berlin
Brussels • Vienna • Oxford • Warsaw

Library of Congress Cataloging-in-Publication Data
Ames, Carol.
Entertainment public relations: communicating with audiences / Carol Ames.
Pages cm
Includes bibliographical references and index.
1. Performing arts—Audiences. 2. Performing arts—Public relations.
3. Performing arts—Marketing. I. Title.
PN1590.A9A53   659.2'979—dc23   2015035395
ISBN 978-1-4331-3054-0 (paperback: alk. paper)
ISBN 978-1-4539-1775-6 (ebook pdf)
ISBN 978-1-4331-3585-9 (epub)
ISBN 978-1-4331-3586-6 (mobi)

Bibliographic information published by **Die Deutsche Nationalbibliothek**.
Die Deutsche Nationalbibliothek lists this publication in the "Deutsche
Nationalbibliografie"; detailed bibliographic data are available
on the Internet at http://dnb.d-nb.de/.

The paper in this book meets the guidelines for permanence and durability
of the Committee on Production Guidelines for Book Longevity
of the Council of Library Resources.

© 2016 Carol Ames
Peter Lang Publishing, Inc., New York
29 Broadway, 18th floor, New York, NY 10006
www.peterlang.com

Printed in the United States of America

This book is dedicated to my past, present, and future entertainment public relations students, who keep me learning as well as teaching; and to Philippe and Charlotte, my rock and my inspiration.

CONTENTS

Acknowledgements xiii

Chapter 1. Introduction to Entertainment Public Relations Jobs
and Media 1
Chapter Overview 1
Defining Public Relations 2
The Title Is Publicist; the Job Is Entertainment Publicity;
and the Field Is Public Relations, Colloquially Known as PR 4
Defining the PR Goal: Why do entertainment
Companies Do PR? 5
Taking Advantage of an Opportunity or Solving a Problem 5
The Concept of the PR Cycle and the Stages of the
Business Cycle 6
Jobs in Entertainment PR 6
Entertainment Media Relations 11
Providing News for the Journalist's Audience 12
Sidebar: The Entertainment PR Toolbox—The Media List 14
The Uses of Digital and Social Media 17
Conclusion 18

	Key terms	18
	Suggested reading and resources	19
Chapter 2.	PR Plans, Audience Segmentation, and Storytelling with Media Releases	21
	Chapter Overview	21
	Entertainment News Stories and Their Origins	21
	Audience Segmentation for Entertainment	22
	Public Relations Objectives	24
	Media Relations Strategy, Tactics, and Tools	25
	Media Releases	27
	Sidebar: The Entertainment PR Toolbox—Media Releases	28
	Conclusion: Repurposing Media Releases as Online Content	33
	Key terms	34
	Suggested reading and resources	36
Chapter 3.	Public Relations Ethics and Uncontrolled vs. Controlled PR	37
	Chapter Overview	37
	The Ethics of the Public Relations Profession	37
	The Conflicting Ethical Precepts of PR Practitioners and Journalists	39
	Professional Codes of Ethics	41
	Sidebar: The Entertainment PR Toolbox—PRSA Code of Ethics (Excerpt)	42
	Uncontrolled and Controlled Public Relations, Then and Now	44
	Entertainment Ethics Online	48
	Conclusion: Ethical implications for the practice of entertainment PR	58
	Key Terms	59
	Suggested reading and resources	60
Chapter 4.	Hollywood Red-Carpet Events—How the World Knows the Business	61
	Chapter Overview	61
	Introduction	62
	PR Objectives of an Event Strategy	62
	The Five Elements of Any Party	62
	An Award Event as a Public Relations Strategy	63
	Sidebar: The Entertainment PR Toolbox—Media Alerts	65
	Parties with Hollywood WOW Factors	67

Who Produces the Oscars, the Emmys, and the
Grammys and Why?   72
Sidebar: The Biz Markets Itself—The Emmy Awards   75
Other Entertainment Industry Events   78
Conclusion: Implications for the Practice of Public Relations 83
  Key terms   84
  Suggested reading and resources   85
Chapter 5. The Network Television Public Relations Cycle   87
Chapter Overview   87
Introduction   88
The Management Structure of a Television Network   88
The Goal of Network Television Publicity   92
Understanding TV ratings   93
Achieving the Ratings Goal and Objectives Using Traditional
Media Relations   95
Sidebar: The Entertainment PR Toolbox—Writing Goal
and Objective Statements for Public Relations Plans   95
Achieving the Goal and Objectives Using Digital
and Social Media   98
The Network Television PR Cycle   102
Conclusion   103
  Key terms   104
  Suggested reading and resources   106
Chapter 6. PR Cycles for Syndicated Shows, Cable Channels, and
Streaming Services, Plus the Celebrity PR
Image-Repair Cycle   107
Chapter Overview   107
Introduction   107
The PR Cycle for Off-Network Syndication or Reruns   108
The PR Cycle for First-Run Syndicated Series   111
Publicity for Premium Cable Series   115
Publicity for Basic Cable   118
Sidebar: The Entertainment PR Toolbox—Press
Statements and the Celebrity PR Image-Repair Cycle   122
Subscription Streaming Services and the Binge-Viewing
PR Cycle   126
Conclusion   128
  Key terms   129
  Suggested reading and resources   130

Chapter 7. The Blockbuster Motion Picture Public Relations Cycle   131
            Chapter Overview   131
            Introduction   132
            Blockbuster Motion Pictures—Expensive to Produce
            and to Market   132
            A Publicity Plan's Background and Situation Analysis   135
            SWOT for Blockbusters   137
            Sidebar: The Entertainment PR Toolbox—Crisis
            Management   138
            Bankable Elements Are Strengths and Opportunities
            for Publicity   142
            The PR Goal for Blockbusters   142
            Audience Segmentation for Film Publicity   144
            Marketing Research for Movies   145
            Blockbuster Releases Are Timed for Summers and Holidays 150
            The Blockbuster Motion Picture PR Cycle   151
            Publicity Types and Media Targets Depend on the Stages
            of a Film's Life   152
            Sidebar: The Entertainment PR Toolbox—Cross-Brand
            Tie-Ins and Licensed Merchandise   154
            Is It a Hit or a Flop?   160
            Conclusion   161
                Key terms   162
                Suggested reading and resources   164
Chapter 8. The Independent Film PR Cycle and the Film Festival
            Circuit   165
            Chapter Overview   165
            Introduction   165
            Independent Films Differ from Blockbusters   166
            Finding the Money to Make an Independent Film   167
            The Independent Film Publicity Cycle   169
            Sidebar: The Entertainment PR Toolbox—PR Proposals
            (RFPs)   169
            Sidebar: The Entertainment PR Toolbox—Prepping the
            Client for Media Interviews   175
            Film Festivals Play Two Roles in the Indie Cycle   176
            Sidebar: The Entertainment PR Toolbox—Guerilla
            Marketing Stunts   178
            Sidebar: The Biz Markets Itself—The Oscar PR Cycle   180

The Typical Distribution Pattern for an Independent Film   183
Conclusion   185
    Key terms   186
    Suggested reading and resources   186
Chapter 9. Sports PR Cycles, Celebrity Endorsements, and PSAs   187
Chapter Overview   187
Introduction   188
Public Relations Jobs in the Sports World   188
The Sports PR Cycle   190
Sidebar: The Biz Markets Itself—The Super Bowl   194
Key Publics   196
Media Targets for Sports Stories   198
Using Social Media and Innovative Technology to
Engage Fans   199
Sports Celebrity Endorsements for Products   199
Corporate Social Responsibility (CSR) in the
Sports World   200
Sidebar: The Entertainment PR Toolbox—Public Service
Announcements (PSAs)   201
PR Problems or Crises in Sports   202
Fantasy Sports: Skill or Gambling?   203
Conclusion   203
    Key terms   204
    Suggested reading and resources   205
Chapter 10. The Music PR Cycle: Singles, the Album, Awards Shows,
the Tour, and Festivals   207
Chapter Overview   207
Introduction   207
Music Industry Media Relations   208
Digital Media—Effective and Mostly Free   211
Masters of Social Media   213
Sidebar: The Entertainment PR Toolbox—Breaking
the Rules   214
The Music PR Cycle   215
Sidebar: The Biz Markets Itself—The Grammy Awards   220
Launching a Tour Nationally and Publicizing It Locally   223
Music Festivals   224
Conclusion   225
    Key terms   226
    Suggested reading and resources   226

Chapter 11. The Video Game PR Cycle: Mobilizing Fan Communities   227
            Chapter Overview   227
            Introduction   227
            Gaming Platforms and Games   230
            The Video Game PR Cycle   233
            Sidebar: The Entertainment PR Toolbox—Navigating
            GamerGate and Other Controversies   235
            Publicizing Blockbuster Games   241
            Publicizing Independent Games   243
            Publicizing Casual Games and Apps   244
            Kickstarter, Early Access, and Other Crowdsourcing
            Platforms   245
            Making Allies of the Gaming Community   247
            eSports, Twitch, and YouTube   248
            Conclusion   249
                Key terms   250
                Suggested reading and resources   251
Chapter 12. Tourism, Attractions, Travel, and Hospitality: Seasonal
            PR Cycles   253
            Chapter Overview   253
            Introduction   254
            Sidebar: The Entertainment PR Toolbox—Pitching   255
            The Goal of a Tourism Plan   258
            Selling the Dream   259
            Nature's Four Seasons Plus High, Low, and Closed   263
            Having News or Making News Year Around   264
            Sidebar: The Entertainment PR Toolbox—Responding to
            Unusual Press Queries   268
            Two seasons: Open and Closed   270
            Stretching One Season to Multi-Season,
            Multi-Activity Attractions   271
            Making One-time Visitors into Regulars   273
            Conclusion   274
                Key terms   275
                Suggested reading and resources   276

            References   277
            Index   291

ACKNOWLEDGEMENTS

This book is the culmination of many years of entertainment industry and public relations experience; of daily reading *The New York Times* and *Los Angeles Times* entertainment and business coverage and reading the daily Hollywood trades, *The Hollywood Reporter* and *Variety*; of learning every day from my entertainment and public relations colleagues and clients; and of being questioned and schooled by insightful journalists such as Michael Cieply, now of *The New York Times*, and Brian Lowry, a living encyclopedia of television.

I am grateful to California State University, Fullerton, particularly to the Faculty Professional Leaves Committee and to Communications Chair Jason Shepard for the semester's sabbatical leave that allowed me the time to complete this book. Thanks also to my CSUF colleagues, especially Dr. Andi Stein, whose book writing is an inspiration, and to Dr. Ed Fink, who first encouraged me to return to academe to share my entertainment expertise.

Thank you to Acquisitions Editor Mary Savigar for encouragement and support and to the wonderful production team at Peter Lang.

I am also grateful to my able, succinct graduate student assistant, Jessica Gray, and most especially to my COMM 465: Entertainment PR students, whose eagerness to learn about the entertainment business inspired me to organize my knowledge for class and then to shape it into this book. To all my readers, I wish you success, great media coverage, and high audience engagement.

· 1 ·

INTRODUCTION TO ENTERTAINMENT PUBLIC RELATIONS JOBS AND MEDIA

Chapter Overview: When you finish this chapter, you should be able to answer the following questions:

- What does the term "public relations" mean in today's entertainment and tourism industries?
- Why does this book use the terms Publicist and Publicity?
- What is the goal of entertainment PR?
- Why do entertainment clients hire PR representation or have on-staff practitioners?
- What is a public relations cycle?
- What jobs can I find in entertainment PR?
- What media will I work with to achieve PR goals for entertainment clients?
- Why will media outlets agree to convey a public relations message to their audiences for no cost?
- What are the public relations uses of digital and social media?
- SIDEBAR: The Entertainment PR Toolbox—Media List

Defining Public Relations

Every show needs an audience. Who are they? Where are they? How do we find them? How do we reach them? How do we motivate them to buy tickets? To bring their friends? To buy extras? To become fans? To become active participants in our fan communities?

"Being entertained" is an audience's experience. So as a concept and an experience, entertainment depends on the presence of the audience and the audience's response—they laugh, they cry, they tell their friends. No audience—no response—no entertainment.

As a business, entertainment also depends on the audience. Without ticket sales to audience members, movie producers wouldn't recoup their $100 million-plus production costs. Without ratings indicating a large audience, television networks and channels wouldn't be able to sell airtime to advertisers. Without buyers for albums and music downloads, the artists and record companies wouldn't be paid for their talent and time.

Stakeholder relationships

In entertainment, working with advertising, promotion, and marketing, the **public relations function** locates and communicates with the audience to motivate the largest possible number of people to commit money, time, and attention to an intangible experience—being entertained. Entertainment PR also fulfills numerous other strategic functions that will be covered in subsequent chapters.

The **Public Relations Society of America (PRSA)** recently modernized its definition of the field: "Public relations is a strategic communication process that builds mutually beneficial relationships between organizations and their publics" (PRSA, 2012). The gold standard in public relations is **two-way symmetrical communication**—communicating back and forth with audiences (Grunig, 2001). This definition emphasizes the "relations" in public relations. Public "relations" means listening and responding to stakeholders' comments, concerns, questions, and suggestions, not just pushing out promotional messages as advertisers, marketers, and promoters often do. In these definitions, **publics** and **stakeholders** mean not just customers. These terms for the wider audience for public relations messages include all of the various constituencies that are affected by and interested in the client, including: employees, stockholders, residents of surrounding communities, opinion makers, various levels of government, and fans.

Entertainment brands and companies—movies, television, music, video games, sports, stars, and celebrities—are at the center of popular culture. To keep them at the center of public consciousness, their entertainment public relations practitioners have been in the forefront in using new media and in taking creative approaches to communications and marketing. Much of the innovation in social and online media usage has come from the entertainment arena, whether it be Ashton Kutcher's April 15, 2009, challenge to CNN to become the first Twitter account with one million followers (Ames, 2012, p. 97), or stars live-blogging with fans. Cutthroat competition between subsidiaries of the major, publicly owned conglomerates means large budgets and do-or-die deadlines to gain audience attention (opening weekend for movies, premiere week for television series). Entertainment communications departments set creative standards that smaller entities in other arenas such as non-profit and community organizations may later try to emulate on whatever scale their own budgets allow.

The U.S. entertainment industry

Most of America's entertainment options are owned and controlled by six major conglomerates: CBS, Comcast (which now holds the majority stake in NBC/Universal), Disney, News Corp., Time Warner, and Viacom ("National Entertainment State," 2006). With their many subsidiaries and entertainment brands, as well as their wide reach, these corporations influence how we live our lives and how we see the world. These companies set much of the public agenda through their own news operations and influence taste and trends through their entertainment operations.

Digital relationships

In recent years, digital technologies such as websites and apps have made it possible to communicate directly with the audience without going through an intermediary such as a newspaper that publishes a story. Today's technology also makes it easier for the audience to send their own messages directly to the company. For example, to complain about sexual innuendo in a television show, a disgruntled viewer is no longer restricted to sending a letter of complaint to the CEO. The viewer can make a negative comment on the company's website or on an industry forum. Or the unhappy viewer can start her very own company-hater website. Today, to go public with a complaint about unsanitary conditions at the county fairgrounds, an attendee doesn't have to write a rational and articulate letter to the editor. He can tweet a nasty comment and a gross photo or post a video on YouTube.

Fan relationships

Now it's also easier for fans to find and communicate with one another. For example, in-person fan activity is no longer limited to attending a yearly Star Trek convention. Message boards, online forums, and fan sites make fandom a year-round, communal experience. Fan opportunities such as live chats with stars and sensitive, responsive participation by a company representative can make these particularly loyal and impassioned customers feel appreciated and special. Direct company two-way communication can make avid fans even more motivated to generate positive word of mouth, which can help ramp up anticipation for an upcoming sequel or a new version of a video game, for example.

Technological advances have made two-way symmetrical PR communications feasible. This gold standard of PR, however, is especially challenging in the field of entertainment, because the number of potential audience members—and therefore of potential audience commenters—is immense. In order to understand the challenges of the gold standard, it's necessary to understand for whom and to whom the entertainment PR person speaks and how messages are transmitted to and from the audience.

The Title Is Publicist; the Job Is Entertainment Publicity; and the Field Is Public Relations, Colloquially Known as PR

In the American entertainment industry, no matter the level of responsibility, the scope, the budget, or the complexity of strategic planning, the ubiquitous name of the job is **publicist**. The work is called publicity or sometimes PR. The name of the professional organization is the **Entertainment Publicists Professional Society (EPPS)**. The name of the labor union, which is part of the International Cinematographers Guild, is the ICG Publicists of Local 600, IATSE. Many academics and communications professionals in other industries hate the terms publicity, publicist, and PR. They always refer to the job as public relations (or now sometimes strategic communications), and they call a person working in the field a public relations practitioner.

Following the custom of the entertainment industry, however, this book uses the term publicist interchangeably with public relations practitioner and PR interchangeably with public relations. This book uses these terms interchangeably with the respect the professionals have earned in a high-risk industry that values the work.

Defining the PR Goal: Why Do Entertainment Companies Do PR?

Public relations activities should be strategic, not ad hoc or random. To be effective, publicity initiatives should be part of a **public relations plan**. Also called a **request for proposal** or **RFP**, a PR plan looks analytically at a specific situation; determines an achievable goal; and defines the strategy, target publics, objectives, tactics, and tools for achieving the goal in a finite time period within an approved budget. Except for the budget, which varies widely depending on circumstances, location, and finances, the elements of a PR plan will be covered as the chapters progress.

The **PR plan goal** should be clear and measurable, and it should support the overall business goal of the company (Scott, 2011, pp. 33–34). Therefore, for entertainment clients, the goal should be delineated in financial terms—either dollar numbers or numbers that are translatable into dollars. For blockbuster movie clients, for example, that means a goal of hitting specified box-office grosses for opening weekend and for the second weekend of release. The distribution arm of the studio, as well as marketing, will be involved in the discussions about the goal, which will be based on historical data for similar films released on similar dates. Like all aspects of a publicity plan, the target is confidential and should not be discussed externally or with the media. For a venue performance the goal can be stated in total ticket sales. A publicity plan for a television series would specify the goal in terms of Nielsen rating benchmarks for the premiere, as well as for each week through the end of the season. Ratings are "dollar-equivalent," because the ratings determine the price that can be charged for advertising in the particular timeslot, as discussed in Chapter 5.

Taking Advantage of an Opportunity or Solving a Problem

A client or company hires public relations representation for one of two reasons: to take advantage of an opportunity; or to solve a problem. Much of the work of entertainment PR is to take advantage of an opportunity: a new product's debut in the marketplace, for example. Even a celebrity—or the career of a celebrity—is a kind of product that benefits from branding and from strategic thinking to take advantage of opportunities, such as invitations to awards events like the Oscars or the Emmys, which offer media exposure to vast audiences.

Entertainment PR problems that benefit from professional counsel include negative advance buzz about a movie, and crises such as a star's arrest for driving under the influence. (See the SIDEBAR in Chapter 6). Ongoing two-way communication with audiences, corporate social responsibility (CSR) initiatives (see Chapter 9), strong branding, and charitable activities are examples of strategic public relations efforts to avert crises before they happen, or to mitigate damage when they do.

The Concept of the PR Cycle and the Stages of the Business Cycle

This book offers a unique contribution to the fields of public relations and entertainment studies. The public relations cycle is a pattern that the author, a seasoned insider, recognized from her 20 years of public relations work in entertainment. Each entertainment industry's **public relations cycle** connects public relations objectives, strategies, and tactics to benchmarks in product development and/or with a recurring calendar of industry events such as major trade fairs, seasons, or stages of a product's development, production, and distribution.

The cycles are different in each part of the entertainment business. In many cases, the cycle is based on the stages of product creation and release, which usually are: development; production; post-production; and distribution (often known in the entertainment business as a premiere). During each stage, the public relations objectives, media targets, target audience, tactics, and tools are different. As one example, during development, the PR objective is industry visibility. Therefore, the target audiences are industry insiders and product fans; the media targets are the trade press; and the main tactics and tools are trade news releases and trade events.

Jobs in Entertainment PR

Jobs in entertainment range from product publicity to corporate communications. In the entertainment industry, most practitioners are hired to take advantage of opportunities.

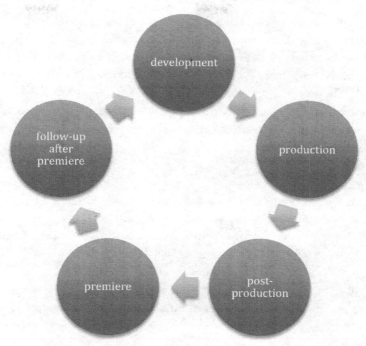

Figure 1.1: Typical stages of the entertainment PR cycle.

Personal Publicist

The job most readers will have seen glamorized on reality television is the **personal publicist**, who represents an actor, director, musician, or celebrity as an individual. The work, which is discussed in greater depth in Chapter 4, includes escorting a client on the red carpet to secure interviews by the most important broadcasters.

The discussion of personal publicity also introduces the concept of the **celebrity PR image-repair cycle**, which is discussed in more detail in the SIDEBAR in Chapter 6. In this cycle, a celebrity's missteps with a DUI arrest, addiction, accident, or offensive comment necessitate a careful public relations program of reputation rehabilitation, i.e., solving a problem for the client.

For example, the movie *Hancock* (2008) stars Will Smith as Hancock, a fallen superhero with a drinking problem and a bad attitude. In the film, a public relations practitioner played by Jason Bateman guides Hancock through a basic celebrity PR image-repair cycle: issuing a press statement with an apology to fans; disappearing from the public eye; and reemerging into the spotlight as a chastened and changed person capable of an immediate success. Most of the cycle is clear in the movie trailer for *Hancock*, which is available on **IMDb.com**, the Internet movie database, a well-respected entertainment industry wiki. The celebrity PR crisis cycle is discussed in more detail toward the end of Chapter 6, along with the elements of a **press statement**, which a practitioner issues in crises and other negative situations to be used as a comment by journalists requesting information.

Product publicity

Less visible product publicity jobs include those at major media companies in publicity, promotion, or marketing departments. The publicists represent entertainment products such as a film; a television show; a music album; a special event; a sporting event, team, league, or venue; a digital content provider such as Netflix; an entertainment website; or a tourism-related business. Additional job functions at major media companies include production publicist for films, called **unit publicist** at film studios (Chapter 7); for television networks (Chapter 5); and for TV syndication companies (Chapter 6).

Corporate communications

Like all major companies, media companies also have **corporate communications** departments that handle PR opportunities such as: corporate image, for example Disneyland's strong anniversary campaigns; business relations; community relations; and charity outreach or philanthropy. The corporate communications staff often also handles certain employee-relations duties including internal newsletters and communications; information distribution; and morale and loyalty initiatives such as employee-training events and social events, for example, the company holiday party.

"Corporate" also often handles PR problems. The **chief communications officer (CCO)** usually oversees crisis communications in consultation with the CEO, the head of legal, and often a specialty, outside crisis agency, such as Sitrick and Company. Examples of crises in entertainment include any death or serious injury on a film set; the mass shooting on opening night in a crowded movie theater showing the Warner Bros. *Batman* sequel; and the January 12, 2012, capsizing of the cruise ship *Costa Concordia*. Not only was there a tragic loss of life when the boat went aground, but the ship was not salvaged until September 17, 2013. The damaged ship lay near shore in plain sight for almost a year and a half. Photographs and video in the media continually reminded travelers of the potential dangers of cruising, so the incident became an ongoing crisis for the entire industry, not just Costa.

Staff publicity jobs

Most media companies have a core of full-time PR people on staff. Young hires start as assistants, because that is where they learn the players, the press, and the main strategies for their part of the industry, before becoming promotable into more responsible and strategic positions. In the film business, a publicist can work for the production company, the studio, or the distributor. Responsibilities can be for one or more specific films, or for an entire slate of films. In television, a publicist can work as a production publicist for a producer. At a network, a publicist might be responsible for several specific shows, the entire prime-time lineup, or the launch of the new fall season.

Numerous other kinds of entertainment companies hire PR staff and/or retain PR agencies to generate audiences for their entertainment products. Record companies use PR for an album or an artist. Producers of live events need to create awareness and excitement to sell tickets to a tour date or a fund-raising event. In sports, public relations people work for the league, the team, or the venue.

In the fields of travel, tourism, and theme parks, public relations is done by hundreds of destination companies, such as Disneyland, and by various business consortia such as local, regional, and state tourist bureaus. Cruise lines typically market heavily with direct-mail brochures to past customers; they also create high-profile special events to celebrate the launch of a new ship.

The senior in-house publicity staffers at entertainment and media companies usually do the most sensitive work, such as pitching feature stories to important and influential media, for example, *The New York Times*. For implementing the rest of the PR and marketing plan, the core staffers usually work with and oversee outside contractors.

PR agencies

Contractors include entertainment PR agencies, the oldest of which is Rogers & Cowan. Agencies may be broad, or they may specialize in only one area, such as film, television, personal publicity, or crisis management.

Some agencies handle only PR and some handle advertising as well. The term **strategic communications** means the combination of public relations and advertising with one team covering both. In entertainment, however, each of the areas is typically so complex and specialized that the work is done by separate teams, perhaps under a president or senior vice president of publicity or marketing.

Entertainment PR subsidiaries of large advertising/communications companies include BWR (formerly Baker Winokur Ryder), with offices in Los Angeles and New York. BWR is part of Ogilvy PR Worldwide, which in turn is part of WPP Communications, a global advertising and public relations agency with more than two thousand offices. Other PR agencies consist of only a few specialists, such as executive speechwriters or crisis communications experts. The field also includes numerous smaller PR firms nationwide that work on campaigns for local entertainment companies and do local campaigns and events for the major media companies.

A public relations agency may hire a junior staffer and initially assign work on several small to medium-sized accounts. Thereby, a junior publicist can quickly gain a broad understanding of a number of companies in a wide swath of the entertainment business. More importantly, the major media companies often look to their agencies for talented up-and-comers to hire when a staff position opens. An agency of record will usually agree to allow its well-trained talent to be poached by a major client, which helps solidify the agency-client relationship.

In addition to the large and small PR agencies, the entertainment business has a number of freelance generalists and specialists who can be retained for short-term projects such as special events.

Professional advancement

To succeed in any public relations specialty, entry-level job candidates should be able to write, pitch, and research, meaning "someone who is good at finding and analyzing information," according to a 2015 survey of PR agencies. Additionally, the agencies desired that a new hire be an articulate, motivated, strategic thinker and team player, who is "client centric." The candidate should also understand social media and PR practices, as well as marketing and business basics (Bates, 2015).

Within entertainment public relations, especially with agency work, people change jobs frequently, moving up the ranks in responsibility and title.

Upward mobility is enhanced by keeping in touch and by being part of industry organizations, such as EPPS, or the Academy of Motion Picture Arts and Sciences, whose current president, Cheryl Boone Isaacs, started as a publicist and became the first African-American woman to head the organization.

People in entertainment publicity keep current on job openings and individuals' availabilities, so they know whom they can hire quickly or recommend to a friend who needs to staff up for a busy period or an increased workload. Because of urgency and deadlines, as well as the need to "know the work" and trust new hires, many jobs are filled without being posted. For speed, some legitimate PR jobs are posted on Craig's List and filled within a couple of days. A job seeker, however, should carefully research a PR company's website and office location. A number of legitimate PR agencies are actually run out of the principal's house, but the interview should be in a safe, public place, such as the ever-popular local Starbucks.

Overview of jobs

Company staff positions allow a publicist to become a specialist in one part of entertainment. Staff positions are the most secure of the jobs discussed above, because they offer ongoing employment and benefits. Jobs at PR agencies, on the other hand, allow a publicist to develop a range of experience and skills, and full-time agency jobs also offer benefits. Agency jobs, however, depend on the agency keeping the client happy and retaining the account. Sometimes at an agency, it is better to work on several clients, in case one big client puts its account under review. The television series *Mad Men* made great drama for many seasons out of an advertising agency's need to keep current clients and woo new ones.

Independent or freelance publicists have the challenge of always finding new projects with clients who can afford to pay (and who actually will pay) for the work. The big advantage of being freelance or starting your own PR firm with one or two other experienced people is flexibility, especially for practitioners who want to be present in their young children's busy lives.

Entertainment Media Relations

The **media** are those in the middle, the go-betweens and technologies used by public relations practitioners to convey messages to entertainment audiences.

Traditionally, **media relations**—working with the press—has been the single most important work of entertainment PR. The goal of media relations is to get non-paid messages to the audience in the form of news articles based on press releases; feature stories and profiles based on exclusive pitches to individual journalists; byline opinion pieces; and calendar listings, among others. Without good relationships with journalists and editors, the PR person used to have no inexpensive way to get the client's story to the audience. Media coverage has the extra advantage of what is called **third-party endorsement**. Because the story has been reported and thereby vetted by journalists and editors, the audience believes it is more likely to be reliable and trustworthy than advertising content. PR uses media relations to augment the number, variety, and ubiquity of messages to the audience beyond what can be paid for by the advertising budget.

Digital alternatives

Up until recently, alternatives to media placements have been expensive. Print advertisements, television commercials (created and placed by the advertising department and the outside ad agency), client brochures, and printed newsletters have all been big-budget costs. The good news now is that digital technology has slashed the cost of creating and distributing newsletters, brochures, and even ads. "Printed" materials need never be printed! They can be created and distributed digitally. "Direct mail" need never be mailed! The brochure can be available on the client website and/or emailed to targeted distribution lists. "Theatrical trailers" aren't just limited to theaters! The "premiere" of a trailer can be teased, posted, and commented about on a client website, featured on IMDb, available on YouTube, and "liked" on Facebook. Using the multiplicity of digital media to achieve public relations objectives is covered in detail in all of the following chapters.

Despite the multitude of company-created messages available on the Internet, however, third-party endorsements through media placements are still important. Nothing has replaced the impact and prestige of a cover story about your client in *The New York Times Magazine* on Sunday.

Providing News for the Journalist's Audience

In order to generate media placements, a publicist must have a relevant entertainment press/media list and keep it updated, because journalists and editors move from job to job and from one beat to another. Important media include: the Hollywood entertainment trades and websites; the entertainment business press; consumer publications that cover entertainment, such as the entertainment sections of major newspapers and magazines, both in print and on line; local and national broadcast media; and for industry issues, controversies, and legislation, the opinion-maker media.

Media distribution lists should target the specific reporter on the specific **entertainment beat**, for example, the television reporter; and publicists should not send news releases or pitch features to people who are exclusively critics.

Journalists and media outlets know their readership or viewership and create content that is **news** (information that is new and of interest) to that specific audience. Therefore, a PR person must know the specifics such as demographics, psychographics, and geographics of the audience each media outlet reaches. When a medium's target audience matches a publicist's desired audience, the publicist can make a successful media placement. If there is a match between the story and a journalist's readership, she will be interested in a news release or pitch. Journalists become annoyed if they are spammed with news releases that aren't relevant to their beat or work assignment and ones irrelevant to their audience.

Therefore, an entertainment media list must be kept updated and current. It can be segmented into at least four parts, representing different kinds of target readers: 1. trade media and entertainment community; 2. business; 3. entertainment consumer; and 4. opinion-maker media. Not everyone on the media list should receive every news release. For example, the **trade media** and entertainment community are interested in news of projects early on, when they are in development. Because everyone in that target audience knows the industry, the readers can understand stories that are technical and specialized. The **business media** are interested in a story at the point a company makes a large financial commitment, such as when a film is green-lit ... and so is the trade press. The **consumer media** are interested in stories about projects that are nearing completion and soon available for the audience to enjoy ... and so are the business and trade press. Each kind of media, however, will take a different angle on a story. The **opinion-maker media** are for trying to influence public opinion or legislation and are typically targeted for byline articles on industry, cultural, or legal issues, such as piracy, controversies about the effects of media sex and violence on children, and First Amendment concerns.

The Entertainment PR Toolbox—The Media List

For each client, the first step in building a media list is to decide on the reach that the client needs. For example, a local, minor-league baseball team, a county fair, or a regional theater benefits from local and regional coverage, as does a musician's tour date in a specific city, such as Portland. On the other hand, the tour as a whole, as well as Hollywood blockbuster movies and network television shows have national campaigns that also target media outlets in all the major entertainment markets.

For Projects in Development—Targeting People in the Business

The Trades

Variety.com, *Variety*
Hollywoodreporter.com, *The Hollywood Reporter*
Deadline.com
Billboard.com, *Billboard*
Spin.com, *Spin*

Entertainment Community and "Hometown" Press

The New York Times
　　– Arts, Briefly
Los Angeles Times
　　– Calendar Section, Sunday and weekdays
KCRW, 89.9, Elvis Mitchell, *The Treatment*, http://www.kcrw.com/news-culture/shows/the-treatment
KCRW, 89.9, Kim Masters, *The Business*, http://www.kcrw.com/news-culture/shows/the-business

For Projects in Production Targeting the Business Media

Entertainment Business Press

The New York Times Business Section
Los Angeles Times Business Section

General Daily and Weekly Business Press

The Wall Street Journal
Bloomberg Businessweek
Forbes

Broadcast Outlets Covering Entertainment

CNBC
Bloomberg News
Access Hollywood
E! Entertainment
Entertainment Tonight
Inside Edition
Marketplace on Public Radio

For Projects Nearing Premiere (Targeting the Potential Audience)

National and Local Broadcast Media

Morning Talk Shows
      Good Morning America
      The Today Show
Late-Night Talk shows
      The Tonight Show Starring Jimmy Fallon
      Jimmy Kimmel Live
      The Late Show with Stephen Colbert
      Late Night with Seth Meyers
National Radio
      National Public Radio, *All Things Considered*
      Ryan Seacrest, *Top 40*
      Terry Gross, *Fresh Air*

National Consumer Press

Entertainment Weekly
Los Angeles Times
The New York Times and *The New York Times Magazine*, Sunday
Parade (Sunday Supplement)
People
US Weekly
USA Today

Long-Lead Magazines

Cosmopolitan
Glamour
GQ

In Style
Redbook
Vanity Fair
Vogue

Local Morning Radio Talk Shows and Drive-Time Shows

Big Boy's Neighborhood, KPWR 106
Good Day LA, Fox, Channel 11, Los Angeles
Similar morning and afternoon radio shows in all major media markets

Local Print Media in Major Markets

Chicago Tribune
The Atlanta Journal-Constitution
Other major local newspapers

Influential On-line Sites

HuffingtonPost.com
PerezHilton.com
TMZ.com

Adapting Your Own Media List

This list is not meant to be exhaustive. Target media always depend on the client or product. A media list must be further refined to include the names and the contact information, including email address and telephone number, for the current journalist on each beat. For pitching stories, it helps to know even more about the journalist. It's important for a publicist to know the favorite subjects and typical angles of individual journalists to prevent pitching a story to someone who always takes a negative slant, for example. Even the hobbies and special interests of **entertainment beat journalists** and their editors will help a publicist develop personal relationships and trust that can facilitate media placement.

Yes, it's time consuming.

Yes, it's tedious.

Yes, you can pay for a list management service such as Cision.

Whatever you do, however, be sure that the information you are using is up to date and targeted.

News catching versus story pitching

Digital and social media capabilities have led to a recent addition to the media relations equation: **news catching**. Besides PR practitioners sending out press releases and story pitches to attract journalists' attention, journalists have started using expert request services such at ProfNet or Help-A-Reporter-Out (HARO), founded in 2007 by the well-known, creative PR expert Peter Shankman (see Shankman, 2007). HARO is now owned by Cision, while ProfNet is owned by PR Newswire.

With the requests and responses facilitated through listservs and Twitter, these services help journalists solicit professors and other experts (and PR representatives) to become sources of information and quotations for stories that journalists already have in development. A 2010 study found that entertainment and lifestyle topics were among the most frequently requested on HARO and that "traditional mainstream media appear to be some of the biggest players in media catching. Social media tactics such as blogs, podcasts, and Web-based forums lag behind their mainstream media counterparts despite outnumbering them" (Waters, Tindall, & Morton, 2010, pp. 251–252). Publicists also make posts, such as requesting donations of items for gift bags from other publicists. These matchups are mutually beneficial to the event client of the requesting publicist and the product client of the respondent. Keeping track of information and source requests on these services is another way an entertainment publicist can broaden media coverage.

The Uses of Digital and Social Media

In addition to communicating with the audience through print and broadcast middlemen, today's technology allows a publicist to reach audience members directly. Social media and company websites let a public relations person communicate directly with desired target audience segments without having to go through media gatekeepers (Scott, 2011, 2012). Therefore, it is essential that public relations practitioners be excellent writers, storytellers, and communicators. These days, public relations materials are often part of **transmedia storytelling** initiatives (stories, contests, and audience-participation tactics utilizing more than one medium) that build anticipation and feed the long-term engagement of avid fan communities. The most important use of digital media is now the possibility of achieving the gold standard of two-way communication with the audience.

Conclusion

This chapter has introduced the work of public relations as it applies in entertainment and tourism, as well as the concept of the public relations cycle. The PR cycle is a series of recurring events or a recurring pattern that allows a publicist to do advanced planning, based on knowledge of recent industry history. In entertainment, most PR seeks to take advantage of the opportunity represented by a new product. The typical PR goal is defined in terms that align with the larger organization's goal, which in most cases can be expressed in dollars, or in a term that translates into dollars, such as television ratings that are used to set the prices for advertising. Sometimes, however, a publicist also has to deal with a problem, such as a client's misbehavior or law breaking.

This chapter also introduces the process of media relations, while the SIDEBAR gives the basics of a media list for entertainment clients. The rest of the book will make use of the concepts introduced in this chapter to go into more depth about the specifics of doing publicity in various subfields of entertainment.

Key Terms—In bold in the text

Public relations practitioners need to know and understand the terminology used in the field, as well as terms used in their clients' businesses. A good self-test is to write out a one-sentence definition of what a term means in the context of the chapter, plus a one-sentence specific example demonstrating how the term applies to entertainment PR. Each chapter's list will demonstrate this exercise using the first term.

Sample two-sentence definition and example

Business Media: The business media write about financial investments and revenue information that may affect the stock price or success of a company. For example, a publicist for Warner Bros. would include *The Wall Street Journal* and the business channel CNBC on the media list for a press release about green-lighting a big-budget installment in the Lego film franchise.

Celebrity PR Image-Repair Cycle
Chief Communications Officer (CCO)
Consumer Media
Corporate Communications

Entertainment Beat
Entertainment Beat Journalists
Entertainment Publicists Professional Society (EPPS)
IMDb.com
Media
Media Relations
News
News Catching
Opinion-Maker Media
Personal Publicist
PR Plan Goal
Press Statement
Public Relations Cycle
Public Relations Function
Public Relations Plan
Public Relations Society of America (PRSA)
Publicist
Publics
Request for Proposal (RFP)
Stakeholders
Strategic Communications
Third-Party Endorsement
Trade Press or Trade Media
Transmedia Storytelling
Two-Way Symmetrical Communication
Unit Publicist

Suggested reading and resources

Bryce, I. (Producer), & Berg, P. (Director). (2008). *Hancock.* [Motion Picture]. Sony Pictures Entertainment. Trailer available on IMDb.com

The national entertainment state: 10th anniversary. (2006). *The Nation.* [Chart of entertainment conglomerates, which is somewhat outdated, but still informative. Instead of General Electric, for example, the parent company of NBC/Universal is Comcast.]

Stein, A., & Evans, B. B. (2009). *An introduction to the entertainment industry.* New York, NY: Peter Lang.

Weisman, A. (2012, October 4). Meet the 20 most powerful publicists in Hollywood (ranked). *Business Insider.* Retrieved from http://www.businessinsider.com/20-most-powerful-publicists-in-hollywood-2012-10?op=1

· 2 ·

PR PLANS, AUDIENCE SEGMENTATION, AND STORYTELLING WITH MEDIA RELEASES

Chapter Overview: When you finish this chapter, you should be able to answer the following questions:

- How do you decide what entertainment to enjoy this weekend?
- How does entertainment marketing segment the audience?
- What are typical entertainment PR objectives and the strategies, tactics, and tools used to achieve them?
- What is special about entertainment-related media releases?
- How can media releases be repurposed and reused as online content?
- SIDEBAR: The Entertainment PR Toolbox—Media Releases

Entertainment News Stories and Their Origins

How do you decide which new movie to watch on Friday night? Or which music festival to attend at the cost of several hundred dollars? Whether you're conscious of it or not, you have been receiving informational and/or promotional messages through the media or through word of mouth. The messages have made you aware of a new movie title, its stars, and its storyline. As your awareness deepens, you consciously search out more details, including the time and place of the specific event or the premiere date, time, and channel of a new television series.

This chapter looks at how those messages in the form of entertainment stories or interviews or mentions are placed in the media where the most likely potential audience members can find them. Whether the messages are public relations, advertising, or promotion, how does a company find the right combination of outreach so that the messages will be read or heard by the particular people most likely to be receptive and take action? When members of the right audience segments become aware of an upcoming entertainment event, for example, they can become motivated to buy tickets or turn the TV to the correct channel on the right night at the right time. Positive stories and feature articles circulating in the media probably originate from public relations-generated content (news releases) and ideas (story pitches to journalists).

This chapter looks at audience segmentation, PR objectives, the media relations strategy, and PR tactics and tools for generating placements of positive messages. The emphasis is on why entertainment PR uses the media release tool, and on how to write effective releases that result in media coverage for your news story.

Audience Segmentation for Entertainment

Before you can communicate with the audience, you need to be able to answer several questions: Who are they? Where are they? How can you reach them? For entertainment, there is often more than one "type" of audience member, for example, men and women. Men and women don't read all the same magazines, where a publicist could pitch feature stories; and they don't watch all the same talk shows, for which a publicist could pitch an appearance by the film's star, who can chat about the movie and show a short clip to get people excited about seeing it.

The main categories of segmentation used for public relations are **demographics**, **psychographics**, and **geographics**. Demographics mean objective, observable, measurable traits, including: age, gender, race, and income. Psychographics mean attitudes, which are subjective, internal, and not easily observable or quantifiable. Examples might be: family oriented, thrill seeking, or romantic. Geographics mean the locations where potential audience members can be found. For most Hollywood entertainment, the overall geographics for PR campaigns are national, with regional and local components.

For a music artist appearing at an arena, the geographics will be regional for the tour date, although first a major tour is launched with a national campaign announcing the tour and ticket availability, followed by more localized fresher campaigns with local angles just ahead of individual tour dates.

Different sub-industries in entertainment use different categories of segmentation based on the demographics, psychographics, and geographics: (Sayre, 2010, p. 167ff) that have been most successful in past campaigns, or based on research about the people most likely to want to attend the project being publicized.

Segmentation for film

The main method of **audience segmentation for film** is based on the demographic categories of age and gender. Film marketers divide the audience into four segments called **quadrants**: men under age 25; men over 25; women under 25; and women over 25. Notice that "under 25" includes only ages 13–25—a very small age range starting with PG-13.

Psychographic segments for film include: fans of the male star; fans of the female star; fans of the director; fans of the genre (action, romantic comedy); and fans of the source material (Harry Potter books).

Segmentation for TV

On the other hand, **audience segmentation for television** follows that of the TV industry's main proprietary or subscription research, the **Nielsen ratings**. Nielsen uses the wider demographic categories of: ages 18–49 for the broad audience; 18–34 when targeting a younger audience; and 24–54 for the daytime audience excluding college-age students. All segments use gender as a secondary element. The Nielsen ratings also: segment by urban and rural; calculate a show's **audience share**, which is the percentage of **households using television (HUTs)** at the time of watching the specific show; and measure a show's **total viewers** in the categories of **live**, as well as **live + 3 days** and **live + 7 days,** which count DVR and video on demand viewing in the days after the show is broadcast.

Geographics

The geographic targets for most television and movies are nationwide, i.e., the domestic, or North American market, although global audiences are increasingly important to the bottom line. Publicity and marketing campaigns including the poster and the trailer are developed in the US and adapted and implemented in international markets.

Buyer Personas

In order to communicate effectively with people in the main target segments of the potential audience, professionals in public relations, advertising, and marketing often find it helpful to create **buyer personas**. A buyer persona is a short biography of a fictional or composite "person" representing one audience segment. The persona should be based on research such as interviews or surveys; and it is usually a composite that includes:

- A name (to make the persona seem real)
- Demographics such as age, gender, race, and occupation
- Geographics (where the persona lives)
- Leisure activities
- Entertainment usage
- Personal motivations for participating in entertainment, and
- Most importantly, details of the persona's media use

The persona's media use is crucial, because the public relations practitioner uses the information for creating a targeted media list to reach that persona.

Public Relations Objectives

Public relations objectives are specified for each important audience segment. Each objective should contribute to reaching the overall goal. For example, objectives and their target segments might include: building awareness for a film among men under 25 or creating visibility in magazines read by women over 25. Other areas for objectives (that would need a specified target audience segment) might be: creating positive attitudes; changing negative attitudes; creating buzz; influencing opinion makers; generating involvement (Sayre, 2008, p. 232); and building to a huge season premiere for a TV show or a blockbuster opening weekend for a big-budget film. Objectives should state a degree or amount of change, a time frame, and a means of measurement. See the SIDEBAR in Chapter 5 for more details on how to write clear, actionable goal and objective statements.

Buzz vs. hype

Buzz is a metaphor for the sound of a lot of people talking in an animated, positive way about the client you represent. Buzz is the excitement that drives people into movie theaters on opening weekend. Trying to quantify and evaluate the "word of mouth" that drives big box office results has always been an elusive art, highly dependent on an industry executive's experience. As discussed in Chapter 7, film industry researchers are currently evaluating the effectiveness of social media metrics as a more scientific way to measure buzz, and therefore as a guide to decisions about modifying or intensifying various elements of a marketing plan.

In contrast to buzz, **hype**, which derives from "hyperbole," means an exaggeration. Both the term "hype" and the practice of "hyping" should be avoided. Marketing messages create audience expectations. Hype creates exaggerated expectations, which lead to audience disappointment. Disappointed customers create bad word of mouth, especially by using social media such as Twitter, Facebook, and Yelp to amplify their negative comments. Therefore, publicists should avoid "hype" and should certainly not refer to what they are doing as "hyping."

Media Relations Strategy, Tactics, and Tools

An effective **media relations strategy** is essential for reaching and motivating audiences. Before the advent of online and social media, it was the primary PR strategy in entertainment. In media relations work, the publicist (representing the client) strives to place news stories in specific media that are read or watched or listened to by a targeted segment of the audience (a buyer persona). Placements as news stories and features in reputable news outlets have extra clout with the audience because of the **implied third-party endorsement** of the story; the reader is positively influenced by the story because a journalist and editor, or a reporter and news segment producer, have judged the story important enough to cover. This third-party endorsement is in contrast to an advertisement, which most readers trust less, because the source is a company that "just paid money" to buy the ad. The clout and prestige, for example, of a cover story in the Sunday *New York Times Magazine*, is "priceless" precisely because it cannot be bought. It must be earned through the newsworthiness of the story, as pitched by an enterprising publicist.

Media relations tactics

Several **media relations tactics** help achieve your objectives. These include:

- Providing a journalist with accurate newsworthy media releases
- Making sure that news releases contain information that is relevant and interesting, i.e., that is news to the journalist's readers or viewers, which means *not* spamming journalists on the wrong beat
- developing good professional relationships and establishing credibility and trust with individual journalists, editors, and broadcast segment producers
- never lying to a member of the media, because a single lie destroys the possibility of future trust
- becoming known as a publicist with interesting story ideas for that journalist's readers
- becoming a helpful resource for journalists, able to provide access to stars and executives
- providing appropriate, usable information to a journalist on deadline
- *always* following through on promises to supply information or access to a journalist; or calling back to give a credible reason why you can't, and whenever possible offering a useful alternative to what was requested
- educating target journalists about the scope and background of your company or client to help stimulate story ideas
- thinking like a journalist, so you understand the journalist's objectives, while nevertheless representing your client's best interest; this means never being manipulated into providing confidential information, gossip, or access to a journalist working on a story with a negative angle about your client—all the while maintaining a positive, long-term relationship

Chapter 3 will go into greater detail about why it is so important to remember that journalists and public relations practitioners have different priorities.

Media relations tools

Media relations tools used to achieve media relations objectives all have to do with the tactics described above for achieving good working relationships with the media in general and with individual journalists in particular. To identify what is newsworthy and to create stories that interest their audiences, the journalists need information, ideas, and story angles. The publicist's job is to provide information, ideas, story angles, and stories to journalists—that is, to help journalists do their jobs. Access to the audience (readership or viewership) is what journalists provide publicists. A good journalist/publicist relationship is symbiotic and mutually beneficial.

The tools the PR person uses to provide information and ideas include: news or media releases; media alerts; online and physical media kits; video and photographs; pitches; and fact sheets. Tools used to provide journalists access to clients or to provide an experience for the journalists include press conferences, media tours/press junkets, and other special events for the press. Creative PR stunts, also called guerilla marketing, are tools to "make news," because their originality attracts broadcast coverage and the possibility of going viral online. Many of these tools are covered in subsequent chapters, particularly in sidebars called "The Entertainment PR Toolbox."

Media Releases

The rest of this chapter focuses on the creation and deployment of the most important and most traditional media relations tool in the Entertainment PR Toolbox—the entertainment **media release**, also called a **news release** or a **press release**.

AP style

Like every journalist, every PR writer should own and use *The Associated Press Stylebook* as the main source for decisions about style. A news release in **AP style** is as ready as possible for easy use by journalists. The exception is when the client organization has its own press release style. For example, the *AP Stylebook* specifies that a person's title should have initial capital letters when it precedes a name, but not when it follows the name. In contrast, a number of entertainment organizations use initial capitals wherever the title appears, and some even put titles and names in bold; these style elements are sops to executive egos, so tread lightly when suggesting a change to the more restrained AP style.

The Entertainment PR Toolbox—Media Releases

You can study hundreds of examples of media releases by going to prnewswire.com and putting the word entertainment in the search box. The elements of a media release are:

- Company or client letterhead
- FOR IMMEDIATE RELEASE (or embargo time and date)
- HEADLINE (plus optional Sub-Heads)
- Social media buttons
- Images: photos, video, and/or logo
- Dateline = CITY, state abbr., Mo. date, year
- Media Release—inverted pyramid news story format
- Lead paragraph: Who, what, when, where, why
- Quote—make it newsworthy, not fluff
- Details, background, supporting information
- Boilerplate = About (insert client name):—standard, approved client description
- PR contact information
- Image URLs for complete photo captions and attributions
- Related links to company or product website

Writing a news story

A **media release** is a complete news story written in AP style by a PR practitioner. A media release appears on a client's official letterhead or media release stationery. It states when a news organization is free to release the information to the audience, usually: **FOR IMMEDIATE RELEASE**. Rarely a release will state that its story is restricted—**EMBARGO:** NOT FOR RELEASE UNTIL 8 A.M., October 2, 2016. These days, it is easy to reach a wide audience quickly by using a news release distribution service such as PR Newswire; by sending the release at the last minute to 24-hour news channels; and/or by sending a tweet with a link to the client website, where the release is posted. Embargos are now usually reserved for such things as the full text of a speech by the president of the United States or by the chair of the Federal Reserve Board.

News stimulants—stars, stars, and $$

Journalists are looking at press releases for news value, so a publicist needs to make sure a release is as newsworthy as possible. Longtime entertainment publicist Rolf Gompertz coined the term **news stimulants** (Gompertz, 1992) to refer to factual details that add extra news value to press releases. Stimulants can include terms such as: new, limited-time, expanded, and many others. Stimulants should be factual, not fluffy adjectives—not hype like "fabulous" and "earthshattering."

To find effective stimulants for a particular release, look back to the PR plan's audience segmentation and buyer personas—the target demographics, psychographics, and geographics. Think about what will excite and interest those target groups. Stimulants in entertainment news releases include: marquee names, such as big stars and some directors; awards and nominations; big numbers such as record-breaking box-office grosses or the highest Nielsen rating for a network timeslot; the names of major media companies; and the names of major companies' CEOs and of some other well-known executives, especially for releases to the trade media.

Publicists writing entertainment news releases have potent news stimulants for their releases, because so many people are interested in—even obsessed with—stars and even lesser-known actors and entertainers. Fans of the various cast members, for example, are targets of psychographic segmentation, so the main cast should all be included in both your headlines and again in the "who" of your news story.

Headline and subheads

The **headline** and perhaps a sub-headline capture the attention of journalists. The headline is used as the subject line, when the release is sent by email to a media list (see Chapter 1).

Here is an example of a stimulating headline: Academy Award-winning Actresses Meryl Streep and Jennifer Lawrence to be directed by Oscar-winner Stephen Spielberg in $100 million-budgeted film adaptation of best-selling novel, *The End of Time*, by Jane Doe.

Although the headline and sub-head grab the attention of the journalist receiving the release, they are *almost never used* in the resulting news story. Each print outlet has its own headline style. Editors want to make the story their own. This means that the attention-grabbing news included in a headline and sub-head must also be included in the opening sentences of the news release.

Social media links

PR Newswire has updated its template to include **social media links** following the headline. These buttons make it as easy as possible for readers (including journalists) to post to their own social media, and perhaps make your story go viral on Facebook or Twitter.

Images

PR Newswire allows you to add **images** and/or a company logo right below the social media buttons. The company's research showed that releases with integrated images get picked up more frequently than those without them. See below for how to attribute images correctly by using image URLs.

Body—your news story

The body of a media release begins with the name of the city where the release originates and the date, which together are called the **dateline**. The first paragraph is a concise summary of the entire story in a sentence or two that contain the **5 W's** of the news: Who? What? When? Where? Why? And sometimes, how? Every journalist needs to know the answers to these questions to write a news story. Remember to include here variations of the same stimulants you wrote in the headline to ensure that they become part of the story.

A PR news release does NOT usually begin with a **hook** or **lead**, sometimes called a **lede**, which is a concise anecdote or quote that a journalist uses to draw the reader into the story. Except when writing a feature-style press release or adapting the news release into a feature for the client's website, PR writers should concentrate on leading with a **summary lead**, the facts of the news as conveyed by the 5 W's.

A news release is written in an **inverted pyramid story format**. This means that the most important information goes at the start (the 5 W's), followed by details, such as a newsworthy quotation, followed by background, followed by less and less important information. This is the same format journalists traditionally use when writing their news stories. When a story is structured as an inverted pyramid, an editor can easily cut the story from the end in order to fit it into the available space in the news hole of the paper. Wherever the story is cut, it still contains the 5 W's.

Approved quotations

The summary lead of a news release is followed by a **newsworthy quotation** attributed to the highest possible person in your client organization. This quote is typically drafted by the publicist, but must be approved by the person to whom it is attributed. Inside a quotation is the only appropriate place for opinion and emotion to appear in a news release. The bulk of the content of the one- to two-sentence quote, however, should be substantive information that does not appear elsewhere in the release, so journalists will have to use the quote to write a complete story. Not: "He's a great guy, and I look forward to working with him," said CEO James Smith. Rather: "His background as a line producer for the *Hunger Games* franchise makes him our ideal choice to head up our new development slate of big-budget films," said CEO James Smith.

Journalists can use a quotation from a press release as a quote in their news stories. In fact, they cannot ethically use information in the quote without attributing it to its source, which means that the publicist's boss or client will see his or her name in print. When the same quotation appears in several similar news stories, the source was most likely a media release (or a press statement, which will be discussed in Chapter 6).

In a press release about a deal between two companies or organizations or about a collaboration between two celebrities, the news release should have a quotation from each. In such cases, a release should alternate which person or company is mentioned first. Hint: Put the other's name first in the headline— which journalists don't use. Then put your own client's name first in the actual release. Then give the other side the first quotation, but have good, newsworthy information in the quote for your client, so that it gets picked up by the press.

A good quote in a news release eliminates the need for a journalist to do an in-person or phone interview, so it saves time for both the journalist and the client. Of course, some journalists will use a news release as a jumping-off point for a longer, more in-depth story. This is almost always a good thing, because it means a longer story and most likely better placement, such as the **front page above the fold**, the most visible placement, when newspaper or trade magazines are stacked, displayed on newsstands, or visible in a coin-operated box. After determining as much as possible the journalist's angle and intentions, the publicist should use her best judgment in setting up telephone or in-person interviews.

Approval process—beware

Remember that all quotations, as well as the release itself, need to be approved by all of the people and organizations involved, *before* a news release is sent to the media list. If you work for a company, stick religiously to its **approval process**. In some of the biggest companies, including entertainment companies, the CEO must approve every release and its timing, before it goes to the media. Senior management never wants to be surprised by something in the media that originated internally.

If you work for a PR agency, the release must be sent up the agency's hierarchy for approvals first. Then it must be sent to the client's point person, who will shepherd it through the company's approval process.

Never skip steps in the approval process. Sending out an unapproved release is a firing offense.

Background and less important information

Background and supporting information follow the quotation. The inverted pyramid format determines the hierarchy for deciding what comes next: most important precedes less important; and most recent precedes earlier. This means that a media release about an executive hire lists her experience in reverse chronological order: previous position; prior position; position before that, etc. The same is true for ordering background information about a star or director's previous projects—unless an earlier project was "most important," for example, winning three Grammy Awards; then most important precedes less important.

Releases about executive hires and promotions should not include personal information unrelated to the performance of the position. Exclude: age, marital status, religion, number of children, hobbies, favorite sports teams, and past accolades, such as high school state championships. In fact, high school is rarely relevant, unless, for example, a band that formed in high school is announcing that the same four people's band has been invited to open on tour for a Grammy Award – winning artist.

Boilerplate

The final text element of a media release is called the **boilerplate**, which means standard verbiage, but in the release it appears as: **About** (fill in the name of the client): Boilerplate contains a client-approved standard description of the client organization, which can be used by the journalist to add accurate information about your client into the story. Boilerplate is especially important when sending a release about lesser-known companies or sending a release to smaller news organizations where a general news reporter or weekend intern—rather than the entertainment beat reporter—may be assigned to write the story. If the release is about two or more companies, include boilerplate about each, by asking the other organization to provide its approved description.

Public relations contact(s)

PR contact information is the last necessary information (and some organizations put it at the very beginning of the release). The information should include a real person's full name, the telephone numbers of phones that are actually answered and that receive text messages, and a frequently checked email address. Since a news release is a service to the journalist, the public relations person needs to be accessible and available.

Image URLs

Instead of identifying each photograph at the top of the release, use an **image URL** that includes complete information: a **caption** stating the news value of the photo and identifying each person; source (the company); **copyright** notice (date); byline (photographer's name).

Related links

A **related link** directs the journalist to sources of further information about the client. This area could list one or more links, for example, to the company website; the annual report; a brochure; a product website, such as a special website created for a film; a press kit; or a YouTube video or channel. Most links will be to company-created material—controlled PR.

Conclusion: Repurposing Media Releases as Online Content

Today people are always plugged in. They are used to searching for and finding information whenever they need it or want it. Internet searches allow the audience to find you and allow you to communicate directly with them without having to go through an intermediary news organization. Therefore, it is important for your client or company to appear high in search results for key words related to your business and projects.

Entertainment companies strive to appear first in the search results for their names and for their intellectual property, such as film titles. Therefore, it is important to post new material frequently that can be easily and quickly found by the searching public. Any media release sent by your organization should be simultaneously posted on your website under the Press tab.

A feature article version of the news story with related color photographs and, if possible, compelling video can be featured on your landing page. Scott advises thinking like a publisher and providing information that interests your customers, as well as using Facebook, LinkedIn, Twitter, and whatever new platforms gain popularity (Scott, 2011). Efficiently repurposing news stories as feature stories gives visitors interesting content to engage them with your client's brand, and new content helps your website rise in the search ratings.

By following the guidelines for content and formatting of media releases in this chapter, you can create interesting, newsworthy stories that your target journalists will want to share with their readers. As an extra bonus, the stories can be repurposed as content for the client's website to answer the questions of customers, potential customers, and journalists.

Key Terms—In bold in the text

Sample two-sentence definition and example

5 W's: The 5 W's are who, what, where, when, and why, plus possibly how, which specify the basic information necessary for a journalist to report a news story and which therefore should appear in the summary lead of a media release. For example, a release about a television series might begin: Emmy Award – winning comedian Jerry Seinfeld will premiere his new half-hour series, *Hello Goodbye*, Thursday, Sept. 27, at 8 p.m. EDT/7 CDT to anchor CBS's new all-comedy, prime-time lineup, it was announced today by CBS Corporation President and CEO Leslie Moonves.

AP Style
Approval Process
Audience Segmentation for Film
Audience Segmentation for Television
Audience Share

Background (in news release)
Boilerplate
Buyer Persona
Buzz
Dateline
Demographics
Embargo
For Immediate Release
Front Page Above the Fold
Geographics
Headline
Hook
Households Using Television (HUTs)
Hype
Image URLs (also photo URLs)
Images
Implied Third-Party Endorsement
Inverted Pyramid Story Format
Lead
Lede
Live
Live + 3 days
Live + 7 days
Media Relations Strategy
Media Relations Tactics
Media Relations Tools
Media Release (also called a Press Release or News Release)
News Release (also called a Media Release or Press Release)
News Stimulants
Newsworthy Quotation
Nielsen Ratings
Photo Byline
Photo Caption
Photo Copyright
Press Release (also called a Media Release or News Release)
Psychographics
Public Relations Contact
Public Relations Objectives

Quadrants
Related Links
Social Media Links
Summary Lead
Total Viewers

Suggested reading and resources

Aronson, M., Spetner, D., & Ames, C. (2007). The public relations writer's handbook: The digital age (2nd ed.). San Francisco, CA: Jossey-Bass.

Associated Press. (2015, or current edition). *The Associated Press stylebook and briefing on media law*. New York, NY: Basic Books.

Gompertz, R. (1992). The Rolf Gompertz instant 3-step copy-test system. From *Publicity writing for TV & film*. North Hollywood, CA: Word Doctor.

· 3 ·

PUBLIC RELATIONS ETHICS AND UNCONTROLLED VS. CONTROLLED PR

Chapter Overview: When you finish this chapter, you should be able to answer the following questions:

- What are the ethical standards of the public relations profession?
- Why do journalists and public relations practitioners sometimes accuse each other of being unethical?
- What do codes of ethics and the FTC say about disclosure?
- What is the difference between uncontrolled PR and controlled PR, and which print, broadcast, and digital media are which?
- What are the ethical dilemmas faced by those doing digital entertainment PR?
- What are the implications of this chapter's analysis for the ethical practice of entertainment public relations?
- SIDEBAR: The Entertainment PR Toolbox—The PRSA Code of Ethics (Excerpt)

The Ethics of the Public Relations Profession

Because what entertainment companies do is so widely known and discussed, it is important to understand what ethical standards are being adhered to—or flouted. The same is true of the public relations profession in general. Sandra Duhé's 2012 thematic review of 30 years of public relations research journals, found only three studies focused specifically on ethics (p. xxiii), as well as a few that raised concerns about legality and risk.

In the first ethics-focused article, Judd (1995) alerted the profession to dislocations and displacements that might be caused by new technologies: "Technology has contributed to changing values which make it difficult to determine which behaviors will be viewed as credible" (p. 35). Judd said that in the context of "the possible conflicts between professional ethics and organizational values, practitioners need precepts which fit the times. As an approach to ethics for the information age, three precepts are proposed: (1) accept responsibility when appropriate, (2) anticipate negative effects, and (3) attempt justice" (Judd, 1995, p. 35). Sweetser (2010) discussed the ethics codes of the **Public Relations Society of America (PRSA)** and the **Word of Mouth Marketing Association (WOMMA)**, and the requirements of the Federal Trade Commission (FTC), and did an experiment that demonstrated that lack of disclosure of the company origin of an online video damaged a company's credibility. The third study by Bowen (2010) looked at the prominence of codes of ethics on corporate websites and found that, "almost 30% of the sample thought that 'communication' with them [their publics] was important enough to be emphasized on the corporate website or in policy. Including ethical principles in communications with stakeholders and working to build their trust over time" (Implications & Conclusions section), was effective, especially as a kind of credibility insurance in times of crisis.

None of these three foundational articles, however, looked beyond postings on corporate websites or the posting of online video to investigate the ethical issues connected with rapid, possibly two-way communication—the conversation model—inherent in current forms of social media, the uses of which the entertainment industry has been exploring and expanding.

Digital communication

Digital communication is changing the ways companies communicate with consumers and especially the ways consumers communicate with companies. Like other industries, the entertainment industry is trying to understand how consumers use social media and how social media influence customers' entertainment choices. Godley (2012) reported on an exclusive study for *The Hollywood Reporter* by Penn Schoen Berland, a market research and consulting firm, whose clients include Universal, Sony, and Paramount. The study surveyed 750 social network users and found that 90 percent of those 13–49 think of social networking itself as a form of entertainment, and that half of them are influenced on what to buy and watch by social media sites. In addition, 33 percent have chosen a movie based on something they read on a networking site, and almost three quarters of respondents post after seeing a movie, perhaps with the idea of influencing others.

In a heads-up to traditional movie marketers, while 40 percent of consumers still are most influenced by trailers—the traditionally most effective means of generating audience interest—and previews, "9 percent of respondents said that comments or reviews on networking sites were the biggest influencer on" moviegoing decisions (Godley, 2012). Godley calls this figure "only 9 percent," but 9 percent represents a large aggregate number of movie customers that are now being reached and influenced by social media at almost no cost to movie marketers, but also with no control by the marketers. In the music business, in which traditional sales and distribution channels have been nearly destroyed by the switch to digital, 70 percent of social media users have been influenced to listen to music based on a posting. As for television viewing, around half of viewers of reality shows and comedies post while watching (Godley, 2012).

In particular, online and digital media support the possibility of two-way symmetrical communication, the long-cherished gold standard for public relations (Grunig, 2001). The messages coming into the company from the public can allow the company to improve products, services, and relationships and to anticipate and address PR problems before they become full-blown PR crises.

The Conflicting Ethical Precepts of PR Practitioners and Journalists

Most communications students take journalism courses before they take public relations courses. Since the decline of newspaper readership, many journalists have moved into public relations positions, particularly because organizations want to post informative, interesting, newsworthy stories on their websites. This fluidity of training and employment is particularly prevalent in entertainment, but it sometimes causes confusion at the most basic level—the definition of a "story." As seen in the previous chapter, a public relations writer uses the same basic format and structure for a media release as a journalist does for a news article: the 5 W's of who, what, when, where, and why written in AP style in an inverted pyramid structure.

Journalistic ethics

The differences between a journalistic story and a public relations story result from the basic requirements of each profession concerning the scope of the preparatory research and the selection of details and quotations in the news release or news story. Newswriting students learn that **journalistic ethics** require that a story be based on **multiple sources** (with transparent attributions), be a **balanced story**, and show both sides of an issue, even in cases in which one side might be described as "fringe" by many reasonably informed and educated people. In fact, a number of tiny minority groups exploit this tenet of journalistic ethics to gain mainstream press coverage, thereby gaining the status of implied third-party endorsement for a fringe viewpoint.

Public relations ethics

Public relations ethics, on the other hand, require that a news release written by public relations tell the client's truthful story from the client's point of view. The PR person does research within the client organization to arrive at the important elements (who, what, why, where, and when) of the story to be written. The PR person selects an informative quotation from a top person in the client organization. It is not part of the PR person's job to include dissenting views, counterbalancing information, or a quote from the company's worst enemy within a media release.

Violations of journalistic ethics

Balance is the job and the ethical responsibility of the journalist or media outlet. This is one reason why many media outlets will not simply print a news release story submitted by a PR person without further research and reporting to provide balance.

Some of the entertainment trade media violate this tenet of journalism ethics and print or post news releases from trusted PR sources with little to no editing, except to create an original headline, and sometimes to add their own byline. Sometimes they do it, because they know and trust the publicist and the entertainment organization; they know that the story—as in-depth as it goes—will be truthful. Sometimes they do it, because they know that other press releases from other businesses have already told other points of view, such as the titles of other films that will open on the same weekend. And sometimes they do it, because their editors require them to meet an onerous daily quota of bylined stories. But whether or not they use the story from the media release, with or without further reporting and additional sources, and with or without their own byline, journalists should not criticize a PR person, who is doing the job she is paid to do. A PR person's job is to tell her client's story and work to get it picked up by media outlets that have readers or viewers with whom she wants to communicate.

Public relations as the source of news stories

Signs that published news stories are based in whole or in part on a press release include: multiple news outlets having the same source and/or the same quotation within a similar story; news stories with one quoted source; and stories that lack a balancing point of view.

A large percentage of print, broadcast, and online "news" begins with public relations sources such as pitches, media releases, and other company-created material, media events, and off-the-record and on-the-record interviews arranged by a public relations person. Having a mutually respectful relationship is mutually advantageous to both journalists and publicists.

Professional Codes of Ethics

The over-the-air broadcast television and radio subsidiaries of media conglomerates are regulated by the **Federal Communications Commission (FCC)**. Other conglomerate activities, including their online presence and publicity initiatives for cable, film, print media, and online and social media, are mostly unregulated.

Truth in commercial speech

The **Federal Trade Commission (FTC)** also requires that **commercial speech**—which includes public relations materials as well as advertising—be truthful. The FTC and industry organizations have been struggling to define "truthfulness" in the realm of digital communication and consumer-generated content.

Both the **Public Relations Society of America (PRSA,** 2009–2015) and the **Word of Mouth Marketing Association (WOMMA,** 2009) have Codes of Ethics. Both organizations also submitted comments to the Federal Trade Commission leading up to its revised "Guides Concerning the Use of Endorsements and Testimonials in Advertising," effective December 1, 2009.

Disclosure required

In section 255.5, "Disclosure of Material Connections," the new FTC Guides clarify that blog entries (and by extension, other forms of consumer-generated content) can be considered **sponsored content** and therefore require disclosure, when a payment is made or a product is provided for review. **Disclosure of affiliation** is required when a company representative posts on a company, product, or fan forum and even when a "street team" kid talks to his friends in order to earn concert tickets (Federal Trade Commission, 2009, p. 53143). "Example 7" under "disclosure" concerns a college student known as an expert in the video game world, who receives a new gaming system from the manufacturer. If he reviews it, "the blogger should clearly and conspicuously disclose that he received the gaming system free of charge. The manufacturer should advise him at the time it provides the gaming system that this connection should be disclosed, and it should have procedures in place to try to monitor his postings for compliance" (Federal Trade Commission, 2009, p. 53143). The FTC Guides put dual responsibility for disclosure on both the provider of a product or payment and on the blogger.

PRSA's Code of Ethics includes honesty and fairness (PRSA, 2009–2015) among its professional values. Honesty and fairness would require disclosure of the origin of social media comments and of payments in money or products to bloggers, Twitter users, or spokespeople.

So both PRSA and WOMMA Codes of Ethics support the disclosure requirements of the FTC.

The Entertainment PR Toolbox—PRSA Code of Ethics (Excerpt)

The Public Relations Society of America's Member Code of Ethics includes the following Statement of Professional Values:

"ADVOCACY
We serve the public interest by acting as responsible advocates for those we represent.

We provide a voice in the marketplace of ideas, facts, and viewpoints to aid informed public debate.

HONESTY

We adhere to the highest standards of accuracy and truth in advancing the interests of those we represent and in communicating with the public.

EXPERTISE

We acquire and responsibly use specialized knowledge and experience. We advance the profession through continued professional development, research, and education. We build mutual understanding, credibility, and relationships among a wide array of institutions and audiences.

INDEPENDENCE

We provide objective counsel to those we represent. We are accountable for our actions.

LOYALTY

We are faithful to those we represent, while honoring our obligation to serve the public interest.

FAIRNESS

We deal fairly with clients, employers, competitors, peers, vendors, the media, and the general public. We respect all opinions and support the right of free expression." (PRSA Member code, 2009–15).

The code goes on to give provisions, guidelines, and examples of improper conduct for these areas:

- Free Flow of Information
- Competition
- Disclosure of Information
- Safeguarding Confidences
- Conflicts of Interest
- Enhancing the Profession

Practicing public relations requires frequent decisions about what is or is not ethical. You can read the full text of the PRSA Member Code of Ethics at: http://www.prsa.org/AboutPRSA/Ethics/documents/Code%20 of%20Ethics.pdf

Broadcast Standards & Practices

In entertainment, broadcast television networks, including ABC (part of Disney) and NBC (part of Comcast), have **Broadcast Standards and Practices (BS&P)** departments that are responsible for making sure that a show's end credits include the names of companies that paid for product placement. The Federal Communications Commission (FCC) requires disclosure. The same end credits run whenever an episode of a show is viewed on a company-connected website.

Company blogs

On the web, Disney Parks Blog has daily, illustrated blog entries by up to a dozen company communications professionals. Using full disclosure, the executives post under their own names, titles, and pictures, so it is always clear that the company—and a specific person at the company—is responsible for the content (Disney Parks Blog, 2016). Overall, major Hollywood entertainment companies are familiar with the rules for disclosure and comply with the rules.

Celebrity endorsements

In contrast, however, paid **celebrity endorsements** on Twitter and Facebook are for the most part currently not being disclosed, even though some A-list celebrities can receive as much as $20,000 for a tweet or update (Bilton, 2013). The FTC may be looking into these violations of rules for dot-com disclosure. Mary K. Engle, the FTC's associate director of the advertising practices division is quoted by Bilton as saying, "'In a traditional ad with a celebrity, everyone assumes that they are being paid. … When it's not obvious that it is an ad, people should disclose that they are being paid'" (Bilton, 2013). When in doubt, disclose.

Uncontrolled and Controlled Public Relations, Then and Now

A myriad of ethic dilemmas—no two exactly alike—arise in the professional workplace. *Real-World Media Ethics: Inside the Broadcast and Entertainment Industries*, 2nd ed., written by entertainment professionals, gives details of numerous, varied situations that require ethical judgments (Perebinossoff, 2016). To help evaluate possible choices and actions, Perebinossoff uses a rubric based on spelling the word ethics: E = Evaluate; T = Truth; H = Harm (as in "do no harm"); I = Investigate; C = Codes of Ethics; and S = Situation (Perebinossoff, 2016). The chapter on "The Ethics of Public Relations" (Ames, 2016) focuses on how confusion between controlled versus uncontrolled PR tools can cause public relations practitioners to act unethically. Distinguishing between controlled and uncontrolled public relations is even more difficult when using social media, resulting in the need for taking a close ethics-oriented look at new media usage in entertainment.

In the past, certain public relations materials were inexpensive, but uncontrolled, and could result in valuable editorial coverage with the implied endorsement of a prestigious publication with respected writers and editors. Other kinds of company communications were controlled, but were expensive and carried no implied third-party endorsement.

Uncontrolled PR

Any public relations material or story that goes first to a media intermediary before reaching the target audience is **uncontrolled PR**. The media outlet takes control of the story and can edit it for length; augment it with further reporting; write a story that contradicts the message of the news release; or simply discard it as uninteresting, unsuitable, redundant, or irrelevant to its readers. Uncontrolled PR includes press releases, media alerts, media events such as the Television Critics Association annual event, press conferences, and interviews including the talk show appearances that are so important for movie openings. In fact, any story or message that can be touched and altered by a journalist, editor, or broadcast producer before reaching the PR person's target audience is uncontrolled. Public relations people nonetheless create and distribute uncontrolled messages, because of the value of the implied third-party endorsement. For example, when people read a profile of a director in The New York Times "Arts" section, they assume the information is accurate and trustworthy, because it has been vetted by respected journalist/editor gatekeepers.

Many PR ethical lapses occur from trying to control an instance of uncontrolled PR—i.e., to manipulate a journalist or media outlet. Western public relations professionals have long agreed that payment to journalists or news outlets for editorial coverage is unethical, because news is uncontrolled PR.

Standards in other parts of the world have been more lax, however. For example, as part of a general crackdown on widespread corruption, China arrested journalists who allegedly conspired with PR people to identify companies susceptible to extortion. Media organizations then extracted large advertising contracts from the companies in exchange for favorable press coverage or for suppressing negative reports (Buckley, 2014, Sept. 12).

Controlled PR

Any material that delivers a company message directly to the customer or audience exactly as it was created is **controlled PR**. Controlled materials include broadcast promos for TV episodes and series premieres, as well as movie trailers. U.S. newspapers label **paid content**—company-controlled content that looks like news articles—as "Advertisement," or "Special Advertising Supplement," or "Advertorial." In addition, glossy four-color brochures, newsletters, and the company's annual report used to be expensive line items in media companies' communications budgets; they were considered worth the money, however, because they delivered a precise message directly to the intended consumer.

Controlled vs. uncontrolled digital PR

These days, digital media have changed both the process of communicating with audiences and the cost equation. A company website or the website for a movie, for example, can deliver controlled content directly to audiences. Social media, such as Facebook, Twitter, YouTube, and others can also be used to deliver controlled messages. And both a website and social media can be used to create two-way conversations with fans.

Twitter and Facebook usage in entertainment reveals the complexity of untangling controlled versus uncontrolled public relations in the digital realm of online and social media. Recognizing uncontrolled PR is extremely complex. The company website and its company postings are controlled.

Consumer response postings, however, are uncontrolled, whether they are made on a company website, a consumer's personal blog, an unaffiliated Facebook page, a fan site, a Twitter account, or a YouTube video. Traditional media stories generated by a client's online or social media presence are also uncontrolled. The FTC Guidelines make it clear that it is illegal and unethical to try to gain control of a message by having someone associated with the company or paid by the company or reimbursed with products by the company post a comment, blog, or video, as if it came from a random, but enthusiastic, member of the public posting an uncontrolled, positive comment. Truth of origin, affiliation, and compensation are essential to ethical and legal public relations.

Social media allow a company to gather many kinds of customer feedback, such as online comments, survey results, Facebook likes, retweets, and even video mash-ups. But what if the customer is saying something that the company doesn't want to hear, and doesn't want other customers to hear? What if, for example, a movie company has spent more than $250 million to produce a potential blockbuster and another $100 million to distribute and market it, but a comment says, "It sucks"? And what if that comment goes viral? The moviegoer's comment is uncontrolled PR, and the situation requires an ethical decision about what to do or not do.

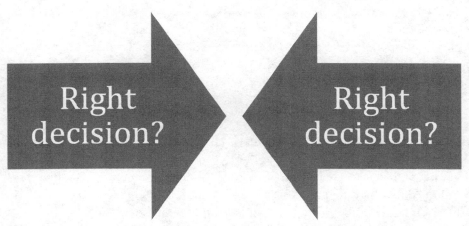

Figure 3.1: Being an ethical PR professional means applying codes of ethics to making complex decisions.

Corporate standards

One solution to the quandary about ethical uses of social media is to see these media in a broader context. Although social media are new, corporate standards are not. New media marketing guru David Meerman Scott (2011) advocates "good behavior" as a standard:

> Have guidelines about what employees can and cannot do at work, but don't try to make a specific set of blogging guidelines. I'd suggest implementing corporate policies

saying such things as employees can't sexually harass anyone, that they can't reveal secrets, that they can't use inside information to trade stock or influence prices, and that they shouldn't talk ill of the competition *in any way or via any media*. ... Rather than focus on putting guidelines on blogs (the technology), it is better to focus on guiding the way people behave. (p. 71)

The New York Times delineated a version of the "behave" standard in early 2012, when a CNN Super Bowl commentator was suspended for what CNN called a "regrettable and offensive," i.e., homophobic, tweet about a David Beckham underwear commercial. In the aftermath, *Times* writer Carr (2012) queried his own media company and learned that: "The rule at *The Times* is that there is no rule, but there is an expectation, as Philip B. Corbett, the standards editor for the paper, told me in an e-mail: 'We expect *Times* journalists to behave like *Times* journalists, and generally they do'" (p. B7). The moral seems to be for people to "behave," to use common sense, and to think before they tweet. Without specific examples of "good behavior" and a code of ethics or a rubric against which to judge a complex situation, however, people may respond emotionally, rather than ethically. Social media technology allows such instantaneous expressions of emotion that the requisite pause to reflect and to make an ethical decision is frequently skipped.

Entertainment Ethics Online

In the past, the corporate headquarters of entertainment companies pre-approved all outgoing press releases and marketing campaigns, a process the author is familiar with from her twenty years as a public relations practitioner in the entertainment business. Any campaign or communication, visual element, phrase, or even word that breached boundaries of taste or ethics had to be justified in advance at the highest levels ... or had to be changed. Today, given the ubiquity and speed of digital and social media, including multiple company and brand websites, Facebook, Twitter, and other social media that require frequent and speedy updating, tight corporate oversight is often impractical and sometimes impossible. While entertainment companies still strive to achieve advanced approval on messages, companies that have been known for the creativity of their marketing and PR campaigns now oftentimes have to trust that their more decentralized communications workforce will hew to acceptable ethical standards.

Companies' digital footprints

Many Hollywood entertainment websites are sophisticated and offer consumers numerous capabilities: to watch trailers, full episodes of television shows, or specially created webisodes; to shop, take surveys, or participate in contests; to read blogs by company personnel, actors, and fictional characters that allow for consumer comments; and/or to post video or links to YouTube and other social media. Entertainment companies' social media may include: Facebook pages for the company, as well as for various products such as individual TV shows, or even for fictional characters; a number of Twitter accounts and hashtags, some for fictional characters; official fan sites (and numerous external and unofficial fan sites); and iPhone or other mobile applications.

The online presence of entertainment companies is now complex and varied. Especially appealing for entertainment entities are live chats with celebrities, while a "Press Room" with news releases posted in reverse chronological order is now a standard feature of company websites. Pettigrew and Reber's 2010 study demonstrated the importance of an online pressroom for gaining media coverage. To make a broad swath of information available to the press, the newsroom on The Walt Disney Company site, for example, includes an archive of press releases dating back to 2001; an archive of videos and photos dating back to 2002; an RSS newsfeed; and a Social Media Index (The Walt Disney Company, 2012). The Social Media Index shows the extent of this entertainment company's adoption of social media. For Disney brands, there are: 423 Facebook pages; 66 Twitter handles; and 115 YouTube channels. There are dozens of others each for ABC, ESPN, and Marvel (The Walt Disney Company, 2012).

24/7 deadlines

As everywhere else in business, the entertainment industry is trying to adapt to the new demands of 24/7 journalist deadlines and a wild-west "post and scoop, then confirm and correct" process, even at mainstream newspaper websites. Throughout entertainment news, there is cutthroat competition for scoops and exclusives. For example, in print and online, the Calendar section of the *Los Angeles Times* competes with the "Arts" section of *The New York Times*, as well as with entertainment coverage in other major national and regional newspapers. In addition, the former entertainment daily trade papers, *Daily Variety* and *The Hollywood Reporter*, now publish four-color, magazine-style weeklies that supplement their 24/7 breaking news websites, variety.com and hollywoodreporter.com. Both sites compete aggressively with deadlinehollywood.com; TMZ.com; perezhilton.com; and dozens of other gossip sites. In broadcast, competitors include daily syndicated shows such as *Entertainment Tonight*, *Access Hollywood*, and *The Insider*, as well as hours of programming on cable channels such as E! Entertainment Television, Bravo, MTV, and others.

One strategy for servicing the needs and demands of this vast news enterprise is for entertainment public relations departments to have as much company-controlled content as possible available online. This helps journalists easily find what they need and confirm facts, whatever time, day or night, weekend or holiday, that they are writing their stories.

Each online company platform for content and communication has a voracious need for timely updates and new material. **Search Engine Optimization (SEO)** means frequently posting new material, using keywords, and establishing links with other sites. Sites that post frequently move up in search results and are therefore seen and visited by more potential customers.

Innovations bring confusion

Each online platform and each piece of content can also present ethical dilemmas, because of ongoing confusion about which elements are controlled versus uncontrolled. For example, the confirmed trend of viewing two-screens simultaneously (TV plus computer, laptop, iPad, or mobile device) has led to such innovations as *The Voice* having a social media correspondent to answer fans' Twitter questions during the show. Afterwards the correspondent hosts a live-streaming, online interview show on nbc.com to facilitate answering fans' questions (Nededog, 2012). This new option, of course, drives traffic to the NBC website, where the after-show is sponsored by Sprint, and where NBC sells other advertising. The site also showcases a variety of controlled content, including the night's lineup with links to program pages. For example, the program page for *Late Night with Seth Meyers* has: an episode guide for full episodes, video, and photo galleries (all sponsored); a shop; social media links to Facebook, Twitter, Tumblr, Pinterest, YouTube, and Instagram (all controlled); and a message board called NBC Peacock Panel (uncontrolled, but requiring registration and a survey, before allowing participation). Like the live streaming of the after-show for *The Voice*, these program-page elements, are examples of the entertainment industry innovating to integrate social media into their television shows and integrate their TV shows into social media.

As reported in the *Los Angeles Times*, social viewing of television has increased 800 percent year over year, according to Bluefin Labs, which tracks social media trends, and "Nielson found that 45% of consumers who used a tablet computer while watching TV were looking for information related to the show they were watching" (Chmielewski, 2012). To ride the trend, a consortium of television station owners in 40 major TV markets launched an app for laptops and tablets from ConnecTV that uses sound recognition to identify the program being watched—even if it is prerecorded. The stations then provide simultaneous supplementary information such as athlete bios and stats, polls, or an online viewing party/chat hosted by a local anchor or sportscaster (Chmielewski, 2012). In the process, these integrations may muddle the distinctions between controlled and uncontrolled PR.

Twitter and Facebook

Twitter represents a hybrid of controlled and uncontrolled PR. Company tweets are controlled. Retweets are controlled; as a bonus, they carry the potential influence of third-party endorsement as they are fed out to the followers of the retweeter. The retweet is essentially the corporate message in its original, company-worded form (controlled). What could be better than a company-controlled message with third-party endorsement? In entertainment public relations, and tweets (and therefore their "endorsed" retweets) can include links to the company website (controlled); a company-posted photo gallery (controlled); a behind-the-scenes, company-created video or blooper reel (controlled); or the official movie trailer, perhaps on the official movie website complete with extra features (all controlled). The consumer is getting the message exactly as created by the company. Additionally on that linked site, the company can include all the usual press kit materials, which traditionally became uncontrolled as they went out to media, but as tweeted or retweeted and linked to the website are controlled! The consumer gets the message—this film is action packed … exciting … intriguing … sweet or. … Publicists can fill in the blanks of their awareness objective statements and deliver their messages directly to their target audience.

Landing pages can also include opportunities to press "Like," thereby linking the company message to Facebook and sending it on direct feeds to Facebook friends (controlled), third-party endorsement included. And to be extra helpful, it is now easy for any film's landing page to include a link that converts consumer interest into a purchase, with a direct link to online, advanced sales of tickets for nearby theaters. This is why Twitter has become such an important tool for publicizing movies and myriad other forms of entertainment. In fact, most entertainment companies no longer print, compile, or distribute physical press kits. Press kit material has all migrated to online availability.

Customer comments

With so much material online, pages can also include opportunities for comments (uncontrolled PR), which can be either positive or negative. Comments can push the boundaries of taste, and at times raise ethical issues for the company. When questionable fan behavior takes place on a company site or in a social medium that links to the company, the company has to choose from possible courses of action, for example: A. no action and no acknowledgment, which can be seen as condoning the behavior or as allowing other members of the online community to verbally discipline the user; B. removing the offending comment, with no explanation, which also condones the comment if others have already seen and retweeted or forwarded it; C. removing the message and making an official statement, disavowing the comment. Because of the "H = do-no-harm" ethical imperative (Perebinossoff, 2016), companies need to take action when negative emotions in incoming consumer messages cross the line into racism, hate speech, or threats of violence.

Sports entertainment riles up fans to extreme emotional highs and lows, and people are now tweeting and posting during the heat of the moment. For example, in late April 2012, when the Boston Bruins lost Game 7 of the first round of National Hockey League playoffs in overtime, various response types were used by stakeholders in different media. A number of irate Boston Bruin fans posted racist comments about Joel Ward, the black Washington Capitals player, who scored the winning goal against the Boston team.

In the aftermath, which was covered widely as perhaps representing the city of Boston's old reputation for being racially polarized (Goodnough, 2012), the team issued a press statement. As reported on BostonHerald.com, the press statement said, "The Bruins are very disappointed by the racist comments that were made following the game last night. These classless, ignorant views are in no way a reflection of anyone associated with the Bruins organization"

(Wedge, 2012). The numerous comments on the online BostonHerald.com article resulted in a number of cases of response type A, letting vehement but not outright racist comments stand and subsequently be soundly criticized by other commentators. In addition, in an instance of response C, one comment was replaced with, "Sorry, but the post that was in this spot has been removed as it did not follow our guidelines," which are, a click-through shows: "The Boston Herald welcomes thoughts and opinions related to its articles. Please stay on topic and be respectful of others. Stick to the issues being discussed, and avoid ad hominem (personal) attacks. Keep the conversation appropriate for all interested readers" (BostonHerald.com, 2012). Companies need to monitor what is being said about them and about others when comments are linked to them twenty-four hours a day.

Deciding on a response

Most large companies now use outside firms to scan and block spam and outsiders' promotional messages. After that filtering, according to a Disney social media manager, the company uses a decision tree matrix to decide how to respond to negative comments, and focuses particular attention on those that are derogatory or that involve safety issues (personal communication, April 24, 2012). Unlike bostonherald.com, Disney Parks Blog, for example, is not a news organization and has no commitment to presenting all points of view, as demonstrated by its comments policy. Its policy is prominently displayed in a bright-colored "Comments Policy" notice at the end of the right-hand column on the home page:

> Thanks for visiting the Disney Parks Blog. We welcome your comments. Please understand that this is a moderated blog. Blog comments will be reviewed prior to posting. As a result, there will be a delay in the posting of comments. Not all comments will be posted. Comments may also be removed after they are posted. (Disney Parks Blog, 2016, February 3)

This level of pre-censorship might seem excessive, or an invitation to abuse or unethical behavior in trying to control what is actually uncontrolled PR. At least in the case of Disney, as noted below, however, a critical comment that is blocked from the official (controlled) page, could likely find an airing on one of the many fan-run (uncontrolled) sites. Therefore, it's important for Disney, or any company, to carefully consider whether it would be best to allow the comment on the corporate site and to make an official response or allow other commenters to respond, rather than to ban the comment so that it migrates to a completely uncontrolled fan site.

One example of a social media response decision matrix is attributable—not to Disney—but to the Air Force. The flow chart guides the decision whether to respond and how to respond, keeping in mind that any response should consider transparency, sourcing, timeliness, tone, and the influence of the blog (Air Force, n.d.). Critics of such decision tools may feel that such pre-planning undermines the very idea of social media—that these new media erase the distinctions between individuals and organizations so that they can "converse" on a one-to-one, equal basis.

The Disney social manager said that most Twitter messages are thought out, planned, and approved several weeks in advance, but managers can tweet live, for example, if there is a possible safety issue at the park or if there are capacity, traffic, or parking issues (personal communication, April 24, 2012). The California parks and their parking reached capacity during the evening of their wildly successful "One More Disney Day" promotion in Anaheim, when the parks stayed open for the extra leap year day from 6 a.m. February 29 to 6 a.m. March 1, 2012. In such cases, live, impromptu (but informed) Twitter messages are effective for communicating updates with Disney's guests, more than 900,000 of whom follow the California Disneyland Resort on Twitter (Disneyland Resort Twitter, 2016, February 3).

Unofficial, uncontrolled sites

For special events, as well as on regular days, a portion of Disney's guests are fervent annual pass holders, who visit the parks often and use official and unofficial apps to be up-to-the-minute on wait times for rides and the locations of Disney characters (Smith, 2011). Although Disney was a bit late to Twitter, there are also numerous official (controlled) and unofficial or fan (uncontrolled) Disney-related Twitter accounts. In fact in 2010 after three years of fan use, Twitter took the Twitter handle @Disney away from a fan named Cheri Thomas, although she seemed to be neither impersonating the company nor trying to mislead others, either of which would violate Twitter's terms of use. A prominent Disney fan blogger wrote, "Obviously, in the end Twitter can do what they want. Disney is always an 800lb monster in the corner and you pretty much have to do what they say or be prepared for the consequences. But this is just uncool and the act of a bully" (Frost, 2010). This blog entry generated three-dozen comments over the next few days. The site where the conversation took place was "The Disney Blog," which sounds official and controlled, but is not. As subtitled in small print, it is "Disney News and Information—By fans, for fans" (uncontrolled). Founded by blogger John Frost, this is one of a number of unofficial (uncontrolled) fan sites that cover everything Disney in obsessive detail.

A question raised by Frost in his May 17, 2010, post, was why did Disney need this handle when they were already communicating on Twitter through numerous others? A few years later, the answer was clear: @Disney (now official, controlled) had 4.73 million followers (@Disney, 2016); and it ranked #2 in a Google search for "Disney" (behind only Disney.com). It tweets information and promotions, short animated video excerpts, and links to other Disney sites and pages full of public relations content (controlled).

Official blogs

Disney now breaks its own news on its own official Disney Parks Blog (Disney Parks Blog, 2016), which was named a finalist as a top corporate blog by Socialfresh in 2011 (Keath, 2011). With an RSS feed and numerous bylined executive posts daily, the Disney Parks Blog now often also posts its own news stories rather than sending news releases to reporters. A new redesign is also anticipated to eliminate the need for Facebook, so that Disney content stays on Disney-owned sites. Disney executives apparently believe that their company has the prominence and active fans to bring the audience to them. Furthermore, on their own blog site, Disney, rather than Facebook, owns the consumer contact information and metrics, as well as the content (controlled). In this regard, Disney's Terms of Use are problematic. Basically, anything posted by anyone on any official Disney site becomes the property of Disney, if the company even allows the comment to be posted. The question then becomes, when does the ability to control become too much control … and therefore unethical?

Twitter spats

Uncontrolled PR such as consumer tweets can damage entertainment brands, including celebrity brands. An example would be the Twitter spats that erupt frequently in the entertainment world, because of "'a combination of self-importance gone awry, the headiness of having followers, the lack of self-censorship and wanting to draw attention to oneself,'" according to Carole

Lieberman, a psychiatrist quoted in *The New York Times* (Considine, 2012). Whether it is Judd Apatow criticizing Howard Stern's relentless satellite radio promotion of his gig as a judge on *America's Got Talent,* or Courtney Love taking on a rumor about her daughter and an older musician, such bashing comments violate Perebinossoff's ethical imperative of H=do no harm (2016), as well as Scott's "behave" imperative not to "talk ill of the competition *in any way or via any media*" (Scott, 2011, p. 71).

One could say that all celebrities are competitors with one another for the public's attention at any given moment. Twitter is a public arena, so all Twitter users are also competitors with every other Twitter user for followers and retweets. Lieberman is quoted as saying of a Twitter put-down, "It's not really to communicate some bone of contention, it's to humiliate the person in front of the whole world. ... Social media in general, and Twitter in particular, is the coward's way of expressing yourself" (Considine, 2012). These are reasons why ethics and many corporate standards explicitly dictate staying positive in messages and responses. Using the "behave" standard, therefore, means following the old parental dictum, "If you can't say something nice, don't say anything at all." Using Twitter to do unethical verbal harm results in consequences from looking like a bully (Love criticizing her daughter) to having a comment taken down, or Love reportedly having to pay damages, after she Twitter-attacked a designer (Considine, 2012).

Social media as megaphones

On the other hand, Twitter can function as a digital version of a bully pulpit to magnify an individual voice—particularly that of a celebrity with millions of followers—to be more equal to that of a large corporation. An example is Kim Kardashian tweeting about personal items being stolen from her suitcase: "Very disappointed in British Airways for opening my luggage & taking some special items of mine. Some things are sentimental and not replaceable," with the report concluding that if the company doesn't find the culprit, "Kim's going to the cops" (TMZ.com, 2012).

In another example, actor Tim Daly used his Twitter to break the news that his *Private Practice* (ABC/Disney) character would not be back for Season 6. His tweet was picked up as a scoop by DeadlineHollywood.com (Andreeva, 2012a). By using Twitter, Daly controlled the disappointing message as much as possible by including a few words akin to a press statement: "It was a great 5 yrs. R.I.P. Pete Wilder" (Daly, 2012). During the next couple of days, the tweet (controlled) generated no public conversations on Daly's Twitter. On DeadlineHollywood.com, however, the article (uncontrolled) generated 10 responses within two days: one positive about Daly; several negative about Daly, or about the show with or without Daly; one highly critical of Daly for not thanking the producer for giving him five years of work, and one highly critical of the producer for not calling Daly personally, but notifying him through his agent. The difference in responses shows the advantage of controlling the message and using a controlled medium.

Avoiding two-way conversations

On the issue of two-way communication, current usage shows entertainment companies pushing messages outward or perhaps posting a provocative question for discussion, but rarely responding to individual consumer questions and posts. Currently entertainment companies do not take full advantage of the possibilities for two-way communication inherent in the "social" of social media. There are few "conversations," at least between entertainment companies and individual fans, though conversations certainly exist among fans themselves. One explanation is that entertainment brands have such a massive audience that individual responses are impossible.

Controlling timing and context

Given this chapter's analysis of the ethics of controlled versus uncontrolled public relations, however, there is another explanation. A company's outgoing messages and online posts are controlled, not just in their content, but also in their timing and their context. To respond to a consumer's social media message, comment, or blog entry, however, means that the company is reacting (playing defense) rather than being active (playing offense). Defense offers less control than offense. In baseball, the rules require that the offense and defense change roles every half inning. But in business, why play defense, if no rules require it?

Responding to consumer messages also requires losing control of the timing of the message. Perhaps the company intended to make the announcement the next week when the star or a specific executive would be available to give interviews. Maybe the plan was to announce the news a month later, when coverage would become part of the PR build-up to the movie premiere. In these cases, as long as the customer comment on a rumor is positive or neutral, it's probably best just to let customers get one another excited, rather than to reply and confirm. If the comment is negative and generates negative commentary, then companies move to a strategy of crisis control.

Responding to consumer comments also cedes control of context. The best context for an important announcement by an entertainment company will probably always be a press event at an attractive (set-dressed) location on the studio lot. This context conveys the glamour of Hollywood and the importance of the company. Also, security guards at the studio gate restrict access to previously credentialed journalists and bloggers. The equivalent context online is the company's own website. In contrast, responding to a consumer comment might put the company response in the context of a fan site or one of the hostile "Company X sucks" sites. It's little wonder, then, that major entertainment companies are reluctant to engage in "conversations" with fans or frenemies, or that when they do engage with consumers, they first use a social media response matrix to guide the why, where, and how.

Conclusion: Ethical Implications for the Practice of Entertainment PR

Hollywood entertainment faces ethical scrutiny. Active, aggressive news competitors follow all areas of the entertainment industry and report on innovations, as well as lapses in judgment and ethics. News oversight and regulatory oversight by the FCC and the FTC, especially since the publication of the new FTC Guides of 2009, help keep entertainment companies compliant in the realm of disclosure of commercial interest or product placement. Nevertheless, undisclosed payments are rampant in the area of celebrity tweets and posts. The codes of ethics of PRSA and WOMMA, Perebinossoff's ETHICS rubric, and other corporate standards, all provide guidance for ethical public relations decision making in any industry or enterprise, including entertainment.

This chapter's findings expand conventional practice of public relations by showing the necessity for ethical decision making and of distinguishing between controlled PR and uncontrolled PR, although the distinctions are especially difficult in the realm of social media. In fact, social media provide numerous, inexpensive new ways to control the public relations message by delivering it directly to customers in the controlled form, timing, and context the company prefers.

There is a tension between the capability of social media to promote two-way symmetrical communication—long the gold standard for public relations—versus the ways that social media allow a company to control the message content, timing, and context. Currently, with major entertainment companies—Disney being a primary example—control is winning out over the two-way conversation model.

Entertainment companies such as Disney have been leading the way by devoting large budgets to social media infrastructure and staffing. These findings regarding the ethical and ethically challenged uses of social media in entertainment can serve as exemplars and warnings for smaller organizations, as they make decisions on how and where to deploy their limited resources while avoiding ethical lapses.

Key Terms—In bold in the text

Sample two-sentence definition and example

Balanced Story: A balanced story is an ethical standard for journalists, which means they should seek input from all of the primary participants in a news story, as opposed to a public relations media release or pitch, which tells the client's story from the client's point of view. For example, when a publicist for a movie sends out a media release about on-location filming in Chicago, in the published story the journalist might also quote angry residents of the neighborhood where streets are closed for shooting.

Broadcast Standards & Practices (BS&P)
Celebrity Endorsement
Commercial Speech
Controlled PR
Disclosure of Affiliation
Federal Communications Commission (FCC)
Federal Trade Commission (FTC)
Journalistic Ethics
Multiple Sources
Paid Content
Public Relations Ethics
Public Relations Society of America (PRSA)
Search Engine Optimization (SEO)
Sponsored Content

Uncontrolled PR
Word of Mouth Marketing Association (WOMMA)

Suggested reading and resources

Duhé, S. C. (Ed.). (2012). *New media and public relations* (2nd ed.). New York, NY: Peter Lang.

Federal Trade Commission (FTC). (2009). 16 CFR Part 255, Guides concerning the use of endorsements and testimonials in advertising. *Federal Register, 74*(198), 15 October, 53124–53143.

Perebinossoff, P. (2016). *Real-world media ethics: Inside the broadcast & entertainment industries* (2nd ed.). Boston, MA: Focal Press.

Public Relations Society of America (PRSA). (2009–2015). PRSA Member code of ethics. Retrieved from http://www.prsa.org/AboutPRSA/Ethics/documents/Code%20of%20 Ethics.pdf

Stein, A. (2011). *Why we love Disney: The power of the Disney brand.* New York, NY: Peter Lang.

Word of Mouth Marketing Association (WOMMA). (2009). WOMMA ethics code. Retrieved from http://womma.org/ethics

· 4 ·

HOLLYWOOD RED-CARPET EVENTS—HOW THE WORLD KNOWS THE BUSINESS

Chapter Overview: When you finish this chapter, you should be able to answer the following questions:

- What objectives can an event strategy achieve?
- What are the five elements of any party?
- How can an award event achieve public relations objectives for a client?
- How do you motivate media to attend and cover an event?
- What industry WOW factors are needed for a successful entertainment event?
- Who produces the Academy Awards, the Emmy Awards, and the Grammy Awards, and why?
- Who benefits from an award show?
- What are the major kinds of events in the entertainment industry?
- What are the implications of an event strategy for the practice of public relations?
- SIDEBAR: The Entertainment PR Toolbox—Media Alerts
- SIDEBAR: The Biz Markets Itself—The Emmys

Introduction

Everybody loves a party, and Hollywood people are no exceptions. The industry parties frequently and on a lavish scale. The kinds of events produced in the entertainment world are similar to those in other communities and other industries, but the scale is usually grander. Entertainment industry events go for the WOW factor.

This chapter looks at the rationale for major television broadcasts of industry award events, which are watched each year by millions of people. The analysis will include a look at the non-profit organizations that produce the entertainment industry events and what these organizations, their industries, and specific people, companies, and entertainment products gain from the events. One SIDEBAR in this chapter explains the structure and purpose of the media advisory, which is used to interest the media in attending an event to file a news story. The other SIDEBAR discusses the strategy and importance of the Emmy Awards within the television industry.

PR Objectives of an Event Strategy

The chapter also looks at the objectives of typical entertainment industry events. Of course an event should leave a positive and memorable impression on attendees. But just as important for a public relations event is gaining media coverage. Media coverage creates awareness for a new product or an organization. Other objectives can include raising money for philanthropic and educational causes and recruiting volunteers and supporters.

The Five Elements of Any Party

Think about what you need to create a memorable birthday party for a 4-year-old.

First, you need to decide on your guest list: who and how many? Here you have to make some difficult choices: At this age, kids already have some favorite close friends, and some others whose parents will be hurt if they're not invited. Do you invite everybody? Do you invite your own friends? The family? You have to remember the wishes and personality of the honoree. Once you decide on the list you can pick the invitations, which can also match the theme. **Element #1: guest list/invitations.**

Next, or simultaneously with deciding the guest list, where will you have it? What **venue**—place—will work for your party? Your apartment? If you're inviting five or six kids, and expect at least one parent of each to stick around, you may need more space. Grandma's backyard? It's bordered by a beautiful, but very spiny cactus garden. The park! The picnic tables right near the swing set and jungle gym will provide enough space for the active energy of your young guests. The parents can sit and chat at the tables. You'll be able to string decorations and balloons among the nearby trees, for festive décor, possibly themed to the birthday child's favorite toy or cartoon character. At the same time, you'll need to think about availability dates of the venue and the timing. The yard or park might be too hot mid-day, but comfortably shaded by mid-afternoon. **Element #2: venue/décor/date**.

Whether they're age 4 or 44, partygoers get hungry and thirsty. At a birthday party, guests expect a cake, and for young children apple juice or another healthy drink. But what else will you serve? For kids' parties, snacks and finger foods are pretty much assumed. For adult parties, the designated time on the invitation often tells the story; 5–7 p.m. implies drinks and hors d'oeuvres, while 7–10 implies dinner. Still better is to state it on the invitation: pizza and birthday cake. An invitee who eats only gluten free or is wheat-intolerant is forewarned. **Element #3: food (and drinks)**.

What will the guests do at the party? Four-year-olds (and lots of older people) aren't so great at conversation—especially when there are bigger crowds and more people and excitement than they're used to. Entertainment gives the guests a focus and makes the party memorable. At the park, the playground equipment may be all you need, or you may want some simple games, or a low-keyed entertainer, such as someone who can twist skinny balloons into amazing shapes. **Element #4: entertainment**.

How will the guests remember the party? At a kid's birthday party, receiving a party bag with the goodbyes eases the sting of having seen someone else being honored with a pile of gifts. **Element #5: souvenir gift bag**.

With these five elements, planned to the scale and budget of the occasion, any party can be enjoyable and memorable for the attendees.

An Award Event as a Public Relations Strategy

Events thrown for public relations purposes have objectives beyond just the enjoyment of the invited guests.

Fundraising objective

An **award event strategy** is used by non-profit, community, trade, and business organizations that have a **fundraising objective** in order to raise money for the organization's survival and its humanitarian or advocacy mission. Organizations in towns nationwide name a Teacher, Humanitarian, Coach, Team Parent, or Business Leader of the Year. The award—often commemorated with an engraved plaque or trophy—is presented at a ceremony at an appropriately sized venue, to which the honoree and others have invited a number of family members, friends, and business associates. The guests pay for the privilege of sharing the honoree's special night, which can include a dinner, speeches, and entertainment. People leave with at least a souvenir program booklet. Profits from ticket sales and ad sales for the souvenir program provide financial support for the organization as a whole, or for a designated special project, such as college scholarships. Usually guests also leave with a commemorative gift ranging from a logo item such as a mug or baseball hat to a more elaborate party bag of items that businesses have donated to the organization in exchange for a tax deduction.

However elaborate or simple any award event may be, the organizers need to consider the five elements: #1—guest list/invitations; #2—venue/décor/date; #3—food (and drinks); #4—entertainment; #5—souvenir gift bag.

Entertainment industry events

Entertainment folks also love to honor their own, especially those who are willing to allow their own names and the names in their contact lists to be used to ensure a large attendance at an event to raise money for a charity they support. Like local organizations everywhere, the entertainment industry parties with a purpose—or at least two purposes.

The first objective is to leave a lasting impression on attendees so that they will think about the organization fondly, donate regularly, and attend again next year.

Media coverage objective

The second, and even more important, objective is the **media coverage objective**. Whether it is coverage in the social column of the local newspaper, on the nightly news broadcast live from the Governors Ball of the Academy

Awards, or in the color-photo pages of the weekly versions of *The Hollywood Reporter* and *Variety*, organizers and honorees love to be "in the news." The public relations tool used to invite the press to an event to achieve media coverage is the **media alert**, which is covered in detail in the SIDEBAR.

The Entertainment PR Toolbox—Media Alerts

The **Media Alert** is also known as a **Media Advisory** or a **Media Tip Sheet**. Whatever it is called, it functions as a press invitation for a print journalist, photographer, or broadcast reporter and camera crew to come to a specific place at a specific time to observe or participate in an event in order to compile the elements of a news story, including photo and video tape opportunities. Note that it is an invitation, and the page layout is similar to that of an invitation, except that it has a headline:

Company or client letterhead

FOR IMMEDIATE RELEASE (send about 10 days before the event)

> ***MEDIA ALERT FOR (DAY OF WEEK), DATE (of the actual event—centered)***

> HEADLINE (in capital letters, centered) Include famous VIP names first and then the hosting organization)

(The remainder of the release is formatted like an invitation):

WHO: Using an indented paragraph format, expand on the news stimulants in the headline, leading with the client organization, and then hitting on the main elements that will interest the press, particularly the broadcast media.

WHAT: A brief description of the event itself, including admission information, if the event is also open to the public, as well as to the media.

WHEN: Day of week, date (same as in the alert line above)

(Time):	Media check-in
(Time):	Arrivals or cocktails
(Time)	Main event
(Time)	Reception

WHERE: Venue name
            Street address
            City, State zip code

INFO: (or WHY, or BACKGROUND, or elements that will be available to the press only by attending.)

MEDIA R.S.V.P. (telephone number and/or special RSVP email address, plus information about credentials, parking, check-in, equipment needed)

ABOUT: (Boilerplate about the organization and/or event)
MEDIA CONTACTS:
name of the PR person(s)
company or PR agency
telephone numbers
email addresses

Awareness objective

News coverage serves a purpose beyond ego gratification. Events are too labor intensive and too expensive to influence only the attendees. The news reports raise the organization's awareness profile in the community, thus achieving the **awareness objective**. By viewers and readers becoming aware of what they have missed, they may also be motivated to donate to the organization's cause this year and/or to decide to volunteer or attend the next year … if there is a next year. Hede and Kellett (2011) reported that research has shown that people rely more on their pleasant memories of an event, rather than on marketing communications, to influence them to attend again. While a one-time event such as an organizational anniversary or a major donor's birthday can be used to raise both awareness and money, one-time events are more labor-intensive than repeated ones.

Having the same event again the next year—continuity—is an important part of an effective event strategy. Events build momentum through their media coverage and through positive word of mouth. In fact, research has shown that word of mouth is crucial to creating awareness for events (Hede & Kellett, 2011). Experienced event planners know how important it is for the inner circle of an organization, such as board members and the honorary event committee, to personally contact invitees to solidify attendance at an event.

Given the importance of fond memories and personal communication, organizations—and their public relations teams—should see a new event as a long-term strategy. An effective event strategy requires an ongoing, multi-year commitment to achieve results of media coverage, awareness, donations, ticket sales, and prestige that are commensurate with the amount of resources, effort, and time commitment required to produce a successful event. The good news here is that each year's event provides a template for the next year's event, so that the organization and the public relations staff can reach higher objectives with somewhat less effort each year, for example: increasing attendees by 10 percent; increasing money raised by 15 percent; and increasing media coverage in broadcast and print, evaluated on placement, prestige, frequency, and reach, as well as on website page views and social media metrics.

For an attendance objective, if this year's event had 100 attendees (10 tables of 10), a 10 percent increase is one more table of ten, which is both achievable and measurable. In certain circumstances, especially in the early years of an event before the chosen venue is filled to capacity, a larger percentage increase may be achievable.

For a financial or net profits objective, as an event becomes increasingly well known and especially after the venue begins to sell out, ticket prices can be increased. So can the price and number of congratulatory ads in the souvenir program booklet.

For a media placement objective, the public relations practitioner can gain more media coverage by reminding outlets of coverage the previous year. Editors and segment producers don't want to miss out on a story that "everybody" is covering.

Parties with Hollywood WOW Factors

Entertainment industry events need the same five party elements as a kid's party. However, expectations are higher, the guests and the news media are more jaded, and therefore budgets are necessarily bigger. Each of the five party elements needs to be magnified and exaggerated so that a jaded industry guest walks into the room and can only say, "WOW!"

WOW Factor #1: Guest list/invitations

Stars, stars, and more stars! People in Hollywood—and everywhere else—want to rub elbows with the glamorous, the famous, and even the infamous. Therefore, the #1 WOW factor for industry parties is star power. Party planners in Los Angeles spend an inordinate amount of time trying to figure out who should be put on the A-list—the list of people to invite earliest and court hardest to attend by going through all their connections and representatives. The producers of a premiere for a major motion picture have an edge in creating the "must attend" buzz that party planners hope will lead to publicists begging for invitations for their clients. Since legal contracts require a film's stars to participate in pre-opening publicity appearances, everyone invited knows that the stars will be at their movie's premiere, helping create interest and anticipation.

Entertainment public relations people would probably agree—off the record at least—that aside from their own clients—only the biggest movie stars and solo music artists at the height of their fame are automatically considered part of everyone's A-list. HBO stars and the stars of the most popular network television hour dramas may have a similar magnetism for attracting great party invitations. For a look at the vagaries of the New York party A-list, see, "'Hey, Why Wasn't I invited?'" (Griffith, 2015).

Here is a conundrum that entertainment industry party producers always face: The less often that a star attends events, the more sought-after as a guest. The most exciting party guest is someone who never goes to parties! Greta Garbo would have been a great party "get" in her time. Before George Clooney's marriage when he was considered one of the most eligible bachelors on the planet, the star was brilliant at rationing his party-going appearances to enhance the news value of events for movies he was involved with and causes he supported. The rest of the time, he was out of sight, off the party circuit, living in northern Italy. For party producers, the bigger the star and the more stars the better. With a firm commitment from an A-lister or two or three, commitments from others are easier, because party guests like to be part of an exclusive crowd that reflects well on their own social status and their self-images.

On her cable show, *My Life on the D-List*, Kathy Griffith made fun of the grip that the concept of the A-list has on Hollywood event planners and social climbers. Down from the A-list mentioned above are celebrities known for being known. Many of these collect substantial appearance fees, for example, just for showing up for 15 minutes and being photographed by the paparazzi outside a new nightclub that wants a reputation for being hot or "in." These celebs-for-hire are often part of the current crop of cable reality "stars." In fact, cast members' contracts for a reality show may include publicity help, because the channel may be partnered with the cast and get a percentage of their income from every source. Is the organization planning the party willing to pay someone to attend? A business wanting to make a splash in the media may be willing to pay. But should a non-profit pay for party guests to attend a party to raise funds?

WOW Factor #2: Venue/décor/date

How can the choice of venue attract A-list guests and make news? One way to make news is to choose a new location, one that has never before hosted an event. This might be a newly refurbished historical property, or a lavish estate that has recently been bought by someone public and publicity minded, such as the CEO of a hot Silicon Beach tech company. Members of the public (and the media and television news viewers) covet a peek at a private place that is usually closed to the public. The ultimate party venue of this type for Hollywood would be the new, or newly remodeled home of a reclusive star of the year's biggest blockbuster film.

Partygoers also like to have a look at a public place when it is normally closed—such as a late-night Halloween party in the medieval wing of a museum. The *Night at the Museum* film franchise shows how evocative "trespassing" can be. In fact, the Hollywood Forever Cemetery hosts a yearly, paid-admission Day of the Dead event, as well as a summer schedule of outdoor movie screenings. Other cemeteries and non-traditional locations may also be looking for ways to raise money for maintenance, perhaps in partnership with a civic-minded non-profit.

A party that offers a look "behind the scenes" also offers news value. A party on a Hollywood studio lot still gives a feeling of being an insider, if just for a night. The partygoer drives up to the gate and for once is waved through by security, because his name is "on the list." Paramount, Sony, and the other Hollywood studios have extensive outdoor street sets or facades that can give party guests a sense of being transported to a different place or time.

Another way to elicit a "Wow" is to choose a more familiar venue, or even a mundane one, such as a parking lot, and completely transform it with décor themed to the party. Many movie premieres take this approach by making the venue look like a scene from the movie the guests have just viewed. In Los Angeles, New York, and other cities with thriving film and advertising businesses, professional set decorators and prop warehouses can supply the expertise and materials needed for such jaw-dropping transformations.

In essence, the setting of the party must be unique, enthralling, and memorable, both to gain media coverage, and to make the party stand out in the jaded partygoer's memory.

The date for events can also be challenging. Major awards events are scheduled in conjunction with the television network broadcasting the event, but tend to be on Sunday evening when the largest home audience can be expected. Movie premieres, as discussed below, are usually scheduled for Monday or Tuesday evening before the film opens on Friday. Industry charity events, such as the Motion Picture Pioneers dinner, are most often scheduled for Tuesday, Wednesday, or sometimes Thursday evening; industry executives can come directly from work, oftentimes attending without their significant others.

Only a few super-glamorous events such as the Carousel of Hope Ball to raise money for Juvenile Diabetes are black-tie/long-gown galas attended by couples and scheduled for Saturday evening. The event features silent and live auctions of jaw-dropping luxury items from a Mercedes to stays in exclusive luxury resorts around the world. Even for such a swanky, long-running event, Barbara Davis, the formidable organizer is quoted as saying, "'You have to make the calls yourself. The people that need to be spoken to, I speak to them'" (Higgins, 2012).

WOW Factor #3: Food (and drinks)

If an event is at a venue such as a hotel ballroom that supplies its own catering, the menu should be top-of-the-line, and if possible include one or more dishes that are inventive or original.

It is easier to have WOW food and drinks, if the catering is hired separately for an unusual venue, although then the overall logistics are more complex. The food can be prepared by a celebrity chef, such as the winner of a prominent cable TV cooking show, or by the chef of this year's hottest new restaurant, or by this year's most sought-after caterer.

One possibility for a WOW is for the food to be themed to the décor of the party, or to reproduce a feast shown in the premiering movie, for example. In any case, the dessert should be spectacular. At a charity dinner, the program with awards presentations and thank-you speeches starts when dessert is served, so the sweet treat—hopefully themed and memorable—helps everyone through the less exciting parts of the evening.

Drinks allow another option for standing out—an original, signature cocktail. Charity and industry fundraisers can add to their bottom line by securing a liquor company to sponsor the event and to create the event's signature drink or a memorable drink presentation, such as a champagne waterfall.

WOW Factor #4: Entertainment

What kind of entertainment does it take to impress entertainment people? This year's newest sensation, such as someone who has never toured, but who is likely to be nominated for multiple Grammy Awards, would create excitement for a younger-skewing crowd. For most charity functions, which tend to skew older, having an arena-quality artist is exciting in a ballroom-sized venue. Another way to go is to arrange a once-in-a-lifetime experience, such as having Cirque du Soleil perform under the stars on a private estate.

Wow Factor #5: Souvenir gift bag

Everybody likes free stuff. Companies like to give gifts to famous people, with the hopes that they will be seen (and hopefully photographed) wearing the gift garment or using the free tech device. Companies can also receive a tax deduction for items donated to a charity, so in a sense, everybody wins. At Hollywood's biggest, most prestigious events such as the Academy Awards Governors Ball, the gift bags can contain many dollars' worth of tech items, certificates for $100 off a massage (that costs $200–$300), and CDs and other popular media products. Part of the job of the public relations team is to line up sponsors for products for the souvenir gift bag.

Achieving PR objectives

From the above examples, it's clear that entertainment world parties are like other parties—only more, more, more so. The public relations team needs to think creatively and plan carefully so that the hard work of putting on an event achieves the planned objectives. For a charity, objectives include raising money and awareness, but even more important are the objectives of making a lasting impression on attendees, and having enough WOW factors to generate media coverage to create awareness in people who were not on the guest list.

Variety and The Hollywood Reporter cover numerous industry events—some of them fairly mundane—by printing photo galleries in their weekly print versions. The editors know that entertainment people—like most people—enjoy seeing and reading about themselves in the news. The most extravagant events are also covered in the consumer press, such as the Los Angeles Times Calendar section or Style section, or in The New York Times Style section, or the advertising column in the Business Section. One example of a WOW event that generated broad media coverage was a Fendi fashion show on October 19, 2007, months ahead of the Beijing Olympics. The opening of a flagship store in Beijing included an extravagant party there followed by transportation for all of the guests to the Great Wall of China, where the ancient wall served as a backdrop and as the runway for a fashion show (Fendi, 2007). News coverage included descriptions of the multi-year negotiation with the Chinese government, as well as the multi-million-dollar cost (Chmielewski, 2007). The WOW factors of this event resulted in worldwide news coverage bringing awareness about Fendi's fashion leadership to huge numbers of people who were not on the guest list.

Who Produces the Oscars, the Emmys, and the Grammys and Why?

The Oscars, the Emmys, and the Grammys are the entertainment industry's most prestigious and most visible awards events. Each event achieves multiple objectives for its organization, within its industry, within the entertainment community, and in the wider world of popular culture, which includes publicity and celebrity.

The Oscars

The **Academy Awards**, familiarly known as the **Oscars**, exist to promote the film industry. The pre-event publicity reminds viewers how much they have enjoyed films in the past and how much they are missing out on if they don't see the nominated films before the broadcast or the winning film, once it is announced. The surrounding publicity tactics for the nominated films and the Oscar winner, as well as for those in the best actress, best actor, and best director categories increase box-office grosses. The publicity also boosts the awareness or name recognition and the individual prestige of nominees and winners, making their names and faces more viable box-office attractions for their future films. Press releases ever after will describe an actor or director as "Oscar-nominated" or as "three-time Academy Award – winning actor," increasing the Stimulants (Gompertz, 1992) or news value of future news stories.

The **Academy of Motion Picture Arts and Sciences** (also known as the **Motion Picture Academy**) is the producing organization. The Oscar ceremony and broadcast, the Governors Ball, and the accompanying week's worth of related events generate publicity in the name of honoring the highest achievements in film in the previous calendar year. The Oscar ceremony is the most prestigious entertainment award and the most widely known. For example, the show is typically the second-highest-rated show on American television, after the Super Bowl.

The prestige of the Oscars derives from how the nominees and winners are chosen—by peers in the film industry. The Academy itself is a membership organization of over six thousand people who are now active or who have been active in the film industry in all kinds of jobs from sound effects editing and costume design to acting and directing. The peer nomination process anchors the Academy Awards in artistry and achievement, rather than popularity, although there have been recent controversies about the lack of diversity among the major categories that may lead to changes in the near future.

The Golden Globes

In contrast, the **Golden Globe Awards** process, which honors both film and television, is run by the **Hollywood Foreign Press Association**, a group of fewer than 100 mostly part-time journalists who cover Hollywood as correspondents for media from around the world (Hollywood Foreign Press Association, n.d.). In the past, the nominations have been criticized for being based on how well known the actors were abroad. The Golden Globes takes place a month before the Oscars. Attendees enjoy the evening, because the ceremony itself takes place in a dinner setting at which people can eat and especially drink during the long telecast. The partying makes for some more spontaneous moments and thank-you speeches than at the Oscars, with its theater seating. In recent years, the Best Film nominations and winners of Golden Globe Awards have been more mainstream than in the past. Some

Oscar prediction pundits have come to see the Golden Globes Best Motion Picture winner as predicting an Oscar victory, but as far as prestige and clout is concerned, a Golden Globe doesn't compare to an Oscar.

Fundraising objective

The Oscars raises money for the Academy from a number of sources. Tickets are sold to the ceremony itself and to the Governors Ball immediately afterwards. As with local non-profits' awards discussed above, congratulatory ads are sold for the souvenir program booklet given to attendees. The biggest source of revenue for the Academy Awards and major awards ceremonies is the sale of the television broadcast rights. Rights sales include not just the deal with ABC television (a Disney company), which has been in place for many years, but also sales to dozens of international television markets.

Non-profit activities

The Academy uses the funds it raises for a number of purposes, both educational and philanthropic. A year after the Academy was founded in 1927, the Academy created its library and research archive, the Margaret Herrick Library, to preserve the history of the Hollywood film industry. The Academy also has an important film preservation project that has preserved and restored more than 600 films. Its newest initiative is the Academy Museum of Motion Pictures, which is expected to become a major tourist attraction and an additional source of income for the non-profit Academy when it opens to the public (estimated to open in 2018) (Boehm, 2015).

The Academy gives grants to schools and non-profits involved with teaching filmmaking, especially programs for minorities and underserved populations. It also gives internship grants and grants to film festivals and film scholars (Academy of Motion Picture Arts & Sciences, n.d.).

The ways that publicity campaigns support the Academy Awards and therefore the initiatives of the Motion Picture Academy are covered in more depth in a Sidebar in Chapter 8.

The Emmys

In the television industry, the **Emmy Awards** are the most prestigious, with a structure, sources of income, and purposes that are similar to those of the Oscars. The producing organization is the **Academy of Television Arts and Sciences** (also known as the **Television Academy**), a membership organization of television professionals. To equalize the playing field among the major television networks, the Emmy broadcast rotates each year among ABC, CBS, NBC, and Fox, which alternate in paying the licensing fee to the organization and in reaping the benefits of the ratings. The network with a particular year's broadcast rights has the opportunity to boost awareness for its own fall primetime schedule, because the ceremony takes place just in advance of most fall-season premieres. In fact, the primary purpose of the Emmy Awards is to boost awareness and therefore viewership of the fall television season, as discussed in the SIDEBAR in this chapter.

Profits from the Emmy Awards support the Television Academy's educational and philanthropic outreach. This includes the initiatives of the Academy Foundation, and especially the Archive of American Television, an online resource available to researchers and fans everywhere that presents in-depth interviews with important television professionals from all areas of the business (Archive of American Television, n.d.). Other projects of the Television Academy include panel discussions and programs for current members and students, an internship program, the College Emmy Awards, and grants and programs for faculty and television departments across the country, such as a Visiting Professionals program.

The Biz Markets Itself—The Emmy Awards

The Emmys are designed to promote the Academy of Television Arts and Sciences, the television industry as a whole, and especially the new fall television season. The announcement of Emmy nominations in June is part of an industry effort to remind audiences, particularly those in the important Los Angeles and New York markets where most voters live, about their favorite shows during the slow summer rerun season. Extra-thick issues of the industry trade magazines—the glossy weekly print editions of *Variety* and *The Hollywood Reporter*—are crammed with expensive full-page, four-color ads announcing: **For Your Consideration**. The ads promote the award candidacies of various stars, writers, directors, and behind-the-scenes craftspeople, as well as series wishing to be considered for best drama and best comedy.

Figure 4.1: Emmy® Statuette.
Photo: ©ATAS/NATAS.

The actual nominations are announced at an early-morning Los Angeles ceremony in mid-July that makes news live on the national morning
shows such as *Good Morning America* and *The Today Show*. The names of
the nominees are covered on every news website and in every newscast

later that day and during the following days. After the announcement of the nominations, trade publicity focuses on the campaigns to gain industry voters for each nominee.

For both the trade and consumer media, publicity focuses on the elements of the upcoming Emmy broadcast. Media announcements naming the host, and then various presenters keep the upcoming Emmy broadcast in the news. News value is sky high, because the nominees in the main categories, the host, and the presenters are news "stimulants" (Gompertz, 1992), as discussed in Chapter 2.

Trade advertising remains intense until the voting deadline. The trades as well as the "hometown" newspapers, the *Los Angeles Times* and *The New York Times*, are pitched numerous story angles and run features about the various nominees, as well as features by multiple critics handicapping the competition in the major Emmy categories.

Meanwhile, the network with the year's Emmy broadcast rights (an opportunity that rotates among ABC, CBS, NBC, and Fox) begins a saturation campaign to make audiences aware of the day and time of the broadcast in the various time zones across the country. Usually the host is a personality on the specific network, so the network PR people are also at work promoting the host. For example, in 2014, when the show was on NBC, Seth Meyers was selected host. On *Late Night with Seth Meyers* on NBC, his segment producers took PR pitches and scheduled a parade of Emmy nominees to talk about their excitement about being nominated, to play a clip from their shows—especially if the shows were returning to NBC for the fall season—and to talk up their upcoming red-carpet appearances.

In these ways, the Emmy Awards broadcast is part of the build-up to the launch of the new fall prime-time television season. Glamorous red-carpet appearances allow celebrities to tout their shows' fall return, or the premiere of a new series. The interviewers range from morning show hosts to representatives of various E! Entertainment Television shows and other cable and reality shows. They also have ample opportunity to promote their own shows.

During the actual Emmy broadcast, continuing series from the previous year receive free airtime through the appearances of presenters; announcements of the names of nominees; clips of nominees' work; thank-you speeches; and interviews of the winners from back stage. The back-stage press conference area, is complete with a backdrop that identifies the event and place, such as the 66th Emmys and the presenting network, NBC (in 2014). The pressroom is often the source of remarks that are more spontaneous than the acceptance speeches, and therefore generate a lot of news traction, for example, when a winner suddenly realizes that he forgot to thank his wife, and makes a bumbling apology that only spreads the news—that he forgot to thank his wife.

These promotional screen appearances on the Emmy red carpet, the broadcast itself, and in the pressroom generate avid comments on social media, further reminding fans to tune in for the fall premieres of their favorite shows. Clips and quotes from Emmy broadcast appearances are played and replayed, discussed and re-tweeted over the following days for further buzz leading up to the fall season premieres. Chapter 5 shows how the Emmy process fits into the network television PR cycle.

The Grammys

In the music industry, the **Grammy Awards** are produced by **The Recording Academy**, again a member organization of professionals, who work in all areas of the music business. The SIDEBAR in Chapter 10 will go into depth about the public relations efforts and effects of the Awards and the award broadcast, especially the creative use of social media. Here, however, the focus in on some of the ways that the Grammys use the funds generated by the award ceremony and the broadcast on CBS. The Grammy organization's main philanthropic effort is MusiCares, which provides monetary assistance and social services to industry people in need. The organization also has a number of educational projects, including a number of music camps and in-school programs under the umbrella of Music in the Schools (The Recording Academy, n.d.). In Los Angeles, the Grammy organization has also gained year-round visibility through the Grammy Museum at LA Live, which is the downtown Los Angeles entertainment district that includes the Staples Center and the Microsoft Theatre (formerly the Nokia Theater).

Other Entertainment Industry Events

Other industry events range from lavish premieres to press and constituent events that last for several days filled with continuous activity and entertainment.

Film premieres

The excitement and glamour of movie premieres have motivated audiences to step up to the box office ever since the studio era of the 1920s and '30s, when premieres were more common than they are now. Back then flashy premieres—and the resulting media coverage in newspapers and weekly pictorial magazines such as *Life*, *Look*, and *Screenland*, as well as in newsreels—created national awareness for a film that might not arrive in a local market until weeks or months later. The premieres were part of the studios' ongoing campaigns to make their stars under contract and their film franchises memorable brand names.

Since the advent of television talk shows, the studios have used TV as a less costly medium to bring the glamour of stars (and a film clip) directly into people's homes. Nevertheless, the studios still rely on a tried-and-true **movie premiere** strategy for their biggest pictures with their most glamorous stars.

Premiere event script

The event script for film premieres has been honed over the decades. Since movies open on Friday night (or Thursday night at midnight, or even earlier in the evening, for some of the biggest recent potential hits), a red-carpet **premiere event** is scheduled for Monday or Tuesday night to maximize the buzz resulting from media coverage. Typically, a premiere follows this format starting in the early evening:

5:00: Red-carpet arrivals. Local evening news crews can broadcast live coverage and tease for upcoming party coverage during their late evening news. Syndicated shows such as *Access Hollywood* tape interviews to be used over the next several days. There will be a holding area for **paparazzi** near the entrance with ropes and security guards to keep the aggressive freelance photographers from getting too close or in a celeb's face. Photos will appear for days and weeks to come in daily newspapers, weekly magazines, and even some monthlies, especially the women's fashion magazines.

7:00: Screening begins.

8:45–9:00: Screening ends. Audience follows a red-carpeted path to an adjacent party venue. (See the above sections on party WOW factors.)

9:00–11:30: Party with buffet food stations and sit-down seating; band and dance floor; other WOW entertainment. Important syndicated entertainment news shows such as *Entertainment Tonight* and *Extra*, as well as cable outlets such as E! Entertainment, have designated interview setups inside the venue near the entrance. Publicists and shows' producers wrangled the stars and celebrity guests to give the shows the most possible options for future coverage and special segments.

10:00–11:00: Fox, CW, and local Los Angeles stations with 10 p.m. newscasts are allowed to broadcast live party shots.

11:00–11:30: Live shots and clips from the red carpet are shown on the local late-night news on the other local stations.

Notice how the elements of the premiere event, except for the actual screening of the film, are geared to achieve the public relations objective of news coverage. The red carpet and the party make broadcast news coverage both convenient and compelling by providing opportunities for candid video and photographs, as well as informal interviews of glamorous celebrities.

Sometimes a studio even throws a premiere event in Los Angeles on Monday night and another in New York on Tuesday night. Afterwards, the cast is already in New York to do the Wednesday and Thursday morning and evening talk shows, a process made easier now, because Jimmy Fallon decided to do his version of *The Tonight Show* from New York, rather than Los Angeles. Publicists know that Thursday evening and Friday morning are when many people make their weekend plans, so the coverage of a glamorous premiere creates top-of-mind awareness and buying intention when people are exposed to a barrage of talk-show appearances, clips, and paid commercials.

Album and tour launch parties

Within the music industry, the closest equivalents to movie premieres are album or tour launch parties. Sometimes the location or the décor is themed to the album, but more often these days the venue is a trendy club, which gets a publicity boost from hosting the music stars and industry bigwigs. The evening is often sponsored by a fashionable liquor company, which provides free-flowing libations. A fashionable DJ keeps the crowd dancing into the night. The key element here is the star power of the guest list. The targeted press includes the music press, gossip sites, and paparazzi. A launch party incident that went viral was Kanye West's drunken rant at a listening party for the launch party of his friend, Pusha T (Nunez, 2013), perhaps confirming the old saw that "any publicity is good publicity," in this case for Pusha T, though perhaps not for Kanye West, whose erratic behavior has sometimes created full-out celebrity PR crises, which are discussed in Chapter 6.

Press junkets

Would you like free round-trip airfare, plus three to 14 days at a nice hotel in Los Angeles, plus lavish meals and entertainment for yourself plus one? That is the offer a studio or a network or group of networks makes to low-paid entertainment journalists and critics from across the country, when they produce a **press junket**. A few newspapers, such as *The New York Times* insist on covering expenses for their reporters to prevent a conflict of interest. Most smaller news outlets have no such qualms. They crave original content and the glamour of Hollywood, so they happily send their media reporters on all-expense-paid junkets.

The public relations objective of producing a junket is to generate the most possible news coverage nationwide without having to produce multiple press events in city after city. Stars and publicists don't want to be on the road for days or weeks on end.

Junkets usually provide reporters with two kinds of story opportunities. The first is a standard press conference format where there are short presentations and introductions of the stars and directors. Then the journalists ask questions. This means that the standard questions only need to be answered once. All the members of the press present can use the answers as quotations in their future stories about the film.

The second kind of opportunity is round-robin interviews. Interview tables are set up around the venue, and the celebrities are escorted from one to the next every five to 15 minutes. The journalists each have a private interview with each star and are able to get individualized quotations. These are grueling for the interviewees. Many journalists ask the same questions that the star has already answered a number of times. The effort, however, is worth the aggravation. A one-day film junket can generate worldwide coverage, because of the attendance of members of the Hollywood Foreign Press Association (that same group of fewer than 100 people whose organization produces the Golden Globes). An example of a multi-day junket is the twice-yearly **Television Critics Association (TCA) Press Tour**, sponsored by the major networks, which is discussed in Chapter 5.

Business-to-business, trade show, and convention events

Business-to-business events are common in every industry. Often they are part of the schedule of a larger event, such as a trade show, that has attracted members of the industry. One such convention in entertainment is **CinemaCon**, a

Las Vegas convention hosted by the National Association of Theatre Owners. Theatre owners and managers from across the USA and from dozens of other countries attend each spring to preview upcoming spring and summer movies and decide which ones to schedule in their theatres and for how many weeks. The four or five days are filled with studio-sponsored presentations. Paramount, Universal, The Walt Disney Studios, Sony Pictures Entertainment, 21st Century Fox (formerly 20th Century Fox), and Warner Bros. usually participate. Each studio has a dedicated day or half day to show its product reels complete with in-person, star appearances, screenings of their most-anticipated films, and social events with free-flowing liquor. WOW factors include the stars, the food, and the gift bags, which can contain anything from film logo merchandise to electronic devices. Sony Pictures' parties are known for featuring dozens of the latest PlayStations, on which guests can try out the company's newest games, one of which may be in the gift bag for journalists.

A second convention with a similar purpose called **ShowEast** is presented in October each year in Hollywood, Florida, by Prometheus Global Entertainment, a media company that owns *The Hollywood Reporter* and *Billboard*, among other publications. This meeting features screenings of films to be released in the late fall and winter, including those from some smaller studios, such as Lionsgate. Except for the biggest Christmas films, those premiering in the fall are often ones the studios are positioning to be competitive in the year's Academy Awards race. The Oscar publicity cycle is covered in the Sidebar on The Academy Awards in Chapter 8.

Another important business-to-business event called the **television upfronts** takes place every May in New York City. Over several days, the five major networks reveal their upcoming fall schedules to advertisers. Each network has a day or half day to announce which new series they will broadcast in the fall, which current shows will be returning, and how they are programming each night of prime time to best compete for ratings. These lavish, multimedia events can end with a cavalcade of stars, who then circulate among the ad agency representatives at a cocktail party and dinner. The quality—and the showmanship—that advertisers and ad agencies see at the upfronts determines, or at least influences, which timeslots for which networks will receive their immediate "upfront" commitments for advertising for the fall season ahead.

Partnership and relationship events

The industry uses events to celebrate ongoing partnerships and cultivate new ones. In television, some of the most important relationships are those between a television network and its affiliates. Most **network affiliate meet-ings** are a combination of pep rally, love fest (unless the past year's ratings have been abysmal), and informational seminar, with large side orders of food and cocktails. For example, in recent years Disney/ABC hosts the affiliates within days of the upfronts. Here the station managers and their senior staff receive their own previews of the new shows and the fall schedule. Social events offer opportunities to interact and chat with the stars. The affiliates are able to judge for themselves how successful they think a series or a night's prime-time schedule will be. Importantly, the network also reveals the kinds of on-air promos, teasers, print collateral, and print advertising co-payments (called cooperative advertising) the network will be supplying to support each series. For many returning shows, the network promises to tape customized promos for individual stations for the fall launch with a popular star of the scheduled series saying the station's call letters, the night, and time of the show in that local market.

Conclusion: Implications for the Practice of Public Relations

A special event is a public relations strategy used to achieve important objec-tives for the client. Typical objectives include: leaving guests with a positive impression and warm memories; increasing public awareness of the organiza-tion or an organization's new product (such as a movie) through media cover-age; and (often) raising money to support the organization's mission.

As discussed in this chapter, all events require careful planning in the areas of #1, guest list/invitations; #2, venue/décor/date; #3, food (and drinks); #4, entertainment; and #5, souvenir gift bag. Entertainment industry parties aim for WOW factors in as many of these elements as possible in order to be memorable to jaded guests and to generate media coverage. The media alert, discussed in the SIDEBAR, is the tool used to invite the press to an event where they can report elements of a story that will interest their readers. Pub-lic relations practitioners in any industry or in the non-profit world can adapt these party principles to their own budgets and priorities.

Events are complex and time consuming to produce. Therefore, they should be undertaken only when they can help the organization achieve important objectives related to its mission or its overall public relations plan-ning and strategy. For example, the Emmy Awards event supports the televi-sion industry's need for publicity to launch the fall television season, while also raising money to support the Television Academy's non-profit philanthropic and educational mission. When planned and executed with care, a special event can WOW both the media and the guests and motivate them to think well of the hosting organization.

Key Terms—In bold in the text

Sample two-sentence definition and example

Academy Awards or Oscars: The Academy Awards are public relations opportunities in the form of a lavish red-carpet event and television broadcast with winners chosen by industry peers who are members of the Academy of Motion Picture Arts and Sciences. For example, the Oscars mean several months of additional publicity for a film and its stars while campaigning for nominations and then for the Awards and participating in a number of media events leading up to the ceremony itself.

Academy of Motion Picture Arts and Sciences, also known as the Motion Picture Academy
Academy of Television Arts and Sciences, also known as the Television Academy
Awareness objective
CinemaCon
Emmy Awards, or Emmys
Event Strategy
For Your Consideration
Fundraising Objective
Golden Globe Awards
Grammy Awards, or Grammys
Hollywood Foreign Press Association
Media Advisory, also known as Media Alert or Media Tip Sheet
Media Alert, also known as Media Advisory or Media Tip Sheet
Media Coverage Objective
Media Tip Sheet, also known as Media Advisory or Media Alert
Motion Picture Academy, also known as the Academy of Motion Picture Arts and Sciences
Movie Premiere
Network Affiliate Meeting
Oscars, also known as the Academy Awards

Paparazzi
Party Element #1/WOW Factor #1: guest list/invitations
Party Element #2/WOW Factor #2: venue/décor/date
Party Element #3/WOW Factor #3: food (and drinks)
Party Element #4/WOW Factor #4: entertainment
Party Element #5/WOW Factor #5: souvenir gift bag
Premiere Event
Press Junket
ShowEast
Television Academy, also known as the Academy of
    Television Arts and Sciences
Television Critics Association (TCA) Press Tour
Television Upfronts (the Upfronts)
The Recording Academy
Venue

Suggested reading and resources

Academy of Television Arts and Sciences has an archive that contains lengthy, in-depth
    interviews with television greats, including public relations practitioners, which can be
    accessed online at www.emmytvlegends.org
Emmys.org is the website of the Television Academy
Grammy.org is the website of The Recording Academy
Oscars.org is the website of the Academy of Motion Picture Arts and Sciences, and contains
    information about its various philanthropic programs, as well as about the Margaret Her-
    rick Library, its non-circulating research library located in Beverly Hills, California.

· 5 ·

THE NETWORK TELEVISION PUBLIC RELATIONS CYCLE

Chapter Overview: When you finish this chapter, you should be able to answer the following questions:

- How is a television network structured?
- How is television regulated?
- What is the goal of network publicity, marketing, and promotion?
- What typical kinds of objectives help achieve the goal?
- What are the Nielsen ratings?
- Why are the Nielsen ratings criticized?
- What traditional PR tactics and tools are used to achieve the goal and objectives?
- How can creative social media tactics harness the energy of devoted fans to achieve objectives?
- What is the network television public relations cycle?
- SIDEBAR: The Entertainment PR Toolbox—Writing Goal and Objective Statements

Introduction

Whether working for a company or for a number of clients through an agency, a public relations practitioner should understand how each client's business is structured and how public relations fits into the overall business. Therefore, this chapter, which focuses on television publicity, describes the management structure of a television network and explains a network's business priorities. It also defines prime time as it applies to different U.S. networks.

Since success or failure in American television is judged by the Nielsen ratings, the chapter talks about how the ratings are measured and how the Nielsens are used by public relations practitioners to define the goal of a public relations plan or proposal.

The next section then looks at typical public relations objectives designed to achieve the ratings goal, as well as strategies, tactics, and traditional and social media tools that are used to achieve the objectives. To aid in learning how to create a PR proposal for a company or client, a SIDEBAR explains how to write goal and objective statements.

Finally, this chapter demonstrates one of this book's original contributions to the field of public relations: understanding the importance of the **public relations cycle**, which depends on the client's area of business. Understanding the public relations cycle allows the publicist to anticipate and prepare for events, occasions, and opportunities that recur in a regular pattern depending on the specifics of the industry.

The Management Structure of a Television Network

A **television network** comprises one broadcast station, called a **network affiliate,** per local market. A network is made up of a **Federal Communications Commission (FCC)**-regulated number of local stations, both those **owned and operated** by the network (**O&Os**) and a number of other affiliated local stations owned by other companies. Affiliates agree to broadcast network programming in specified day parts, and use the network brand, logo, advertising, and promotional material. Network-originated programming usually includes the national news and prime-time shows, plus a morning show and a late-night show, plus a daily soap opera or two, plus whatever sports and specials, such as the Oscars, for which the network holds the broadcast licensing agreement. These days the networks are subsidiaries of larger, parent media organizations.

Definition of a TV network

The term **television network** properly refers to only those entities that are licensed to broadcast over the public airwaves through affiliates in each of the local television markets. Networks originally included only ABC, CBS, and NBC, but now also include CW and Fox, as well as PBS, which is the non-commercial public television network. These days, most viewers do not receive their network television through the air via antennae on their roofs. Instead, viewers often receive all varieties of television through cable or satellite systems, which also carry hundreds of cable channels. Others view television programming through streaming services such as Hulu and Netflix, which allow viewers to watch individual episodes whenever they wish. For public relations purposes, however, it is important to understand the definition of the distinct category—television networks.

Prime time

The term **prime-time programming** refers to what is scheduled on the six television networks during specific hours of the evening. For ABC, CBS, NBC, and PBS, prime time is 8–11 p.m. M–Sat. and 7–11 p.m. Sun. on the east and west coasts; for the CW and Fox, prime time is an hour shorter and ends an hour earlier (8–10 M–Sat; 7–10 on Sun.). In the central and mountain zones, the entire prime-time schedule is shifted one hour earlier.

Management structure

The management structure of a television network is complex, but fairly typical of other businesses in the entertainment industry. The Network President oversees everything and is responsible to the parent company for financial results. **Government and Community Relations** monitors laws and community issues; lobbies politicians regarding legislative and FCC initiatives; and oversees charitable giving.

The **News Division** produces the national news and hour news magazine shows broadcast in prime time. It also shares news footage created by a global workforce of correspondents and camera crews with local affiliate news operations.

The **Programming Department** is responsible for overseeing the development and production of all network programming except news. Within the programming department, **Development** is responsible for new programming until it is scheduled on the air. The development staff takes pitches, reads scripts, and looks for material in other media that might be adapted for television series, movies, or specials. Development executives decide which ideas "go to script"; give notes and oversee revisions; and order the pilot and oversee casting. Different members of the development staff are responsible for the various categories of programs, including: comedy, drama, movies for television, reality, and children's programming. When staffing a series pilot, special, or television movies, development executives work with their in-house **Casting** department and outside casting agents hired by the production company to find the right actors for each role.

Current Programming (comedy, drama, reality) is responsible for series once they are on the network's schedule. Executives read the script of each episode; give notes; suggest changes to the producers, recommend writers for the "writers table"; recommend and approve casting of guest stars; and view dailies and rough cuts.

In-house and external **production companies** come up with series ideas, develop material and pitches, pitch programs to their assigned network development executive, and hope the network will want to "go to script" and then order a pilot, paying a negotiated fee for preproduction, production, and post-production, which includes editing, sound, music, and any special effects.

Business Affairs and Legal negotiates the deals (license fees) with production companies and write the contracts. When a series is scheduled, the network pays the production company a per-episode "license fee," which allows it to broadcast the episode usually three times within two years in the US (**the licensing agreement**). After a series has aired 80 to 100 episodes, the production company may then sell it "into syndication" to local stations and cable channels, a business model that is discussed in the next chapter.

The **Advertising Sales** department negotiates with advertising agencies representing various brands to sell national advertising time on the entire range of network programming on all affiliates across the country. **Broadcast Standards and Practices (BS&P)** is responsible for keeping all programming content within the bounds of "community standards," mandated by the FCC so that local affiliates will not face fines or have trouble with their license renewals. BS&P reads and gives notes on all scripts of all programs. An executive is in charge of the bleep button on all "live" programs, which are broadcast with a few seconds of tape delay so profanity and nudity can be bleeped, cut, or blurred. BS&P also reviews and accepts or rejects all advertising for broadcast on the network, after reviewing it for false claims and other problems.

Scheduling decides when to broadcast each series and each new or repeat episode, by moving programs like chess pieces in relation to what competitors are doing. **Research** analyzes the Nielsen ratings and other data for each episode of each series, as well as conducts its own research in connection with the development and current programming departments. Research does focus group testing of program concepts in the early stages of development. It also audience-tests pilots and later episodes in computerized facilities that can measure the viewers' physical responses, such as heart rate, and compile their answers to detailed survey questions about individual characters and scenes.

The **Broadcast** department is responsible for the actual "airing" of the East and West Coast network feeds of programming that go out to the local stations and to cable and satellite systems.

The in-house divisions of **Marketing** oversee marketing to all constituents, including viewers and affiliate stations. These in-house departments include **Advertising**, which oversees and pays for the creation of all paid advertising that is placed in other media for the network itself and for individual shows. This includes **print advertising** (in newspapers, magazines); **outdoor advertising** (billboards, bus stops, buses); radio commercials; and television ads that appear on other networks and cable channels.

On-Air Promotion creates, edits, and schedules all show promos for broadcast on the network, including shooting special material that may involve coordinating cast availability with the Programming and Publicity departments.

Public relations

Publicity is in charge of getting free (unpaid-for) media coverage, including maintaining a vibrant presence on social media. External agency publicists and internal network publicists may interact with the above-mentioned departments while doing research and executing publicity plans. Knowing what the various departments do allows the PR person to work efficiently and go to the right department and the right person for information and background and to set up executive interviews with the media.

Members of the publicity department and their external PR agencies write press announcements, create media kits, organize bi-annual press tours and satellite press tours, and schedule cast member appearances on talk-shows and at events. Publicity also organizes the appearances and programs for affiliate meetings, up-front advertising sales presentations to advertisers, and special charity events that involve senior management and stars.

In connection with Publicity, the **Affiliate Relations** department organizes annual or bi-annual affiliate meetings, usually in Las Vegas or Los Angeles. These multi-day business/entertainment extravaganzas are geared to create excitement about the network schedule and make the managers and owners of the affiliate stations feel good about continuing as part of the network. The agenda always includes lots of entertainment, stars, and parties, as well as opportunities to hear from senior management. These speeches and presentations are researched, drafted, and coordinated by members of the network publicity staff, PR agencies under contract for specific shows, or outside PR consultants, such as speech writers and multimedia specialists.

The Goal of Network Television Publicity

As discussed in Chapter 1, a client typically hires public relations representation for one of two purposes: to solve a problem or to take advantage of an opportunity. Unless there is controversy or a flaw, product launches and product publicity are done to take advantage of an opportunity. In the business model of network television, each new television series is a new product. Each new series represents a major investment in development and production, as well as a major opportunity, just as launching a new digital device represents an opportunity for a consumer product company such as Apple or Samsung. On a smaller scale, each episode of a television series also represents an opportunity to gain additional viewers and take market share from competing networks' shows in the same timeslot, as well as from all the other available entertainment options.

Successful public relations practitioners understand that their goal for their publicity plan must align with the client's goal. Since entertainment is a business, the goal should be stated as money or as something that equates to money. Typical goals for entertainment businesses are, for example, the number of digital downloads of a song or album during the first week of release or the total box-office result for the first weekend of a blockbuster film's release.

Ratings equate to money

For broadcast television, ratings determine the amount of money networks can charge advertisers for each 30- or 60-second commercial during a timeslot.

Thus, ratings are a money equivalent that can be used to state the goal of a public relations plan.

Understanding TV Ratings

Nielsen sells its proprietary **Nielsen ratings** to industry subscribers. Nielsen ratings are based on data from more than 40 thousand households nationwide every week and from 1.6 million viewing diaries for four specific month-long time periods known as **sweeps**. Sweeps take place in November, February, and May, and less importantly in July. The ratings during each specific timeslot of sweeps periods determine the amount the network can charge advertisers for a 30-second commercial in the corresponding timeslot the next year.

Demographics

For network television the **public relations objectives** should be stated as ratings. Ratings are broken down into categories of **demographics**, which are measurable or visible attributes of an audience, such as age, gender, race, and geographical location.

Demographics for network prime-time programming focus on age, gender, and urban versus rural. The important demographics for network television are ages 18–49, and secondarily ages 18–34. These are the ages targeted by most consumer product companies, because people in these age ranges typically have income and are in the accumulation stage of their lives. Viewers over 50 "don't count" and aren't counted, because advertisers believe they buy fewer discretionary products, such as smart phones and pricey vehicles. People younger than 18 are considered to have most of their purchasing power controlled by parents (18–49).

Possible flaws in the Nielsens

There is a long history of questioning the Nielsen ratings: Is their sample really representative? Do people in homes selected to be Nielsen families try to game the system by lying in their viewing diaries or by leaving their television tuned to PBS so they seem more cultured? Does the company accurately count "out of home" viewing, such as in college dorms and sports bars? In response, Nielsen has continually updated its technology and how it monitors viewing.

Since the advent of digital viewing, however, there has been a crescendo of criticism related to the Nielsens' ability to keep up with changing viewing habits. Viewers, especially younger people, time shift by recording shows on a DVR and watching later—usually skipping commercials. Therefore, Nielsen now measures "live" on-schedule viewing, also called **linear viewing**, but also measures **live +3** days and **live +7** days. These ratings count those who record their favorite shows and watch them later at night or on the weekend. Various Nielsen technologies have included set-tuning meters; people meters with individual buttons for each household member; handwritten diaries; and A/P or Active/Passive meters for viewing via DVR and **VOD (Video on Demand)**.

All of these data collection techniques still miss counting audience members who view **OTT**, **over the top**, such as through subscription services such as Hulu Plus and Netflix. In particular, Netflix does not enable the embedded codes on their offerings that would enable Nielsen to count their viewership, so currently no one outside of Netflix knows how many viewers watch specific shows via Netflix.

Because of the controversy about who is watching and how the viewership can be counted, a number of competitors are once again, as in the past, challenging Nielsen's dominance. For example, comScore, which measures not just viewing on laptops and computers, but also on mobile and other digital devices, found, "the total digital viewership for television networks increased by a range of 8 percent to as much as 30 percent" (Steel, 2015a). In late 2015, comScore merged with Rentrak, which measures viewing via data from set-top boxes, so that the merged company could better compete with Nielsen, "by measuring how people consume media across a proliferation of screens—mobile, desktop, television and more" (Steel, 2015c).

Using viewing data from all devices could mean a substantial increase in the rate a network could charge for each 30-second commercial—if the measurements can also show how many of those additional viewers are also watching the commercials. Until the networks and the advertising agencies can agree on which are the most accurate measurements of overall viewing—including watching the commercials, skipping them, or fast forwarding through them—comScore/Rentrak and other rating services' data will augment, rather than replace, the Nielsen ratings.

The scorecard

Every morning, Nielsen's **overnights**, which are preliminary ratings from a smaller sample from the major urban markets, give network executives the scorecard from the previous night's competition. Recently, however, publicity departments began publicizing overnights only for "live and special events. The live-plus-three ratings that encompass DVR and VOD viewing within three days of a program's premiere truly are becoming the new industry standard" (Littleton, 2015a). Live events, such as awards shows and major athletic competitions, are more likely to be viewed live than dramas and comedies, which can be recorded and viewed later without damaging the viewing experience. Game scores and names of award winners, however, are so widely covered in social and traditional media that delayed viewers are likely to come across "spoilers."

The weekly **nationals**, based on a larger sample, are the ratings numbers that are announced widely in the media. There are also local ratings for each station in each television market. Anyone working in television publicity needs to understand ratings, and especially to know what the client network's ratings expectations are for each timeslot. The goal of a public relations plan for network television should be expressed in terms of target Nielsen ratings, or percentage increase in Nielsen ratings.

Achieving the Ratings Goal and Objectives Using Traditional Media Relations

PR plan objectives delineate pathways to achieving the overall **public relations goal**. The objectives are often targeted to individual audience segments defined by gender, age, and urban vs. rural. Network PR objectives include high pre-season awareness; high sampling of the premiere; high ratings; increasing ratings from week to week; increasing desirable demographics; winning the time slot; and beating year-ago ratings for the same timeslot. The SIDEBAR explains how to craft clear, focused goal and objective statements for effective public relations plans.

The Entertainment PR Toolbox—Writing Goal and Objective Statements for Public Relations Plans

A goal statement for a network's prime-time public relations plan might read: To increase the ranking of the network to #1 in prime time from #2 for the new TV season, as measured by the Nielsen ratings. The goal specifies the direction of the desired change to be achieved by the PR plan; it specifies the outcome (#1), the magnitude (#2 to #1); the time frame or target date (by the end of the TV season, which runs from September to May); and the means for measuring or evaluating the success of the plan (the Nielsen ratings, which translate into dollars).

A public relations plan should include clear, measurable objectives that support the overall goal. Objectives should also be in the form of statements that specify the target audience segment. Examples of objectives are:

- To increase age 18–49 ratings for this May's Sweeps by 10% versus last season
- To achieve high 18–34 awareness for big season finale (this May), as measured by three weekly surveys leading up to the finale
- To have a strong May presentation to advertisers, as measured by advertising sales versus the same period following the previous year's upfront presentations

Figure 5.1: Sofia Vergara (left) and Kerry Washington (right) pose for the photo press on the red carpet at the 65th Emmy(R) Awards on Sunday Sept. 22, 2013, in Los Angeles. (Photo by Matt Sayles/Invision for the Television Academy).

In addition to leveraging the media opportunities of the Emmy cycle discussed in the previous chapter, television publicists utilize both traditional and social media to achieve the PR goal and objectives.

Traditional media

In traditional media, the publicist can pitch and arrange for: star appearances on morning, afternoon, and late-night talk shows; interviews on other broadcast outlets, especially the nationally syndicated entertainment news shows such as *Entertainment Tonight*, *Access Hollywood*, and various shows on the E! Entertainment cable channel; print magazine cover shots, and fashion shoots; photo and interview coverage in fall television preview issues; and feature articles and interviews, among many others.

Broadcast and print coverage of television is facilitated by multiple days of press conferences, Q&As, and **round-robin interviews**, which are one-on-one interviews with cast members in conjunction with industry events such as Emmy week activities.

Television Critics Association (TCA) press junkets

The **Television Critics Association's (TCA)** two-week-long July and January **press junkets** are called junkets, because the participating networks pay the expenses of most of the television critics and journalists. As mentioned in Chapter 4, only a few publications, such as *The New York Times*, insist on paying their journalists' expenses as a matter of ethics to prevent the appearance of bias or conflict of interest. For most of the media, however, the TCA meetings are paid working vacations for two in beautiful Southern California when the rest of the country is sweltering in July's humidity or freezing in January's snowstorms.

Each TCA event has a day hosted by each network and usually half days hosted by major cable channels to present and promote their fall or winter lineup—and to wine and dine the journalists for breakfast, lunch, dinner, and usually a themed late-night party, including a souvenir gift bag, as discussed in Chapter 4. A typical day's schedule looks like this: Each morning, the publicity staff of the day's host network checks in with the journalists and gives them a press kit. The kit contains a main press release and announcements about each show on the prime-time schedule (prepared by public relations). The president of the network, the head of programming, and the head of marketing give talks (drafted by PR) and multimedia presentations (created by PR). The executive presentations give the highlights of the schedule, including introducing new programs with sizzle reels and clips and announcing changes in timeslots, with the rationale for the changes. They will also introduce the stars and show runners of the new series and some of the continuing series. Anyone who speaks will also take questions from the press. The journalists can use everything that is said in the presentations, panels, and Q&As as quotations or background in future articles for their home publications.

Later in the day, after a hosted lunch, the members of the media are given separate tables around the room, and publicists escort the stars and panelists from one journalist to another in a series of **round-robin interviews**. Each journalist has the chance to quickly make a personal connection and get individual quotes, although in reality, most of the questions and the answers are repetitive. Over the course of the day and the two weeks, journalists take notes and write as much as possible on their laptops or tablets. The material that they collect at the TCA junkets can be used over the coming weeks and months to provide features, interviews, and industry overview articles for their home publications. For the publicity staff, such events are work and time intensive, but the results are hundreds of articles all across the country for weeks to come, as well as clips and sound bites on entertainment news programs and local news channels.

The daily trades (variety.com, hollywoodreporter.com, and deadlinehollywood.com) cover the TCA with news stories that report the tenor of the critics' reception for each new series. The buzz generated by the TCA events is crucial, especially for new series. The enthusiasm—or not—of the attending journalists and critics is a key element in the strong launch of a new series and a new season.

Achieving the Goal and Objectives Using Digital and Social Media

Digital media have greatly multiplied and enhanced our ability to communicate with audiences. Digital tactics to achieve a ratings goal can include posting video on YouTube or on the website; encouraging customer-generated content, such as Vine videos; creating podcasts; setting internet radio interviews; and posting on a show's Facebook page or even a character's page. Especially important is creating an endless variety of online public relations – created content for the show's pages on the network's website. The web content, which is available 24/7 whenever someone is searching, can include feature stories, blogs, quizzes, fun lists, contests, surveys, and opportunities for two-way conversations.

Two-way conversations

Conversation (i.e., symmetrical two-way communication) has long been the gold standard for public relations, as discussed in Chapter 1. While it may be possible for an organization with a very small constituency, such as a niche non-profit, to respond to every incoming digital message, conversations are more challenging for organizations such as television networks that need to speak with the mass audience. Social media, and especially Twitter, can nevertheless offer many of the benefits of two-way conversation. Social media community managers can respond to a typical message such as a common question, or thank an individual for a typical compliment, or offer a bit of information about the series that will interest thousands of people, in addition to the specific recipient.

Conversations are especially important for encouraging active fan communities. Super fans can help create awareness and repeat viewership for a show; create a social viewing phenomenon that promotes live viewing; make a show trend on social media each week; rescue a series from cancellation; and even bring a series back from the dead. Typical social media tactics include online Q&As; prompting the cast and fans to live tweet during the initial east- and west-coast broadcasts of an episode; and Twitter contests, among many others.

Tweets and retweets

Twitter is a boon to public relations, because a retweet forwards the company's message exactly as the publicist wrote it. This cuts out the uncertainty that arises when a message such as a press release is sent to a traditional media outlet, which is then free to edit it and shape it. Beyond Twitter, Facebook, Snapchat, and whatever other new apps become popular, a good public relations plan includes communicating with avid fans across various social media platforms and at live events such as ComicCon to harness the fans' passion and make them feel like an integral part of the show community.

Social media engagement

People throughout network television are aware of the importance of social media. Series **show runners**, who are usually the head writers with the title executive producer, often follow and participate in social media. Marlene King, the show-runner of *Pretty Little Liars*, is quoted as saying, "'I pay enormous attention to it. … I am on social media live every night when the show airs and the next day as well looking at the feedback we got regarding the episode'" (Rancilio, 2014). Shonda Rhimes, who executive produces *Scandal, How to Get Away with Murder*, and *Grey's Anatomy* has around 800,000 Twitter followers (Rancilio, 2014). The trend toward live, social viewing of certain television series continues to grow. For example, *Empire* started its second season in Fall 2015, by achieving "a record 1.3 million tweets when it aired on Sept 23. The large Twitter audience coincided with a huge live TV audience. About 16 million people saw the premiere, according to Nielsen" (Manjoo, 2015).

A Twitter feed can act as a huge, real-time focus group of the audience members that are most passionate and therefore do most to spread the word and share their excitement, which is a pretty good definition of the slippery term, **social media engagement**. A competitor, Google, asserts in its own self-promotional materials that people's engagement is more important than the number of people exposed, and that brands should, "super-serve the most important people for their brand first and use the resulting insights and advocacy to then broaden their reach and make the entire media and marketing plan work better" (Levy, 2015, Introductory section).

A Nielsen study using brain scans of viewers confirmed claims that Twitter activity "is an accurate indicator of the overall audience's interest in a show, right down to the specific scene" (Goel, 2015). For those doing public relations for television clients, there are other reasons to generate Twitter commentary about a client: "In a study Twitter conducted with Fox, the network found that people who noticed tweets about *Empire* said they were far more likely than people who had seen no tweets to say they were interested in next watching the show in real time" (Manjoo, 2015). Real-time viewing means watching TV on TV, ads included, which is what advertisers want.

In addition, people who saw tweets were more interested in time-shifted viewing, possibly because "people who notice a conversation about a show decide to catch up by watching previous episodes online" (Manjoo, 2015).

Fans and fan communities

Television brands were some of the earliest to realize the power of fan engagement and fan communities. For example, *Star Trek* fans, called Trekkies, held yearly conventions and fostered fan-created content focused on a long-since-canceled TV series. Eventually their passion led Paramount to create Star Trek films and spin-off series, such as *Star Trek: The Next Generation* and the many later sequels, prequels, and reboots. In late 2015, CBS announced that it would mark the 50th anniversary of the franchise in 2016 by creating a new 2017 "Star Trek" series. The new series would be available only to paid-subscribers of the digital platform, CBS All Access. The CBS press release quoted Marc DeBevoise, head of digital media, as saying that the franchise's "devoted and passionate fan base" ("New 'Star Trek,'" 2015) would be a driver of the new business model. Incidentally, the corporate owners, called Paramount at the time, had used the 25th anniversary of the franchise to drive the development of a new television network by launching the series, *Star Trek: The Next Generation*. The network, called UPN (United Paramount Network) later merged with the Warner Bros. network called the WB to form what is currently the CW. The power of a devoted fan community, if properly cultivated and appreciated, can be leveraged to launch multi-million-dollar brand extensions and innovative business models.

Social media measurement

Using social media to engage fan communities for a television series also has the advantage of being an easily measured element of a public relations plan. It is relatively easy to compile **social media metrics**, such as numbers and the percentage increase of YouTube views, Facebook likes, and Twitter followers. One can also access **social media analytics**, such as graphs that pinpoint helpful information about individual tweets and posts, such as the number of likes and clicks. Here is a brief summary of the ways TV publicists are using social media right now. PR can create two-way conversations with the mass audience in a number of ways:

1. Have a website that answers most of people's questions.
2. Use Facebook for Q&As that answer representative questions.
3. Use Twitter to retweet fans' posts.
4. Use Twitter to answer or respond to representative comments or queries.

5. Be inventive, creative, and outrageous to get people talking among themselves on social media.
6. Offer special opportunities to die-hard fans, and they will do much of the PR for you through social media word of mouth.

Both traditional media coverage and social media engagement contribute to achieving the PR ratings goal for a network television series, and both can be used strategically throughout the PR cycle.

The Network Television PR Cycle

A **public relations cycle** is a pattern that is repeated regularly over time. Since it repeats, there is often no specific beginning or end, especially when considering network television. Chapter 4 has already discussed the place of the Emmy Awards in launching the important fall television season. The network television season traditionally follows the school calendar. Its first day (season premiere) is in the fall; its last day (season finale) is in May; and summer is vacation time (the production companies go on hiatus and the networks program reruns). Therefore, it seems logical to start in the fall and discuss the following repeating public relations opportunities: September pre-season publicity; the Emmy Awards; season premieres; November sweeps; Christmas hiatus (reruns, holiday specials); January mid-season replacements and premieres; February sweeps; spring break; May sweeps, season finales, and the **upfronts** (the presentation of the new fall schedule to advertisers); summer hiatus and campaigns for Emmy nominations; August campaigns for Emmy votes; and again the pre-season publicity culminating in the Emmy Awards, and the next new season's premieres.

Throughout the cycle, the PR goal for a TV series is to be the No. 1 show in its time period (based on the ratings), or at least to improve the ratings versus those for the same timeslot last season.

PR Objectives

Objectives for any TV series include: high pre-season awareness; high sampling of the premiere; high ratings with desirable demographics; and increased ratings that mean the show wins the timeslot, beats week-ago numbers, and beats year-ago numbers. Objectives for all shows—new and returning—include a strong debut, which is facilitated by publicity opportunities afforded by the Emmy nominations for returning shows, and the other Emmy-related publicity opportunities discussed in the Sidebar in Chapter 4.

To take advantage of awareness created by the Emmy Awards, most series have their fall premieres during the week right after the Awards. The overnight Nielsen ratings immediately tell network executives which returning series had strong audience retention and which new series had strong awareness leading to sampling.

Then the key objectives are audience retention for the second week and a build in ratings, as word of mouth spreads after the launch. Strong showings in the three main sweeps periods (November, February, May) are essential to ensure renewal for a next season.

Renewals are announced and new series are introduced to advertisers during one week in May called the **upfronts**. Each network has a day or half day to impress the New York advertising community with the strength of its schedule and especially its new shows for fall by doing extravagant multimedia presentations and executive speeches (prepared by PR), as well as introducing the new and returning stars (travel, accommodations, hair, and makeup arranged by PR).

Strong ratings for the season finale, especially ending with a cliffhanger, help the audience remember the show during the summer rerun season. Once a show is renewed, it enters the Emmy Award part of the cycle.

To publicize the new fall season, tactics may include:

- TV—Book stars on the talk-show circuit
- Radio, social media—Reach demos through contests
- Events—Cast members participate in charity events
- TV & events—Cast participation in Emmys and big wins
- Print—Feature articles, cover shots, and fashion shoots
- PR stunts—Creative tactics

Thus, the public relations cycle begins all over again for the next Emmy Awards and the premiere of the fall network television season.

Conclusion

This chapter explains the management structure and business priorities of network television, because it is the business of a public relations practitioner to know the client's business. Only then can public relations plans be aligned with the client's business goal. In the case of network television, the goal is high Nielsen ratings in the desirable age demographics of 18–49 and especially the younger, 18–34 demos, with more emphasis on urban markets versus rural ones.

Because network television requires a national audience, media relations work includes producing complex events that bring television journalists together from across the country—the TCA meetings in Los Angeles in July and January. Network publicists also produce affiliate meetings to cultivate and inform the owners and managers of local stations, and the upfronts in New York in May, when the networks showcase their fall schedules and new shows for the advertising community.

In addition to media relations work with traditional media, television publicists also make masterful use of the network and a show's website, as well as reach out via social media in new and inventive ways.

Finally, the chapter outlines the **network television PR cycle**, which generally follows the school calendar. During the summer, the Emmy Awards cycle discussed in Chapter 4 kicks into high gear to maintain audience awareness over the summer. Understanding the Emmy Awards cycle and the network television PR cycle forms a strong basis for understanding the complexities of public relations for the other television business models to be discussed in Chapter 6.

Key Terms—In bold in the text

Sample two-sentence definition and example

Advertising Department: At a television network, the Advertising Department creates and pays for all of the print, outdoor, and other ads and commercials not on the network itself that promote the network's shows, as opposed to PR placements, which are not paid for. For example, the ABC Advertising Department might create and pay for an outdoor campaign of bus stop ads and billboards for *How to Get Away with Murder*.

Advertising Sales Department
Affiliate Relations
Broadcast Department
Broadcast Standards and Practices (BS&P)
Business Affairs and Legal Department

Casting Department
Current Programming Department
Demographics for TV ratings
Development Department
Federal Communications Commission (FCC)
Government and Community Relations Department
Licensing Agreement
Linear Viewing
Live +3
Live +7
Marketing Department
Nationals (weekly ratings)
Network Affiliates
Network Owned and Operated Stations, also known as O&Os
Network Television PR Cycle
News Division
Nielsen Ratings
O&Os, also known as Network Owned and Operated Stations
On-Air Promotion
Outdoor Advertising
Over-the-Top Viewing (OTT)
Overnights (fast ratings)
PR Plan Objectives
Press Junket
Prime Time
Prime-Time Programming
Print Advertising
Production Company
Programming Department
Public Relations Cycle
Public Relations Goal
Public Relations Objectives
Publicity Department
Research Department
Round-Robin Interviews
Scheduling Department
Show Runner
Social Media Analytics

Social Media Engagement
Social Media Metrics
Sweeps
Television Critics Association (TCA)
Television Network
Upfronts
Video on Demand (VOD)

Suggested reading and resources

Littleton, C. (2015b, February 11). TV's new math: Networks crunch their own ratings to track multiplatform viewing. Retrieved from http://variety.com/2015/tv/features/broad-cast-nets-move-closer-to-developing-ratings-that-consider-auds-delayed-viewing-hab-its-1201430321/

· 6 ·

PR CYCLES FOR SYNDICATED SHOWS, CABLE CHANNELS, AND STREAMING SERVICES, PLUS THE CELEBRITY PR IMAGE-REPAIR CYCLE

Chapter Overview: When you finish this chapter, you should be able to answer the following questions:

- What is the difference between off-network syndication and first-run syndication, and how are they publicized?
- What is the difference between basic cable and premium cable, and how are they publicized?
- How do Netflix and Amazon publicize their paid subscription, made-for-binge-viewing, original series?
- SIDEBAR: The Entertainment PR Toolbox—Press Statements and the Celebrity PR Image-Repair Cycle

Introduction

This chapter discusses the publicity cycles for television programming that diverges in various ways from the network model discussed in the previous chapter. Keeping the network model in mind, each section will delineate both the similarities and, more importantly, the differences in the PR goal, strategies, and overall cycle. This chapter covers publicity for off-network syndication, first-run syndication, premium cable, basic cable, and original programming for streaming services.

As discussed in the previous chapter, a network is made up of one local station in each television market. The parent network has the right to broadcast its national programming in certain timeslots, including: prime time; the evening and late-night national news; a morning show, such as *Good Morning America*; perhaps a day-time serial (soap opera); late-night talk shows; and whatever sports programming the network has the rights to. Local stations, however, are on the air 24/7. Each station fills all the other slots with programming from a variety of sources; each sells local advertising on those shows; and each has to publicize, promote, and advertise that programming locally.

Very few local stations have the financial wherewithal to create much original programming of their own, beyond their local evening and late-night news broadcasts and in some larger markets a local morning talk show (Barnes, 2015c, June 29). Instead, the stations license the rights to broadcast series that have been made available by license holders for **syndication**, meaning for individual sales to individual stations. Syndicated programming falls into two main categories: **off-network syndication** (reruns) and **first-run syndication** (new, original programming).

The PR Cycle for Off-Network Syndication or Reruns

Off-network syndication refers to reruns of programs that were originally produced by an outside production company or an in-house production company for a network, usually to be scheduled in prime time. The network pays a licensing fee that offsets most of the cost of production, and usually gains the rights to three broadcasts of each episode, the premiere and two reruns. After that, ownership and rights revert to the production company.

After a production company has produced 80 or more network episodes (about 18 per season for four or five seasons), the series can be "sold into syndication" by the producer. This means a big payday for the producers, actors, writers, and directors, who receive **residual payments**, as specified by their guild or union contracts, each time an episode is broadcast anywhere globally.

The off-network syndication PR cycle

For a syndication sale, the production company's marketing department coordinates a campaign that involves the sales force, as well as publicity, advertising, and promotion. Publicity will prepare a public relations plan that will take the series from the beginning of the sales process right through the on-air launch and beyond—the **off-network syndication PR cycle**.

First, the production company prepares a sales kit that highlights the strengths of the series with comparisons to similar series that have achieved excellent local ratings for stations. The Nielsen ratings for various demographics that the series has achieved on the network are of primary importance in enticing a high syndication sale price. These series have already proven themselves successful ratings magnets. The job of the sales force is to show each potential station buyer how this series will increase its ratings in its intended local timeslot, and therefore be well worth a high purchase price.

PR strategy

For off-network syndication, the publicity plan is based on the audience's familiarity with the series, its stars, and its "world." There is a pre-sold audience of fans. In addition, a wider potential audience is "aware" of the series. Even if viewers haven't watched it in its network timeslot during the multiple years of its network run, they have probably come across articles or clips or interviews or Emmy-season publicity. The title, the stars, and the characters have become familiar. The goal of off-network syndication publicity is great ratings in each local market. The main public relations strategy is to use viewers' familiarity with the show to trigger their intention to view it in a daily local timeslot.

As part of the sales process, the production company commits to the kinds of publicity and promotional support it will provide for the local launch and on an ongoing basis over the course of the years covered by the sales contract. Production company support usually includes the involvement of the actors in filming special local station tags for the show. For example, to support the local stations that purchase *Big Bang Theory* in syndication, the production company, Warner Bros., may commit to shooting a series of station identifications, such as, Sheldon or Penny saying, "Watch me on *Big Bang Theory* here on WPWR, my Fox Chicago 32, weeknights at 6 p.m." Warner television publicity may also promise a satellite press tour that will allow purchasing stations' local morning talk show anchors, such as those on Fox's *Good Day Chicago*, to interview the stars live on the air in the days leading up to the launch. The syndication sales force visits the various local stations in each market, and presents the ratings argument as well as the publicity plan, as it tries to achieve the highest possible per episode license fee.

Sale to multiple platforms

These days the syndication sales arrangements can be complex. While new episodes may continue to be created for the original network's prime-time schedule, the reruns can be sold simultaneously to several types of media outlets that are not direct competitors, for example: local broadcast; superstations such as WGN America; basic cable such as TBS; and subscription video on demand, such as Hulu Plus. For example, in February 2014, *Elementary*, the updated Sherlock Holmes detective series broadcast in prime time on the CBS network, was sold with contracts totaling $3 million per episode to WGN, Hulu Plus, and unnamed broadcast outlets (Rose, 2014).

Big Bang Theory was sold in off-network syndication in spring 2010. Local stations paid a total of $500,000 per episode, and in addition, TBS paid $1.5 million per episode, so the series sold for more than *Seinfeld*. The series debuted in off-network syndication in the fall of 2011, but Warner Bros. continued creating new episodes for CBS prime time for many years afterwards. Happily for the local stations, publicity generated for new network episodes also supports the syndicated episodes by helping maintain awareness and familiarity.

Reruns as lead-ins

Most local stations programmed *Big Bang Theory* as part of their lead-in to prime time. Usually a station's local evening news and local late-night news are its biggest profit centers. Therefore, each station is particularly concerned to have strong, promotable shows in the lead-in time slots. Network affiliates, for example, want strong network series in prime time, especially in the hour leading into their local late-night newscast. Local stations pay the most for an off-network series that can be a strong bridge between the evening news and the beginning of prime time. Meanwhile, TBS used *Big Bang Theory* as the lead-in to *The Conan O'Brien Show* at 11 p.m., sometimes scheduling a block of *Big Bang Theory* episodes running back to back for the entire evening.

Name recognition

Publicity for the launch of *Big Bang Theory* built on name recognition for the show, i.e., brand-name familiarity or awareness for the title and for the stars. The local stations, which had paid a high price, marketed the series and timeslot aggressively using: on-air promos; features on local news broadcasts and local morning shows; PR generated feature news stories, as well as paid advertising, in local newspapers; and heavy local radio promotions, such as contests and giveaways.

When *Big Bang Theory* launched in off-network syndication in the fall of 2011, a typical trade magazine article proclaimed that it was "off to a bang-up start" (Block, 2011). This article and others clearly came from a Warner Bros. publicity press release, because only Warner Bros. would have access to this level of detail about the ratings. It reported a 13 percent improvement over the stations' timeslots in the previous year, making it second only to *Two and a Half Men*.

Because the public relations goal for off-network syndication is higher Nielsen ratings (higher for each individual station than the syndicated series in the timeslot the previous year), both the public relations and the sales plan for *Big Bang Theory*, as well as the strategy of leveraging pre-sold audience awareness, have to be considered successful.

The PR Cycle for First-Run Syndicated Series

First-run syndication refers to series made up of all-original episodes—not previously broadcast on a network—that are created especially to be sold to a large number of individual local stations, usually to be run five days a week in the same daily timeslot (called **strip syndication**). First-run shows include *The Ellen DeGeneres Show*, entertainment news shows such as *Access Hollywood*, and game shows such as *Wheel of Fortune*. Both the off-network and the **first-run syndication PR cycles** involve sales of a show to one station in each local market, but the source and type of programming are different, and the strategy of the publicity plan is different. The PR goal, however, is again the same— higher Nielsen ratings in each station's timeslot versus the previous year.

The main strategy for achieving the ratings goal for a new, first-run syndicated series is to create a snowball effect—maybe even an avalanche—of interest by local stations. The sales people want to make station managers feel that they'll miss out on the next big thing (the next Oprah), if they don't sign on quickly before their cross-town rivals make a deal. When stations pay a high licensing fee, they are motivated to schedule the show in a good timeslot and also to work hard to publicize it locally, thus giving the show the best possible shot to meet its ratings goal.

Timeline for first-run syndication

First-run series are developed independently of a network, so there is no network-financed pilot. The public relations process is usually more than 15 months from announcement of the series in the spring of calendar year one to the premiere in the late summer of calendar year two. The early publicity is of interest mainly to the trade press, which keeps score on the sales of various new competitors. PR broadens to the business press in the winter of year two and then to consumers in the summer of year two, leading up to the premiere. Let's look at the typical steps in the 15-month process of launching a new first-run syndicated series that will broadcast a new original episode five days a week on various local stations across the country.

Development

In spring of year one, an independent production company such as Warner Bros., Paramount, or King World develops a project and announces casting. Sometimes the announcement is done with great fanfare at an elaborate PR-arranged press conference, trying to keep the format and host(s) of the show a surprise until the big reveal—something that was always difficult to pull off and is almost impossible in the age of social media.

Once the show is announced, during summer and fall of year one, the production company creates a sample reel of the projected show. Because of the high cost of production, especially for a show shot before a live audience, the reel is usually not a full-length pilot, but rather a sample of the projected format and segments called a **presentation**. The sales force uses the presentation and other publicity and sales materials to begin selling the series to the most likely stations—stations that have a ratings weakness in a morning, afternoon, or late-night timeslot, compared to their cross-town competitors.

The snowball strategy

By early winter, the producer's sales force "clears" some stations—gets tentative deals. Publicity uses press releases to announce these **clearances** and the percentage of the country that has been cleared in order to create a sense that the snowball is rolling and an avalanche is gathering. Because the targets are station managers, not general viewers, this publicity is aimed at trade publications. When clearances gain some momentum, PR announces a "firm go." It's never actually a very firm go, however. These original programs are expensive to produce, and the producers have to put out new episodes five days a week year around. To be profitable, they need to be in good timeslots in large markets and in a large percentage of the country. So a production company looks closely at the contracted commitments from stations before finally deciding to commit to production.

NATPE

The end of January each year is make-or-break time for nascent first-run series. The **National Association of Television Programming Executives (NATPE)** trade show provides an opportunity for the production company's sales force to meet with multiple station managers and programmers from across the country to lock in new sales and to firm up previous tentative commitments. After NATPE many shows die a quick death, because it becomes clear to the production company that clearances are insufficient to generate a profit.

Pre-Production

If the sales process has been successful, the production company announces it will produce the show. The planning process goes into high gear, and publicity broadens to the business press, because now the company is committing to a large investment in production, possibly for years to come. The producing company sets up a dedicated production office and staffs up with segment producers. It leases a sound stage that will hold a sizeable live audience, builds a set, and hires a crew.

In the summer of year two, the publicity focus widens from the trade and business press to the consumer press. The challenge is how to create awareness and viewing intention among viewers for a new, never-before-seen daily series. Part of that burden is on the host, who has been chosen from the start for name recognition and audience appeal. A host who has been a star in another area of entertainment, such as the well-known and well-liked Ellen DeGeneres, becomes the publicity focus, similar to the way off-network publicity leverages the star power of series regulars. Publicity will pitch the host to magazines, newspapers, and other television shows, particularly early-morning and late-night talk shows.

On the pre-production front, segment producers are on the lookout for the perfect guests for the show's premiere week, which will define the style of the show. Segment producers take pitches from industry publicists and agents representing talent, and/or they search out ordinary people with extraordinary life stories. The segment producers are thinking about who or what will make compelling television, which usually coincides with what the show's public relations staff and PR agency will find easily promotable.

The publicity build-up

The publicity increases in the weeks before the premiere. Usually new first-run series debut in late August or early September, just as kids are back in school. This gives the new show a head start on the fall season. It also allows the show to offer a publicity platform to Emmy nominees and those promoting network series for the new fall season. This premiere schedule means that segment producers can book more high-profile guests for the first weeks' shows than might otherwise be interested in an unproven talk show. In addition, the Emmys can provide an opportunity for the host to be seen on the red carpet, or as a presenter—depending on his/her industry clout. So here again, even for a series that has just debuted, the Emmy Award PR cycle represents an outside opportunity that every savvy industry publicist will take advantage of.

Daily publicity

Once a five-day-a-week, first-run series is on the air, every single weekday, the publicity and promotion departments highlight the next day or two and the next week's guests, and they tease their surprises. This hamster wheel of press releases, pitches, radio promotions, and press interviews needs to keep spinning as long as a first-run series is on the air.

Radio promotions can be especially effective for first-run TV series, because both the television station and the radio station are local. Radio advertising sales departments have accurate, audited figures on both their number of listeners and their listener demographics, so it is relatively easy for a TV station marketer to figure out which radio station and which timeslots to use to reach the desired demographics.

In connection with radio contests, public relations practitioners need to understand the legal distinctions the Federal Communications Commission and state laws draw between **legal contests** and **illegal lotteries**. A lottery, which is mostly illegal—except for those run by a state lottery authority—has three characteristics according to the FCC. It is "any game, contest or promotion that combines the elements of prize, chance and consideration" (FCC, n.d.). "Consideration" means that participation requires buying something (a bar of soap or a car) or paying a fee (lottery ticket). That is why one so often hears the disclaimer, "No purchase necessary."

A legal radio contest can have two of the three elements, such as a prize that can be won by chance, or a prize that can be won by demonstrating a skill, such as identifying a song. The rules for legal contests are complex and may vary by locality or state. Therefore, the syndicating producer will usually work with a specialty marketing firm. For example, MerryMedia has run nationwide and local contests and promotions for off-network series, such as *Modern Family* and *How I Met Your Mother*; and for first-run series such as *Dr. Phil* and *Rachel Ray* (see merrymedia.net). Syndicators use contests as a way to keep awareness and intention to watch high over the lifetime of the series, especially for sweeps periods.

Contracts and cancellations

How long will that be? That depends on the ratings—of course. Shows with weak and fading ratings face cancellation. For example, on October 29 of the second season of *Anderson Live*, the syndicated talk show hosted by CNN anchor Anderson Cooper, the production company announced that the show would last only through the end of the season, because of its weak ratings (Andreeva, 2012b). *The Queen Latifah Show* was also canceled early in its second season, and again production continued into the spring after the announced cancellation (Kenneally, 2014) to fulfill contract terms and give stations time to plan how to realign their schedules. Ratings had been increasing, but apparently not fast enough to make up for costs. Other series languish and get moved to less desirable timeslots late at night, meaning lower ad rates. Less income means that continuing to run the series no longer makes sense for the station, and if the stations start backing out, the production company will decide to cancel the series.

Publicity for Premium Cable Series

Cable television has two publicity templates based on its two main business models: **basic cable** is supported by advertising; **premium cable** is supported by paid subscriptions.

Premium cable, which includes HBO, Showtime, and others, is based on a subscription model, not on advertising sales. Viewers have to sign up specifically for the premium channel and pay an additional fee on top of the fee for basic cable delivery. Rather than being concerned about ratings and advertising dollars, premium cable channels have the goal of increasing their subscriber base by generating new subscribers and keeping current ones based on the quality, exclusivity, and prestige of their offerings.

The history of premium cable

In the early years of cable, premium channels were movie channels. Today, it's hard to realize that there was a time before cable delivery to individual households. With only three commercial networks plus PBS, and a scattering of independent local stations in large markets, the public had limited opportunities to see big-budget studio films: first was the theatrical release; then a dozen years later, crowd pleasing studio films began to be bought by a network and scheduled with lots of publicity, fanfare—and commercials—first for NBC *Saturday Night at the Movies* (1961) and soon for movie nights on ABC and CBS. While old black-and-white films, such as those starring the Three Stooges, were syndicated to local stations, newer foreign films and critics' favorites could only be seen in art film revival theaters in the biggest cities or as part of a university film series. By the 1980s, with the development of new technology, studios made many films available for individual purchase on videotape at high prices (often $129 or $99). This exorbitant pricing led to the era of video rental stores.

In that context, premium cable offered a compelling buying proposition. By winning contracts from studios to show their latest films soon after the theatrical release, premium channels had easy-to-publicize, "must-see" offerings of titles audiences were eager to watch, because the publicity for the theatrical release was still fresh in people's minds. The subscription price for an entire year of HBO often cost less than the purchase of one home video, and a family could watch numerous new-to-them movies each month—all uninterrupted by commercial breaks.

Soon, however, the studios were licensing more movies to the networks and newer movies were being syndicated to the local stations. The premium channels were running out of movies to purchase, and they needed to do something different to keep up their subscriber bases. Thus, HBO, Showtime, and other premium channels began to create original, exclusive programming:

original movies; original, hour-long drama series; and original half-hour sit-coms.

The premium cable PR cycle

The **premium cable PR cycle** focuses on promoting each piece of original programming as a must-see, must-subscribe event. Under the slogan, "It's not television; it's HBO," the public relations practitioners use two primary strategies to achieve the goal of increasing subscribership. First, they leverage the name recognition of the movie stars, film directors, and feature film writers that the programming executives entice to become part of an exciting project "That's not TV," because these people are too important and too rich and famous to sully their careers with "just television." Securing this level of talent can then be used to create buzz and "must-see" excitement. Usually HBO has debuted its series in June, right as the network season ends. Each premiere is supported by a full-out publicity campaign and a lot of advertising, as well as a push for major reviews that can then be used as pull-quotes in advertising and as bait to pitch stories for feature coverage.

HBO and the Emmy PR cycle

When it was just making original movies, HBO successfully lobbied the industry to end the programming ghetto of the Cable Ace Awards and make cable programs eligible for the Emmy process. Once eligible for the Emmys, which are televised nationally, rotating each year among the major networks, HBO moved to a new publicity strategy to generate and maintain premium subscriptions. HBO has made masterful use of the Emmy cycle to achieve free media placements and wider audience awareness.

HBO's typical summer debut strategy makes a movie or series ineligible for Emmy nominations during the current summer. The prestige of the cast of movie stars, however, makes them exciting and welcome on the red carpet and as Emmy presenters, and they will be eligible for the next year's Emmy Award cycle. At that point, HBO pulls out all the stops to mount extensive, expensive Emmy campaigns to generate nominations and then wins in the movies-for-television and miniseries categories. Much to the chagrin and the dismay of the networks, HBO regularly outpaces all the networks put together in the movie, miniseries, and hour-drama categories and in the related acting and directing categories. During the Emmy cycle, HBO is everywhere in the news, with more media coverage coming to HBO for winning bragging rights for more Emmys than the networks.

Only a few savvy trade journalists, such as Brian Lowry, formerly at *Variety*, have written about Emmy issues related to non-network originals (Lowry, 2014) and about the uneven Emmy playing field resulting from premium cable's much higher budgets and much shorter production seasons. HBO seems determined, however, to use the Emmy nomination period to publicize its current summer offerings to gain subscribers and to use the Emmy bragging rights to generate new subscribers who will want to catch up through reruns before the debut of the next season of an original series.

Publicity for Basic Cable

In contrast to the premium cable model, the business model of basic cable is based on advertising sales, and the prices for ad time are determined by the Nielsen ratings compared to all of the competition, just as for network television (see Chapter 5).

Figure 6.1: Outdoors at Nickelodeon Animation Studio in Burbank.
Photo credit: 2015 Carol Ames.

Basic cable channels include A&E, Bravo, E! Entertainment Television, ESPN, HGTV, Nickelodeon, TNT, USA, and a multitude of others, which are included with the monthly fee for cable service from the local provider, such as Comcast or Charter, or from a satellite service such as DIRECTV. Each channel competes with all the others on a local cable system to determine the sliver of customers' basic cable fee that the provider will pay them for offering their programming. For example, in 2015 Comedy Central reportedly received 22 cents per subscriber, per month for its entire lineup (Weiner, 2015b, p. 45). In most cases, the cable channels are also advertiser supported. Their advertising rates depend on the number of viewers they can draw compared to all other options, including the networks.

Niche strategy

To compete, most channels focus on a **niche audience**, a narrow audience of viewers with specialized interests, rather than the mass audience that network television must reach to support its expensive programming. To reach its target niche, a basic cable channel achieves buzz by emphasizing the sensationalistic elements of its programming, for example, the blood and gore of a horror series or the outrageousness of a reality series.

Off-cycle premieres

Cable channels promote their original drama series much as the networks do. The main difference is that basic cable originals often debut off-cycle from the network school-year cycle, usually scheduling two short seasons per year. For example, USA has successfully found an audience for slick dramas with attractive, well-dressed casts (*White Collar*, *Suits*) by publicizing and promoting split, 16-episode seasons, often with 10 episodes debuting in June and the final six debuting in January. Both periods are times during which the networks program mostly reruns, for which they do minimal publicity. The television critics and feature writers are eager for something and someone new to write about, and the basic cable publicists take advantage of the lull, just as we saw above with HBO and Showtime.

Taking a page from HBO's "prestige" PR playbook, in 2007 AMC (originally named American Movie Classics) debuted its first original drama series, *Mad Men*, which went on to become the first basic cable series to win an

Emmy for Best Drama Series. *Mad Men* and other AMC series, such as *Breaking Bad* and its later spinoff, *Better Call Saul*, also hitched much of their publicity to critical praise and the Emmy Award PR cycle.

Masters of digital media

The use of digital media for publicity came to the forefront during *Mad Men's* lengthy run. By the final season, publicity was using the full capabilities of the website, with a wide variety of content: posts, games, interviews, photos, and most importantly—press releases, which on the website become content marketing (Norris, 2015). The company didn't reply to fan queries on the website, but the information was available for all who clicked on it. *Mad Men* also had what they called a "social club." It was actually a newsletter—meaning that the company messages went directly to fans without going through a media intermediary (Norris, 2015). *Mad Men* PR focused much of its digital efforts on Twitter. The *Mad Men* Twitter account was activated early in the life of Twitter and sent more than 4,000 tweets to more than 200,000 followers. Spring 2015, during the final season, the show actively used #madmen and #endofanera. It exploited the full capabilities of Twitter's 140 characters by including links to complete stories, photos, and videos. Posts of famous quotes from past episodes and seasons aimed to trigger **nostalgia**, a longing to revisit and reconnect with old experiences or old friends.

The Royals, which was E! Entertainment's foray into scripted programming, premiered March 15, 2015. The show's robust website had trailers, photos, sneak peeks, and behind-the-scenes features. But they also entertained people and got tongues wagging with some creative digital tactics. In December 2014, Britain's real Queen Elizabeth gave her traditional yearly Christmas Address. *The Royals* immediately uploaded a profane and forthright Christmas address by Elizabeth Hurley, the show's star (J. N. Barnes, 2015). It went viral on the website, Facebook, and YouTube, with the caption, "Queen drops the F-bomb" ("Queen Drops," 2014). The viral publicity must have boded well, because E! renewed *The Royals* for a second season already in January ahead of its mid-March premiere (Wagmeister, 2015). In this kind of situation, the public relations strategy is to create a buzz—to make news so as to cut through the clutter to let people know that the E! Entertainment cable channel theretofore known for celebrity news coverage was ready to make its mark on scripted programming.

The reality TV PR cycle

For reality programming, basic cable uses formats without expensive professional casts and without scripts written at Writers Guild minimum fees. These unscripted, but highly manipulated, series can make regular people into instant celebrities. Creating celebrities is the primary programming and public relations strategy used to achieve cable's PR ratings goal, which again is high ratings versus the show in the timeslot the previous year. By creating its own celebrities, a cable channel not only gets inexpensive programming, but its contract usually makes the channel a partner in the potential celebrities' outside projects—cookbooks, speaking engagements, fashion lines, and so forth. This strategy also creates a plethora of cross-brand promotional opportunities for both the channel and the newly minted celeb. The Kardashian juggernaut is an example—or the template—for the basic cable public relations and business model for reality programming, and for the **reality TV PR cycle**.

During development of a reality series, the cable producer with a concept for a show holds interviews or casting sessions to find real people who are "interesting." This usually means people who are self-confident, talkative, gossipy, un-self-aware, and attractive, odd, sexually ambiguous, or easily identifiable as a type (or cliché), such as the volatile fat woman. Various combinations of cast members (often friends and family) are considered for the cast, until a core group is found that has lots of potential for emotion and conflict. The typical show then explores a special niche of American culture (a **sub-culture**) that most viewers would not have access to in daily life: rich, bored housewives in Southern California (*The Real Housewives of Orange County*), for example; would-be avant-garde fashion designers (*Project Runway*); or a southern family that made a fortune creating duck calls (*Duck Dynasty*). A cast member can become a "celebrity" or gain notoriety by behavior that shocks or amuses viewers, because it is outrageous or extreme.

Leveraging social media followers

Publicists work with the cast members to help them gain media attention. Social media are especially useful, because the cast can, for example, be encouraged or required to live tweet during the east- and west-coast premieres of each episode, so that viewers feel as if they are getting the inside scoop. Bravo has a talk show, *Watch What Happens Live*, that features cast members from the evening's reality offerings. Additionally, Bravo can have the cast members of their various shows follow one another on social media, thus adding the other shows' fan bases to their own social media followers. It's no surprise that for years Kim Kardashian ranked No. 1 in followers on Twitter. She or her social media team understood the value of retweeting fans and of selective direct replies to fans to give the sense of a two-way conversation. At this writing, Kim Kardashian West still ranks No. 14 in followers (Twittercounter, 2016).

Making news and the celebrity crisis

Because cable channels are small operations with limited staff, each channel is hoping to develop an inexpensive reality series that strikes a chord with the public, i.e., that *makes* news. That way a limited publicity staff can gain lots of free airtime, free newspaper coverage, and spiking social media analytics as the antics of the new celebrities dominate the 24-hour news cycle, talk shows, and private and social media conversations. For the cable channel, a best-case scenario presents itself when a secondary cast member becomes an audience favorite. The channel can then spin that person or a couple of those people off into an additional series of their own. This has happened multiple times with the Kardashian franchise (*Kourtney and Khloe Take the Hamptons*; *Khloe and Lamar*), for example, and with *Here Comes Honey Boo Boo*, a spinoff of *Toddlers & Tiaras*.

It's not surprising that these newbie celebrities can develop a sense of entitlement that makes them feel immune to norms of behavior and even above the law, for example, by driving under the influence of alcohol or drugs. When they step over the line by tweeting a racist remark or doing something that injures another person, the public relations practitioner may be able to calm the situation by using the **celebrity PR image-repair cycle** described in the SIDEBAR. The cable channel may put the series on hiatus until the crisis cools down, which forces the cast to disappear from public view, as suggested by the celebrity crisis cycle. If the series retains enough advertiser support and the offending celebrity appears contrite enough, the channel may return the series to the schedule.

The Entertainment PR Toolbox—Press Statements and the Celebrity PR Image-Repair Cycle

Since much of the content of both first-run syndicated programs and basic cable series, such as afternoon talk shows and early evening entertainment news series, covers celebrity crises, including DUIs, brawls, accidents, and addiction, this SIDEBAR delineates appropriate public relations responses to negative events and details the celebrity crisis PR cycle.

The positive stories in circulation in traditional media and social media often originate from public relations activities, such as a publicist distributing a press release (complete news story); issuing a media alert (an invitation for the press to come to a specific place at a specific time to gather material for a story); or pitching an exclusive angle for a story to one specific journalist.

The public relations objective in a negative situation, however, is for media and public interest in the story to fade away as quickly as possible. Therefore, practitioners *almost never* write a press release, pitch a story, or hold an event such as a press conference about a negative situation.

Therefore, the negative stories that circulate usually come from news reporting and research by journalists, from gossip sites such as www.perezhilton.com, or from muckraking sites such as www.tmz.com. Without good public relations management, the Bad and the Ugly may quickly develop into PR crises. **Hyperturbulence**, a term adapted from management research, is defined as, "what happens when complexity and change exceed the collective adaptive capacity" of those affected (McCann & Selsky, 1984, p. 460). In public relations, hyperturbulence means a situation spiraling out of control, going from bad to worse. Rather than fading away, new details keep emerging. The controversy grows and widens, as it did with golfer Tiger Woods's career-hobbling sex scandals prior to his divorce and his eventual return to professional golf.

Such negative situations demand an active, thoughtful response, not evasion. Journalistic ethics require news stories to include comments from all direct participants; at the very least, a print news story must say, "Star so-and-so did not immediately respond to a request for a comment," which means the journalist made at least a half-hearted attempt to verify the story at the source.

Therefore, a **press statement**, which can be used as a quotation by journalists, is usually the first step in the celebrity PR crisis or image-repair cycle. A well-crafted press statement:

- Is limited to one to three carefully worded sentences
- Provides accurate information
- Can be used by the media as a direct or indirect quotation

- Offers no opportunity for follow-up questions or further comments
- Should work to cut down on media speculation and hyperturbulence

This is an example of an effective press statement regarding a celebrity: "Patrick Swayze passed away peacefully today with family at his side after facing the challenges of his illness for the last 20 months." The statement was released by his publicist, Annett Wolf, and appeared in various news reports attributed to her or to a spokesperson for the family.

When comedian Robin Williams committed suicide and there was a media frenzy speculating about the reason, his widow, Susan Schneider, issued a press statement that included the information that Williams had been in the early stages of Parkinson's disease. The statement was widely quoted and referred to and seemed to quell speculation, as least partially because it allowed reporters to focus their follow-up stories on Parkinson's disease (Rothberg & Brown, 2014), rather than on speculating about the reasons for the suicide.

The most frequent types of negative or problematic situations in entertainment seem to be celebrities' arrests for driving under the influence of alcohol or drugs. In these cases, the celebrity crisis cycle, which can also be called the celebrity image-repair cycle, is usually some variation of the following: A negative incident occurs. The celeb's personal publicist quickly issues a press statement that apologizes to fans and family for disappointing them, mentions rehab or a period of rest and recovery from "exhaustion," and asks for privacy during this trying time.

Some things that should **never** be in a press statement:

- "Lindsey (Lohan) has entered Promises Rehab in Malibu," because the **paparazzi** (freelance photographers) will stake out the rehab center to get any possible photograph.
- After a DUI, "He'll be available to answer questions as soon as he is released," because he is likely still under the residual effects of the narcotic and is likely to be loose-tongued or angry at the police having dared to arrest a big star like himself.
- After an injury accident: "The pedestrian stepped in front of her car," because a client should never, ever appear to be blaming the victim.

After issuing a press statement, the publicist wants the celeb to disappear from public and media view. The movie *Hancock*, mentioned in Chapter 1, has the PR practitioner, played by Jason Bateman, tell the down-and-out superhero, played by Will Smith, to accept his jail sentence and serve his time, to "make them miss you." In cases of addiction, rehab serves the double function of removing the celeb from the public eye and hopefully also curing the addiction.

The next steps in the image-repair process are the most difficult for the publicist to manage. When reappearing in the public eye, the celebrity should be a new, better person who has learned a lesson from the experience. To complete the image-repair cycle, the celeb should demonstrate his/her transformation by having an immediate, spectacular success that focuses media and fan attention on the new news, not the old misstep.

This culmination of the image-repair process after his sex scandal was exemplified by Kobe Bryant leading the U.S. Olympic Basketball team to a gold medal in China; or after her breakdown and dismal, follow-up performance on the 2007 MTV Video Music Awards, Britney Spears making a successful comeback and launching a successful album.

When a reality celeb's transgression crosses certain lines, however, image repair may be impossible. One of those lines appears to be child sexual abuse, in connection with *19 Kids and Counting*, which was taken off the air in May 2015 due to allegations about past sexual misconduct of their oldest son and then canceled in July (Battaglio, 2015). Another line appears to be child endangerment. For example, when the mother in *Here Comes Honey Boo Boo* was reported to be seeing a convicted child molester, the TLC channel could not repair the damage (Hamedy, 2015) and canceled the series. In these cases, the tainted celebs find their audiences melting away, their series canceled, and their 15 minutes of fame used up—gone.

To sum up, basic cable can maintain and increase ratings (and therefore ad sales) with publicity that highlights sensationalism and outrageousness, either in subject matter (*The Walking Dead*) or in behavior (any part of the *Real Housewives* franchise). On the other hand, the public relations strategies for both basic cable and premium cable can, when possible, focus on prestige (*Mad Men*). This means assembling a high-profile, high-status cast and team, including creators and directors with classy entertainment pedigrees—preferably from successful feature films. The prestige strategy helps gain feature article and talk show coverage, helps assure getting great reviews that gain viewer attention, and later helps hitching a show's publicity to the power of the Emmy Awards PR cycle.

Subscription Streaming Services and the Binge-Viewing PR Cycle

Streaming services, which deliver programming via digital downloads through the Internet, include pay services such as Netflix, Amazon Prime, and Hulu Plus. Streaming also includes free services such as YouTube, Hulu, and the websites of program providers, such as ABC, CBS, and NBC, which offer their most recent episodes for viewers to catch up on. This section, however, focuses on publicity for pay or premium streaming services.

The public relations goal for pay streaming services such as Netflix and Amazon is to increase the subscriber base, which equals dollars each month by generating new subscribers and retaining current ones, just as with premium (subscription) cable, such as HBO. The main public relations strategy of subscription streaming services is to create must-see interest in shows for which a service holds exclusive streaming rights.

Originally these businesses licensed rights from television producers and movie studios and sent episodes and movies on DVDs to subscribers on a mail-and-return basis. As broadband speeds improved, they began providing TV episodes and entire movies as streaming downloads that could be accessed instantly on a subscriber's whim.

The binge-viewing PR cycle

Concurrently, customers began to **binge view** television programs. A 2015 Deloitte survey of two thousand people found that 68 percent over age 14 had binge viewed TV, and 31 percent said they watched "three or more episodes of the same series in a single sitting" at least once a week (Day, 2015). Other bingers consume entire seasons of television series, and even multiple seasons or the entire library of series episodes in chronological order, as soon as they become available.

The typical publicity for a rights acquisition deal that will foster binge viewing starts with a press announcement. For example, Netflix announces that it has acquired the rights to a past season of a current network series or to all of the seasons of an old television series. Media outreach, such as interviews with cast members, and coverage depend on the prestige of the series.

The Netflix announcement in mid-October 2014 of the acquisition of all 10 seasons of *Friends*, for example, received extensive press coverage, even though the series was being shown in off-network syndication for years. This splashy acquisition received wide coverage in the 10 weeks leading up to its availability for streaming on January 1, 2015, with one online commentator saying, "we can fully expect subscriptions to go through the roof between now and then in anticipation of the big day" (Hill, 2014). The publicity strategy for old series is to trigger emotions such as nostalgia; and the desire to enjoy binge viewing a complex story that evolves over dozens of episodes viewed in sequence, instead of the random grab bag of episodes from multiple seasons that syndicators play at the usual rate of one per day.

By making large numbers of episodes available all at once, these streaming services are riding the trend wave of binge viewing. Previously, one had to purchase an expensive, special edition, whole-season set of DVDs to indulge in binging, except for the rare occasion when a cable channel offered a weekend marathon of a fan favorite, interrupted by lots of commercials, of course, and not necessarily in chronological sequence.

The demand for new product

But what happens to Netflix and Amazon Prime when the availability of old series doesn't keep up with viewer demand? What happens when the networks invest in competing pay streaming services such as Hulu Plus and license the recent seasons of their series exclusively to that service first? How does a pay streaming service maintain and increase its subscriber base, if it can't license interesting, exclusive product?

Adapting to the increasingly limited amount of recent, high-quality programming available for them to license, both Amazon Prime and Netflix took the initiative to produce their own original series. Netflix made news by taking the financial risk of producing entire seasons before making their original series available for download: *House of Cards* (February 2013) and *Orange Is the New Black* (July 2013). Both series debuted to critical acclaim, which helped to generate a lot of media coverage the weeks of the premieres and afterwards.

Driving new subscriptions

Taking a page from HBO's PR playbook to sign up new subscribers and keep current ones, the streaming services leverage the power of positive reviews as the central public relations strategy for original series. Earlier in the chapter, we saw that premium cable hopes that advanced publicity will get viewers to sign up ahead of the first episode so that they don't feel that the train has passed them by, or subscribe to watch reruns of season one ahead of the start of season two. In contrast, much of the publicity and coverage for streaming originals is timed for the week *following* the premiere (Luistro, 2015). With streaming content, the early episodes are always available to be viewed in sequence, whenever a new subscriber signs up or a current subscriber decides to dive in.

Debuting in February, *House of Cards* was eligible for the Emmy cycle in 2013. Netflix made history by winning an Emmy for Outstanding Direct-ing for a Drama, the first prime-time Emmy for a web-only series. Again, the Emmy PR cycle, including "historic" nominations, red-carpet appearances, and on-air mentions helped drive subscriptions.

Another new Netflix series using Twitter extensively to create advance awareness was *Unbreakable Kimmy Schmidt*, a comedy created by Tina Fey and Robert Carlock. It began streaming 13 episodes on Netflix on March 6, 2015, but the premiere was preceded by a Twitter account purporting to be written by the character Kimmy herself. It focused on the Rip Van Winkle aspect of her return to the contemporary world after years as a captive, with tweets such as this one cited by Luistro (2015): "Who has a tape player? I am totally going to buy the first season of Moesha for my birthday #Kimmy Schmidt ("Unbreakable," 2015). The Netflix series used Kimmy's point of view to stim-ulate interest ahead of time, because its downloadable, on-demand availabil-ity eliminated having a specific timeslot when millions of viewers would be watching and tweeting, such as during the premiere of a Bravo basic cable episode. The constant availability of content from a streaming service, how-ever, offers the option of incorporating critics' rave reviews into the publicity plan for the first season.

Conclusion

The goal of public relations efforts should correspond with an organization's overall goal, which for most companies is "profitable revenue growth" (Scott, 2011, p. 139). In the world of television, revenue depends on two distinct business models. The first model is based on advertising sales, the price of which is determined by the Nielsen ratings for each station in each timeslot versus every competitor. This determines the revenue—and therefore the PR cycle—for network television (Chapter 5) and for off-network syndication, first-run syndication, and basic cable programming, all covered in this chapter.

The second revenue model is based on subscribers who pay a monthly fee. This is the revenue model—and therefore the PR cycle—for premium cable, such as Showtime and HBO, and of streaming services such as Netflix and Amazon Prime. These premium services need to maintain their current subscribers and generate new subscribers by publicizing their exclusive content.

This chapter has delineated the similarities and differences in creating effective publicity for non-network television programming. The SIDEBAR focused on negative situations and demonstrated the creation and uses of the press statement as part of the celebrity PR image-repair cycle.

Key Terms—In bold in the text

Sample two-sentence definition and example

Basic Cable: Basic Cable means the channels that come with a customer's monthly fee for hookup, which may include dozens of channels that are supported by advertising, but aimed at niche audiences. For example, Bravo and E! Entertainment Television are basic cable channels that have a number of shows such as the "Kardashian" franchise and "Real Housewives" series that use sensationalism and social media as the primary PR tactics.

Binge Viewing
Celebrity PR Image-Repair Cycle
Clearances
Contest (legal)
First-Run Syndication
First-Run Syndication PR Cycle
Hyperturbulence
Lottery (illegal)
National Association of Television Programming Executives (NATPE)
Niche Audience
Nostalgia
Off-Network Syndication
Off-Network Syndication PR Cycle

Paparazzi
Premium Cable
Premium Cable PR Cycle
Presentation
Press Statement
Radio Promotions
Reality TV PR Cycle
Residual Payments
Streaming Service
Strip Syndication
Subculture
Syndication

Suggested reading and resources

Weiner, J. (2015a, June 18). Comedy Central in the post-TV era: The network is in the middle of a creative renaissance—And a business-model crisis. Retrieved from http://myti.ms/1GuiWM9

THE BLOCKBUSTER MOTION PICTURE PUBLIC RELATIONS CYCLE

Chapter Overview: When you finish this chapter, you should be able to answer the following questions:

- What is a blockbuster motion picture?
- Why do a background and situation analysis for a PR plan?
- What does a SWOT show about blockbusters?
- What are bankable elements of a blockbuster?
- What is the goal of a PR plan for a blockbuster?
- How is the audience segmented when marketing films?
- What kinds of research do motion picture publicity and marketing use?
- What are the typical distribution periods for blockbusters?
- What is the blockbuster PR cycle?
- What are the stages between a film being just an idea and its release to the public?
- Is it a hit or a flop?
- SIDEBAR: The Entertainment PR Toolbox—Crisis Management
- SIDEBAR: The Entertainment PR Toolbox—Cross-Brand Tie-Ins and Licensed Merchandise

Introduction

Blockbusters are usually studio-produced films with big stars, big production budgets, big marketing budgets, and big box-office grosses. Whatever the projected production budget of the blockbuster film (say $200 million), the industry norm is to allocate an additional 30–50 percent for marketing (in this case $60–$100 million more). Most of the marketing money is allocated for television commercials in the days leading up to the release. A smaller portion is allocated for publicity spread out from the first announcement of a project being put into development through the second week of release. If a film then seems to have Oscar potential, additional money is allocated for the Oscar cycle, detailed in a SIDEBAR in Chapter 8. Throughout the process, in order to amplify the effect of the money spent on expensive television commercials and print advertising, the publicity campaign is multifaceted, intensive, inclusive, and often highly original. All possible lines of communication in traditional and new media are established with the potential audience, from talk show appearances to guerilla PR stunts to innovative uses of social media.

Before talking about the PR cycle, this chapter demonstrates how researching background and doing a situation analysis and a SWOT analysis form a solid foundation for creating a public relations plan. Motion picture publicity uses different age criteria to segment audiences than those discussed in the chapter on network television, so this chapter shows how to use film segmentation into age quadrants. It also discusses typical types of film industry research that help determine the best strategies and tactics needed to reach and communicate with targeted audience segments. Then the chapter looks at the blockbuster motion picture public relations cycle by dividing the PR activities related to the behind-the-scenes life of a motion picture into stages: development, green lighting, pre-production, production, post-production, pre-release, and opening weekend, with possible follow-up publicity during the first week of release.

By the end of a blockbuster's second weekend of release, everyone in the entertainment business knows the answer to this question: Is it a hit or a flop? This chapter will help readers answer this question for themselves by using readily available information to arrive at an "insider" understanding.

Blockbuster Motion Pictures—Expensive to Produce and to Market

The term "blockbuster" technically refers to a movie that has *already* made a lot of money at the box office. Certain movies, however, are referred to as blockbusters before they are even made, because everyone at the producing studio believes the film *will* make a lot of money. Because of this strong belief in the film's potential box-office prospects, the studio is willing to commit to big budgets for production and marketing.

Industry terms

Blockbusters are usually **studio films**, meaning that they are developed, financed, produced, and distributed by a major Hollywood studio. Smaller production companies simply do not have the financial wherewithal to risk so much money on a single film. Other terms for the same category include big pictures, action films, teen movies, franchises, sequels, remakes, and superhero movies. **Franchise films** are follow-ups to an initial blockbuster and are created using the same main characters and similar, but slightly different plot lines, such as the "Ironman" franchise.

Another prevalent industry term is **tent pole**. In an outstanding article on movie marketing, Tad Friend writes, "The larger studios can lose more than a hundred million dollars on a film fairly easily, yet their occasional tent-pole blockbusters can generate six hundred to eight hundred million dollars in profits. And tent poles spawn sequels that give the studio some assurance of profitability in years to come" (Friend, 2009). Just as an actual tent pole holds up the roof of a camping tent, a movie tent pole is predicted to make so much money that it will figuratively hold up the roof of the studio by paying for overhead, repairs, and salaries.

These high-profile movies can easily cost more than $100 million to develop and produce—costs that have to be paid up front to writers, directors, and especially stars. In industry accounting terms, these people are called **talent** or **above-the-line** personnel. Their salaries often make headlines, especially when leaked to the press, because in Hollywood above-the-line salaries are supposed to be confidential. Ahead of the film's release, the studio must also pay the hundreds of behind-the-scenes workers who build sets, run temporary electrical lines, and do costuming, to name just a few of the production jobs that are called **below-the-line**.

Industry unions

For the movies made by major studios, minimum payments for above-the-line talent and for the wages of below-the-line workers are highly regulated by industry union contracts, as are hours and working conditions. Hollywood unions are often called guilds. Examples include the **Screen Actors Guild (SAG)**, the union for actors; the **Directors Guild of America (DGA)**, the union or negotiating entity for directors; the **Writers Guild of America (WGA)** for writers; as well as the **International Alliance of Theatrical Stage Employees (IATSE)**, which represents many categories of below-the-line employees.

Publicity

Some Hollywood publicity positions are also union jobs under IATSE. This union is known as the **Publicists Guild of America**, Local 818 of the International Cinematographers Guild, Local 600 of IATSE. The complexity of this union's name gives just a hint of the complexity of the work rules governing the creation of major Hollywood motion pictures!

The main thing for future members of the entertainment industry to remember is that you can get many jobs, especially on independent films (discussed in Chapter 8) without being a union member. If you get a job that is covered by a union contract, however, you will be required to join the union and pay union dues—and you will receive the generous employment, health, and pension benefits the unions have negotiated on behalf of their members.

As mentioned above, the majority of the marketing budget is spent on advertising—in industry terms, the **media buy**. A few years ago, Tad Friend said of the media buy, "Between seventy and eighty per cent ... is spent on television advertising (enough so that viewers should see the ads an average of fifteen times)" (2009). As mentioned above, television advertising is always the biggest part of the advertising budget. In contrast, film marketers spend "eight or nine per cent on Internet ads, and the remainder on newspaper and outdoor advertising" (Friend, 2009). These days, they probably spend a higher proportion on Internet ads, because so many viewers watch television programming in ways that allow them to skip commercials.

Friend (2009) also estimated that, "Studios typically spend about ten million dollars on the 'basics' (cutting trailers and designing posters, conducting market research, flying the film's talent to the junket and the premiere itself)." These basics include executing the elements of the PR plan. The rest of the chapter will cover the basics of what a publicist does to help ensure that a film made with a big budget actually lives up to its wishful designation by becoming a box-office blockbuster.

A Publicity Plan's Background and Situation Analysis

As first discussed in Chapter 1, a **Public Relations Plan**, also called a **request for proposal or RFP**, begins with sections giving background and a situation analysis of the client that forms a foundation on which to build other effective elements of the plan. These other elements include: the PR goal; the audience segmentation; the objectives for various audience segments that together will help reach the goal; and proposed strategies, tactics, tools, and activities to be used to achieve the objectives and reach the goal.

Researching background

To write the **background** and **situation analysis**, the publicist does research. What incidents in the client's recent history give clues on how to proceed? What other current elements of the client's company and the client's product contribute to the context within which the publicist will execute the PR plan? For a blockbuster film, for example, background might include relevant recent history, such as the current overall health of the industry-wide box office; the client studio's recent success or disappointment with a similar or different genre of film; the source of the film's story or material (such as a best-selling book); the development history of the film (such as whether it moved speedily through development or languished for many years and why); the recent box-office grosses of similar films; the box-office results of any prior installments of the same franchise; and the kind of media coverage the studio has been receiving, among many other possibly relevant details.

For Disney's 2015 live-action *Cinderella*, for example, the situation analysis probably mentioned Disney's ongoing success with merchandise sales, especially princess dresses, and particularly the retail frenzy of parents trying to obtain the Elsa dress from *Frozen* for their daughters to play in or to wear to themed parties. A mention of this in the situation analysis could have led to the emphasis on the theme of fashion in the resulting public relations tactics.

For a blockbuster, the situation analysis might also include information about the past successes of each of the stars, the director, the screenwriter, and the producer. Such information should include any Academy Award wins and nominations, as well as box-office grosses of their recent films and of films in which they played similar roles in the past. The situation analysis should

Figure 7.1: Four-year-old Princess Aurora (Sleeping Beauty) in one of her several Disney princess dresses.
Photo: 2015 S. Humphrey.

also include notable positive and negative media coverage, to guide media relations priorities and choices.

PR playbook

According to Friend, "For marketers, much of the science of marketing is determining which old movie your new movie is most like, so you can turn to that movie's playbook as a rough guide" (2009). Doing research for the background and situation analysis sections of the public relations plan helps public relations practitioners figure out which metaphorical **playbook** to consult. A publicist can consult an actual plan used by her own studio in the past. Sometimes publicists are also able to network with friends at competing studios about elements of past publicity plans. Because of confidentiality agreements, however, competitors probably cannot reveal any hard dollar figures. These days, however, a few quick Internet searches for past media coverage of relevant film titles will help outline a fairly reliable PR playbook. If a story was in the media, it most likely originated in the PR plan.

Situation analysis

A publicist's ongoing, up-to-date knowledge about the industry is essential for developing an effective situation analysis. For example, in late summer 2014, a *New York Times* headline read: "Movies Have Worst Summer Since 1997" (Barnes, 2014b, p. C1). The article attributed the box-office doldrums to the familiarity of so many of the summer movies (many sequels, franchise films, and remakes) and their seemingly standard-issue marketing. The article also pointed out a few bright spots—films with fresh marketing that hit pay dirt at the box office. For *Lucy*, a surprise blockbuster starring Scarlett Johansson, "Fresh marketing may have made the difference: Universal Pictures backed *Lucy* with an unusual black-and-white ad campaign that stood out against a sea of uninspired billboards" (Barnes, 2015b, p. C6). The article also mentions a couple of other films that cut through the clutter by executing unusual and creative campaigns. The marketing and publicity executives who created the inspired campaigns had done their background research and situation analyses months ahead of the summer. Noting in advance that many cookie-cutter films would be competing with their client films, they created PR and marketing plans that made their clients stand out.

SWOT for Blockbusters

After doing the background and situation analysis, the next step is the **SWOT**, which stands for strengths, weaknesses, opportunities, and threats. **Strengths** and **Weaknesses** are internal to the client studio or film and therefore can be somewhat controlled. A good PR plan shows how to take advantage of a client's strengths, such as a star's large fan base, and compensate for or downplay weaknesses, such as a convoluted plot. **Opportunities** and **Threats** are external to the client, and exist out in the world or society. A practitioner has little control over them; however, a threat analysis can foster thoughtful preparation.

External opportunities

The key is to be aware of outside opportunities, both those known in advance, because they recur regularly, and those that come up unexpectedly, with which PR must seize the moment. Again a good PR plan outlines how to leverage or take advantage of external opportunities, for example, using the industry buildup to the Oscar PR cycle (Chapter 8) as part of the publicity for a well-made blockbuster released during the Thanksgiving to Christmas holiday season.

External threats

On the other hand, a PR plan needs to be aware of external threats, such as a strong competing film premiering in the same general time period, or possible disruptions of publicity activities due to extreme weather. For example, a blizzard could hamper media coverage of a film's New York City premiere scheduled for 10 days before Christmas, so PR plan activities always need to be planned with an eye on the weather, and a Plan B in mind.

Any negative situation that is not handled with finesse can spiral downward into a crisis. The SIDEBAR gives guidance on how to be prepared.

The Entertainment PR Toolbox—Crisis Management

Negative situations can arise—an accident on a film set or a fire on a studio lot, for example. If the public relations practitioner is not adept, or if the client tries to ignore the situation or asks the publicist to lie to or stonewall the media, even a minor incident can escalate into a crisis. The best way to avoid a crisis is to follow the Girl Scout Motto: "Be prepared," which means: "Willingness to serve is not enough; you must know how to do the job well, even in an emergency" (Girl Scout Traditions, 2015).

Crisis management, meaning preparation for a crisis and doing the job well in an emergency, requires public relations practitioners to:

- Understand potential risks. For example, every company has a risk of fire. Every company in Southern California is at risk for earthquake damage. When there is a regional emergency such as a crippling blizzard or flood, journalists quickly call large employers and prominent companies to check for deaths, property damage, and closures. Be prepared in advance with press statement templates into which you can insert verified facts.
- Be prepared with an emergency communications plan, including internal and external emergency contact numbers, emergency assignments, internal sources of reliable information, and a familiarity with possible holding areas for the media. During an emergency, it is prudent to keep the press from wandering around, interfering with emergency personnel, and interviewing random bystanders who may speculate wildly without any real information about what has happened.
- Communicate internally and act quickly.
- Do not agree "to wait awhile" or "to wait until everyone can meet" to communicate with the media. The ostrich approach will not work, because the media needs a quotation from a company source to round out any story. "No comment" makes it seem as if the client is hiding something.
- Have one spokesperson to avoid media confusion and the possibility of appearing self-contradictory—of being unreliable.
- Issue a press statement that specifies the facts as they are known at the moment. Then issue statement updates as new verified information becomes available. (See the SIDEBAR in Chapter 6 on press statements.)
- Tell the truth.
- Do not speculate.
- Express compassion for victims and their families, rather than listening to those who advise against any comment for fear of admitting responsibility and therefore being liable for damages in future lawsuits. Remember the humanity of those who have been injured.
- Do not try to deflect blame, especially by blaming a victim.
- Provide alternative visuals, which means **B-roll**—pre-prepared video footage of company images other than, for example, the burning building. Each time a TV station updates or teases the story, the

> news producer needs a visual behind the news anchor. Unless you provide some alternatives, the same footage of the building burning, people fleeing, or someone bleeding on the ground will play in a loop as endless as a Vine video.
>
> Public relations practitioners who follow these precepts will be prepared to represent their clients well, even in an emergency.

In the face of unexpected threats, PR should be ready to move quickly, as happened after the off-set death November 30, 2013, of the popular star Paul Walker during the filming of *Furious 7*. The film's PR team moved quickly to communicate with over-25 fans through traditional media, and with under-25 fans through social media. After a hiatus, Universal announced that production would continue with the cooperation of Walker's brothers, and PR kept in communication with Walker's grieving fan community (Zal, 2015), through the film's successful release on April 3, 2015.

Internal strengths

For major studio films, strengths usually include the star, the director, the pre-sold value of the title (fans), and an early summer release date. An additional strength of Disney's 2015 live-action *Cinderella* was hiring Academy Award–winning costume designer Sandy Powell. Recognizing this strength, the PR team successfully pitched the fashion angle and received outstanding media in both general publications and fashion magazines, such as *Vogue* and *Glamour*. The fashion angle also led to coverage of Powell's design for the glass slipper and to Disney having nine famous shoe designers re-imagine the glass slipper (Wicks, 2015).

Music can be another strength that leads to media coverage. For example, Lionsgate received a lot of media coverage at the end of July 2014, when it announced that the Grammy-winning artist Lorde was going to curate the soundtrack and write an original song for *The Hunger Games: Mockingjay—Part 1, The Rebellion Begins*. Closer to the premiere, Lorde publicized the film by doing numerous radio and print interviews (McFarlane, 2015). While Lorde did not receive an Academy Award nomination for "Yellow Flicker Beat," as many expected, the music angle continued to generate media attention for *Mockingjay* throughout the campaign and long afterwards.

A good publicity plan leverages the power of each of a picture's strengths. *Gone Girl* was a best-selling thriller by Gillian Flynn before it was made into a film starring Ben Affleck, with its screenplay also by Flynn. Because of the book, the film had a pre-sold audience, and the title was already familiar, so much of the publicity was geared toward exciting "knowledgeable fans" (Welc, 2015). In Gompertz's terms (see Chapter 2 SIDEBAR), such strengths are stimulants that a publicist can use to increase news value (Gompertz, 1992) and gain coverage.

Internal weaknesses

Weaknesses are internal. For a blockbuster, weakness might include: a little-known lead actor; a young director with no blockbuster experience; a casting change from a previous film in the series; a convoluted or muddled storyline; a running time over two hours; and any cast or behind-the-scenes controversies or misbehavior.

Leveraging opportunities/solving problems

Chapter 1 showed that clients hire PR practitioners for two main reasons: to take advantage of an opportunity or to solve a problem. In this context, the S&O of a SWOT equal PR opportunities and the W&T of a SWOT equal PR problems.

PR opportunities for a blockbuster include: one or more bankable elements (see below), which include stars and other above-the-line participants; pre-sold elements, such as title or story recognition; pre-opening buzz; a big opening; big box-office numbers; a strong second weekend; and Oscar buzz. *Furious 7* made the expensive media buy of a Super Bowl XLIX commercial that aired two months ahead of the release date. The commercial made news and kickstarted the final stage of the campaign. One headline declared, "The 'Furious 7' Super Bowl Trailer is Better Than the Super Bowl" (Rosen, 2015). Public relations was able to leverage the commercial as a PR opportunity (S&O) by treating the ad and the response to the ad as news angles to generate headlines for days to come.

PR problems for big movies include: production delays; cost overruns; a director or star quitting or being fired; an unhappy star; star misbehavior; and any production accident that causes death, injury, or production delays. Thus, the accidental, off-set death of the film's beloved star, Paul Walker, was a PR problem that needed and received masterful PR handling by the public relations practitioners for *Furious 7*.

Bankable Elements Are Strengths and Opportunities for Publicity

Another term used in the film business is **bankable**. Bankable elements are so well known to the public and probably have such a record of generating massive box-office grosses that a bank would literally write a letter of credit guaranteeing financing. A studio often functions as its own bank, but its financial executives look closely at bankable elements before deciding to give a green light to produce a high-budget film.

The most convincing bankable element is a charismatic star with a strong box-office track record in a similar type of film. Another bankable element is a widely known story, such as *Cinderella*. One of the strongest bankable elements is being a sequel or part of a franchise. The bank can look at box-office results from the previous, very similar films in the series to evaluate **box-office potential**, which means the likelihood of being able to pay off the investments of more than $100 million for the production budget and additional marketing costs of $30 to $50 million, and leave a substantial profit for the studio.

For the public relations plan, a film being bankable also means opportunities for wide media coverage. If the movie is based on a best-selling thriller such as *Gone Girl*, for example, the title is **pre-sold**. It already has fans and awareness, so journalists know that their readers are already interested in stories about it. The bankable elements make gaining media coverage easier. In fact, sometimes a film has so much advance interest that the publicist's job becomes turning media away or trying to delay media coverage until close to the premiere.

Taken together, the background, situation analysis, and SWOT provide the foundation on which to build an effective PR plan.

The PR Goal for Blockbusters

The next step is defining the goal of the PR plan. The goal should be put in business terms that are understandable to the entire organization (as discussed in Chapter 1 and elsewhere). Therefore, the goal should be stated in terms of money or something that easily equates to money. For films, the goal is

THE BLOCKBUSTER MOTION PICTURE PUBLIC RELATIONS CYCLE 143

specified in terms of the expected (or hoped for) **box-office gross**, which is the total dollar amount of ticket sales. Only a portion of the gross, however, comes back to the studio/distributor, with the rest going to the theater that shows the film to the public.

Here is a general guide for the **box-office split**, between the studio/distributor and the theater of total ticket sales (the gross) for a blockbuster film:

- 1st week: 90% distributor   10% theater
- 2nd week: 80%   20%
- 3rd week: 70%   30%
- 4th week: 60%   40%
- 5th week: 50%   50%
- 6th week: 40%   60%

The box-office split helps explain why studios want a potential blockbuster on as many screens as possible for the first couple of weeks: most of the box-office take early in the run comes back to the studio's coffers.

What's in it for the theaters, which have to send so much money back to the distributor? Popcorn. Soda. Red Vines. Premium in-theater dining is also now available in some theaters. The theater itself keeps 100 percent of the receipts from the sale of concessions during the entire run of the film. Theaters love movies that **have legs**, meaning that they keep running week after week. Theaters love a Disney movie that stays popular for an entire holiday season and beyond. The theater keeps earning its popcorn money and earns larger and larger percentages of the box-office gross as the weeks go by.

Despite the box-office split, the client studio and the marketing team agree to use the total box-office gross for the opening weekend and for the domestic and global markets as their goal.

As indicated above, the goal is decided by looking at the playbook. This means researching the box-office results for other similar films of the same genre; those with the same star; and those that were released on similar weekends in the recent past. Internally, however, it takes the accountants much longer to determine the amount of actual profit or loss that contributes to the bottom line and earnings per share of the company's stock.

Beating expectations

Ahead of weekend premieres, many media outlets publish articles or items about the dollar expectations of openers. On Mondays, media compare the actual results versus expectations and discuss possible reasons for discrepancies. The bottom line is that any film that doesn't meet or beat expectations for opening weekend begins to look unsuccessful. By the end of the second weekend, everyone in the business will be able to declare if a film is a hit or a miss, as discussed toward the end of this chapter.

Audience Segmentation for Film Publicity

To achieve the public relations goal, you have to know who the potential audience members are in order to plan how to communicate effectively with them. As discussed in Chapter 2, audience segmentation is done to separate the entire potential audience into discrete categories based on logical criteria. If done properly, members of a segment will have enough in common in media use and lifestyles that they can be reached with similar PR tactics and tools. Film marketers segment the audience using **demographics** (easily distinguishable characteristics), categorizing first by gender and then age.

Quadrants

For most films with a PG13 or higher rating, particularly blockbusters, the standard film industry audience segmentation is into four categories called **quadrants**: men under 25; men over 25; women under 25; and women over 25. Compared to the age categories used for television (18–49 for the mass audience and 18–34 for the younger audience, as discussed in Chapter 5), the young categories for film skew much younger. For superhero and action films, as well as many other franchises and sequels, the young male segment is of supreme importance, in part because young men who love a movie will see it multiple times in the theater, driving up box-office results.

Movies that achieve the highest grosses, however, reach all segments and are called **four-quadrant films**: "a film's budget is usually directly related to the number of quadrants it is anticipated to reach. The most expensive tentpole movies, such as the 'Pirates of the Caribbean' franchise, are aimed at all four quadrants" (Friend, 2009). Director Jim Cameron has created the two biggest megahits of all time, the only two movies to date to gross more than $2 billion worldwide: *Avatar* has earned $2.788.0 billion and *Titanic* has earned $2.186.8 billion (boxofficemojo.com, 2015). These four-quadrant movies had something for everyone—for both men and women and for those under and over 25.

Psychographics

After the PR plan's initial audience segmentation, additional research during a campaign may lead to refinements that include other elements of demographics such as race and income. Research may also reveal possible target categories based on **psychographics**, including taste, emotional preferences, and mindset, such as being romantic, thrill seeking, or family oriented. Research may also point toward making special marketing efforts directed at niche targets, such as males 17–22 who are attending college. This may be a perfect target audience for a fun-in-the-sun, gross-out comedy premiering for spring break in late March or early April. It is also an audience that can be reached as a group via college radio stations and newspapers, sports programming, satellite radio, Comedy Central, and YouTube.

Buyer personas

A **buyer persona** is a short profile of an imaginary customer who typifies an audience segment. Based on research such as focus groups or test audience questionnaires, a buyer persona keeps the PR and marketing plans focused by answering these questions: Who is our customer? How do we reach this customer through traditional and social media channels?

Quadrants are the primary audience segmentation section for a blockbuster public relations plan. Secondary segments are specialized target groups based on prior box-office anomalies. For example, the outsized audience of "church-going African American women" for Tyler Perry movies has led to many underestimates of those films' potential box-office results (Friend, 2009).

Not every anomaly is based on past performance of similar films. Therefore, refinements and niches are added later if research indicates that publicity activities targeted to specific subgroups are likely to help box-office results without breaking the budget. Even though the marketing budget for a blockbuster is substantial, all publicity and marketing activities need rationales showing why they are cost effective. Everyone should be able to answer these questions: Why are we spending money on this? Why are we spending time doing this?

Marketing Research for Movies

With mega-investments at stake, the film studios and their public relations agencies do internal research. They also pay for a variety of external, proprietary research to aid rational decision making. Research falls into two broad types: quantitative and qualitative. **Quantitative research** is based on quantities or numbers—items that are countable, scalable, or subject to statistical analysis, such as the results of surveys or percentage of people from each quadrant in a test screening. **Qualitative research** looks at ideas and qualities that cannot be expressed as numbers, such as the intensity of emotions or the depth of identification with a star. Qualitative research includes focus groups, case studies, and ethnographic field research using the model of anthropology.

Different types and methods of research are used at different stages in a film's life cycle from development through production and editing right up through the release. Q Scores are used during casting. Focus groups help in developing the central concept for the poster and other marketing materials. During post-production, test screenings with audience feedback questionnaires and focus groups help refine the editing or indicate adjusting plans for the final marketing push before the premiere—particularly the television media buys, which are the most expensive element in a campaign. Tracking polls and social media metrics are also used ahead of the premiere, while CinemaScore research is done opening day. Taken together, research results help producers and marketers make some of their decisions about what to do, when to do it, and what it all means for a film reaching profitability. The following section talks about film research at various stages of the life cycle of a film.

Development research

During the development process, a studio may sequentially hire new writers or teams of writers. While working with a writer(s), the producers may also hire a **script consultant**. These days some script consultants may claim to have an algorithm to apply to a script that compares it to a proprietary database of scripts of hit films (Barnes, 2013). One such company claims that with, "a rich database of historical comparisons, we will provide you with actionable results within an industry context" (Worldwide Motion Picture Group, n.d.). The use of script consultants is a hot-button issue within the industry. Scriptwriters hate being second-guessed by studio executives or by market research. They bristle even more at the thought of their creative ideas being second-guessed by a bot (Laporte, 2013). All of this is to say that the use of big data and data mining may be on the upswing in the film industry, but is not yet pervasive.

During development, and especially as a film nears the green-lighting stage, the studio's marketing department researches the background, situation analysis, and SWOT, and may advise the production executives and producer on what stars or other bankable elements would be strengths to buttress future media coverage and audience awareness. Adam Fogelson, chairman of STX Entertainment is quoted as saying, "'Only make a film you already know how to sell,'" because he "believes that seventy-five percent of a movie's success is due to its marketing and its marketability" (Friend, 2016, p. 38). This means that the marketing plan and the PR plan need to be solidly researched, inclusive, and creative.

Q scores

For casting the starring roles during development and for casting secondary roles during pre-production, studios purchase research called Q Scores. Based on proprietary research by an outside company, **Q Scores** assign a single number in each global market to stars' likability, a combination of name recognition and appeal. Studios equate high Q scores with box-office potential. Likability is a strong stimulant for generating good publicity. To generate publicity abroad, a second or third lead is sometimes cast with an actor who is relatively less known in the United States, but has a high Q Score in Germany, Great Britain, or another important film market.

As of 2014, the star with consistently the highest American Q Score was Tom Hanks (Maglio, 2014). Another example of a star with high recognition and appeal might be Brad Pitt, while a star with high recognition but low appeal—resulting in a lower Q score—might be Mel Gibson, after a drunken, racist rant. Actors who consistently star in blockbuster films command astronomical salaries, because their presence in a film is supposed to mean bankability, i.e., to guarantee box-office success, based on past performance and Q Scores. Which comes first, the chicken or the egg?

Production research

While a film is in production, the marketing team creates the central selling concept, the image and slogan, that the poster and the trailer will use to generate buzz and advance awareness. Focus groups are commonly used to tease out people's emotional responses to various combinations of taglines and images for the poster or to evaluate response to various rough cuts of the trailer. **Focus groups** are small groups usually of eight to 12 people selected to be representative of target quadrants. Typically, they are gathered in a research room with a professional moderator, often a psychologist, while the marketing team watches from an adjoining room through one-way glass. The entire session is taped for later review. Because focus groups are dynamic and results complex, studios typically hire one of a very few well-known consultants to conduct and interpret the research.

Post-production research

During post-production, which is when the film is being edited, test screenings may be done for two different purposes at two different points: the rough-cut stage and the final-cut stage. Companies such as Nielsen NRG, OTX Research, and Entertainment Research and Marketing, LLC are hired to recruit audiences and compile and synthesize research results. They recruit viewers in busy pedestrian areas such as malls by offering free tickets. At the screening, the research company hands out and collects audience questionnaires and sometimes follows the screening with a focus group for further feedback.

The **audience questionnaires** for both types of screenings have several elements in common, each with a specific purpose: Demographic questions (age, gender, race, income) help identify or refine the audience segments and niches that marketing and publicity will target. A rating question asks for an evaluation of the film from Excellent (1) and Very Good (2) down to Poor (5). A second important question asks whether the viewer would recommend the movie to friends, with the choices ranging from Yes, definitely (1) and Yes, probably (2) down to No, definitely not (4). Studios and marketing people are hoping that the scores for "the top two boxes" for both of these two crucial questions are 80 percent or higher (Friend, 2009). The rating score equates to how well a film opens. Positive recommendations equate to positive word of mouth after opening day.

Rough-cut screening

At a rough cut test screening—perhaps before the music and all of the special effects have been added—the film may be screened to see how it "plays in the room" and to try to settle disagreements between the production team and the studio about further edits and changes. The studio executives—including the heads of marketing and publicity, the director, editor, and the producer—sit in the back of the audience. They carefully monitor the visceral responses of the first people outside the film's orbit to see the film. If it's a comedy, does the audience laugh in the right places for the right reasons? If it's horror, do they scream and gasp? What about the ending, the most problematical section of most films?

The rough-cut questionnaires often have a number of additional open-ended questions asking the responders to describe what they liked and disliked about the film, the characters, and the story, including favorite and least-liked scenes. They are also asked to comment on the ending. The studio might select from the well-liked scenes when cutting the trailer or TV ads. Strongly disliked scenes may be re-edited, cut, or even re-shot at great expense.

Final-cut screenings

In contrast, the primary purpose of final-cut screenings, which occur close to the release date, is to test the effectiveness of the marketing. At this stage, the film is what it is, but last-minute adjustments can be made to the mix of media buys, the story angles being pitched, and the personal appearance schedules of the stars. Again getting a majority of responses in the top two boxes of the two key questions is important to support the distributor's intention to keep spending money in the run-up to the premiere. Again the questionnaire asks for demographic information. It also asks the respondent to rank the elements that influenced the decision to attend, such as the individual stars, the story, the director, the genre, the trailer, the advertising, etc. And it asks how important various media ads, articles, and star appearances were in the decision to attend. Results are used to tweak the marketing and publicity campaigns during the pre-release period, or to pull back on spending if the film looks like a complete dud.

Not everybody connected with films is onboard with the importance of test screenings or the accuracy of results taken from a small sample of viewers who didn't even have to pay to see the film: "Opinion surveys—'idiot cards,' as some unimpressed directors call them—indicated that 'Fight Club' would be the flop of the century. It took in more than $100 million worldwide" (Barnes, 2013).

Pre-release research

Tracking is another kind of research done weekly as the release date approaches. "Conducted among people who've seen at least six movies in the past year" (Friend, 2009), **tracking surveys** compare awareness of a film's title among likely moviegoers to awareness of competing titles that will open the same weekend. Again results are used in attempts to predict opening weekend box-office results and for adjusting media buys and publicity efforts. In recent years, studios have added a number of other approaches to tracking, including "pulling data from IMDb, Flixster, Twitter, and Fandango's pre-sales in assembling their predictions" (Lang, 2014a). According to *The New York Times*, "studios have started using Facebook 'likes' and online trailer views to mold advertising and even films" (Barnes, 2013).

Opening weekend

Studio executives have always done informal and formal exit polling to understand what actual paying customers think. In recent years, **CinemaScore** aggregates letter grades from exit polls of opening-day attendees. The grades help studios forecast the total box-office gross of a film. One executive is quoted as saying, "'The CinemaScore shows likability and playability and length of the film's ride. It's not always right, but it's a pretty good indicator. I rely on it'" (Busch, 2014). Other companies, including PostTrak, and often the studios themselves, also do exit polling of paying audiences on opening night.

The types and uses of research in the movie business are continually evolving, especially as the uses of social media metrics become more sophisticated and pervasive. In the past, industry research was a closely guarded internal secret, but now news of results reaches the press almost as soon as the studios receive it. For example, CinemaScore releases results via Facebook and Twitter. Therefore, these days, on the one hand, public relations practitioners have to be prepared to respond with a press statement (see the SIDEBAR in Chapter 6) when queried about negative research results. On the other hand, they can make news with stories about positive exit polls. For example, they can schedule additional television and radio interviews with stars to take advantage of the word-of-mouth buzz generated by people leaving a movie, loving it, and wanting to tell their friends about it.

Blockbuster Releases Are Timed for Summers and Holidays

Traditionally, big-budget films open in the late spring and early summer with the Memorial Day and July 4th weekends considered the most desirable timing. Films usually open on Friday, and the biggest ones often stretch the weekend by opening with shows Thursday night at midnight. Sometimes theaters have several screenings into the early morning hours to accommodate long lines of excited fans. A holiday weekend with an extra day for moviegoing allows a studio to beef up its opening weekend box-office numbers, the better to make box-office news.

Alternatively, a studio will claim the weekend prior to the three-day holiday. That way the box-office figures for the second weekend get a boost from the extra day, the importance of which will be discussed in the later section about hits and flops. For the big summer weekends, studios announce the scheduling of their most high-profile films two years or more in advance in order to "claim the territory," which is called **planting the flag** (Friedman, 2007, p. C5).

Other coveted opening dates include, for holiday and family-themed films, the weekend before Thanksgiving and the second weekend in December as kids are getting out of school for the break. An attractive target date for a high-profile romantic comedy is the weekend before Valentine's Day. This is the one time that American men can reliably be induced to see a "chick flick."

Over the years, the competition to claim a coveted weekend and stick to it despite production delays or complications with special effects has led to a number of Darwinian face offs of blockbuster versus blockbuster between May and July (Lang, 2014b, p. 37). According to Surowiecki, "releasing all the tent-pole movies in the summer guarantees a crowded marketplace, which cannibalizes the industry's sales" (2015). As a result, in recent years some distributors have cautiously moved toward widening the release calendar for their biggest films. This is especially good news for the publicity staff and entertainment PR agencies. The pre-release period for a blockbuster is time and staff intensive. Having an extra week or more to concentrate on a single film can mean placing more feature stories and gaining better premiere party coverage, as well as other additional media placements. The extra publicity efforts can boost opening weekend box office.

The Blockbuster Motion Picture PR Cycle

The **blockbuster PR cycle** is a multi-year process with two key dates: the date the movie is green-lit and the premiere date 18 months or more later. The development process can stretch from a year to beyond a decade. **Green-lighting**, which is official approval to go into production, can only occur when enough bankable elements are attached and available. The studio and its financial people must feel comfortable committing to a multimillion-dollar budget and a schedule for producing and opening the film on an opportune weekend, as discussed above. The essential elements for green-lighting include: the stars, the director, an acceptable final draft of the script, an approved budget and production schedule, and the projected premiere date. Most importantly for readers of this book, the outlines of approved marketing and public relations plans must be in place. A studio does not spend $100–$200 million to make a film, unless and until it knows how to sell it.

The sections that follow describe the various stages in the life of a block-buster in terms of the public relations objectives, target audiences, tactics, and tools that are characteristic of each stage.

Publicity Types and Media Targets Depend on the Stages of a Film's Life

Development = trade publicity

Studio development executives take pitches for movie concepts, stories, and scripts from producers and writers. If the studio becomes excited about a proj-ect, it puts the project into **development**. The studio makes deals with the producers and writer, and the writer begins to be paid for drafts, as specified in the Writers Guild contract. Press releases and media pitches that can be considered news during the development stage include: the sale of a pitch "in the room"; the sale of story rights to a true story or a big book; and the sale of a **"spec" script** (a script that a writer completed on speculation without having a deal in place to be paid by a producer or studio). A star "interested" in the project, or committing to the project, and a director being attached are also news.

During development, the target audience for PR-generated news is the entertainment industry. Competitors want to know who is doing what at which studio in order to jockey for position with their own projects. The target media used to reach the audience are trade outlets such as variety.com, hollywoodreporter.com, and deadlinehollywood.com. The usual PR tactic is to write a press release geared to the trade audience.

During the development process, various writers, directors, and stars may be attached and announced to the trades, but then fall out of the proj-ect due to conflicting time commitments or "creative differences." In fact, sometimes a film languishes in development (which some in the industry call "development hell") for many years. Only finding a bankable combination of elements available within a specific time frame will move a project forward out of development and into production.

Green-lighting = adding business media

The section above specifies that an acceptable marketing and publicity plan is one of the necessary elements that must be in place for a studio to green-light a blockbuster movie. One industry executive was quoted as saying, "'You start selling a film the minute you decide you want to make it. ... You're continually in the process of selling the film (nowadays). You have to know your pitch'" (Sperling & Littleton, 2005, p. S1).

At green-lighting, the target audience for PR broadens and now includes both the trade media and the business media. When a public company such as Paramount commits a huge amount of money to produce and market a blockbuster, the readers and viewers of the business media want to know the rationale for the decision and the prospects for eventual profits. The decision to green-light can affect the stock price immediately or when the film becomes a hit or a flop.

Pre-production = adding some consumer publicity

Pre-production is the period between green-lighting and the actual start of physical production. During this time, a production office is opened on location, secondary cast is auditioned, the crew is hired, and specific locations for individual scenes are scouted. Since a large portion of a very large budget will be spent making the film, the announcement of the location where the film will shoot for several months is also trade news, business news, and local news in the area of the shoot. Other news angles during pre-production, such as hiring the production designer, costume designer, and the cinematographer, are more limited to the trade media, unless the person is an Oscar winner or a well-known name in a wider field such as a Grammy Award-winning pop star or a world-renowned couture designer. In those cases, the publicist uses the specific news stimulants to try for broader news coverage.

Cross-brand tie-ins that can add potential for publicity and promotion have probably been explored before green-lighting, but are locked in, if possible, during pre-production so that products can be placed in the movie for a fee (**product placement**). The studio must sell merchandise rights as soon as possible as well, so that licensing companies can manufacture and ship products in time for the film's opening. Tie-ins and merchandise licensing are discussed further in the SIDEBAR.

The Entertainment PR Toolbox—Cross-Brand Tie-Ins and Licensed Merchandise

The public relations objective of a **cross-brand tie-in** is for two brands that partially share an audience segment to mutually widen each other's audience reach, first through co-advertising and second, when possible, through news coverage. Which brand's new sports car will James Bond drive? The answer can be worth millions in direct payments to the production company; more millions when the car company co-advertises the film in a major campaign timed for the film's release; and further millions when the news media pick up the car angle for news and feature stories. For optimal effectiveness, a cross-brand partnership needs to be locked in two or more years in advance, during development or pre-production. The product company and its advertising agency need time to create an integrated campaign (Friedman, 2007).

Early deals are also necessary for **merchandise licensing**. The owner of the **intellectual property (IP)**, in this case, the studio or perhaps a partnership between the studio and, for example, Marvel Comics, sells the right to produce a specific category of merchandise related to a film for a specific period of time. The goal is to find reliable partners to create well-made products that are in the stores ready for purchase during pre-release and afterwards. Logo T-shirts, baseball caps, and backpacks worn by avid consumers are like moving billboard and peer endorsements. The logo items serve as additional reminders, which amplify advertising and PR messages about the film's opening.

Usually a film based on a new concept that is untested in the marketplace is not able to generate merchandising deals. It's too risky for the licensing company and for retailers. What happens if the film is a flop? The merchandise manufacturer (the licensee) and/or retailer would be stuck with unsalable merchandise touting a movie that no one saw, or worse yet, that became a bad joke. (*Cowboys and Aliens*, anyone?)

On the other hand, when a film is based on a pre-existing property such as a Marvel comic, or is a sequel to a huge hit, merchandisers line up to make deals. They know that fans will be avid buyers. A company called Kernel has been working with studios to sustain the fan excitement that now accompanies the release of a trailer or a franchise film, sequel, or pre-sold film, such as *The 5th Wave*, based on a young adult book. In partnership with Sony Pictures, Kernel started more than a year before the premiere using its website to sell tickets, "bundled in packages that can include a future download, or a poster, or a script, or even a blue Burton backpack just like the one Ms. Moretz [the star] totes in the film." (Cieply, 2015, p. B6). The early, exclusive merchandise is a way of cultivating and activating the superfans who can so effectively sell a movie through their own word-of-mouth excitement.

Disney movies are an exception to the licensing disinterest in most original movies for a couple of reasons: Disney has such a strong reputation for creating quality originals; and Disney has its own stores to sell and support the merchandise, including those at the Disney theme parks worldwide that hawk film merchandise as "memories" of family fun.

Figure 7.2: The Disney Store in Shanghai, China, next to the iconic Oriental Pearl Radio and TV Tower.
Photo credit: 2015 Carol Ames.

There are dozens of categories of products ranging from costumes and sleeping bags to infant toys that can be licensed to support a children's film. Anybody who took lunches to school probably carried a Disney-themed lunchbox at some point during childhood.

Website as publicity

A dedicated **movie website** allows the publicity department to function as a publisher. The PR team creates, controls, and distributes news directly to potential audience members to be viewed whenever and wherever they want it. The website should be up and running during pre-production. The green-lighting news release and the start-of-production news release can be featured stories on the website, before being archived in reverse chronological order under a Press tab. As with any website, it is crucial for the publisher, i.e., the publicity department, to post new material frequently to help the site rise in the search engine rankings. If used well, the movie's own website along with its listing on IMDb.com, its listing in Wikipedia, and its Facebook page should be among the top search results.

The best movie websites keep the viewer engaged by offering a variety of content, for example: character bios, video clips, photo galleries, sweepstakes, fun surveys, and moderated comment areas or blogs. The website can tease the release of the teaser trailer and then debut it. In fact, Friend points out that movie studios have a huge advantage over other product producers, because they can give away free samples in the form of a trailer or commercial (2009). As the premiere approaches, the site should feature any special events with lots of photos, as well as a convenient link for finding theater locations and purchasing tickets in advance.

Production

Production is the period when the director, cast, and a crew of close to 200 craftspeople are shooting the film. Usually a film is shot on location, often at a great distance from the Hollywood studio. For hands-on PR work during this crucial period, the studio hires a **unit publicist**. It is the Unit's job to be on the set every day during production.

With the studio's approval, the Unit writes and distributes a **start-of-production media release**, which announces that production has started and where the film is being shot. The release includes the title, major cast, producer, director, writer, and company credits. It also includes a short synopsis of the film's story. Sent to the trades, a start-of-production release alerts the industry that a new product is on the way.

During production, the Unit handles long-lead stories and exclusive behind-the-scenes shoots for various entertainment news shows, such as *Entertainment Tonight* and *Access Hollywood*. **Long-lead magazines** are the monthlies such as *Vanity Fair, Esquire,* and *Vogue* that decide on their main stories and choose prospects for cover photos many months ahead of the issue date. The Unit selectively leaks stories to favorite journalists. On the other hand, these days, part of the Unit's job is to deter crew and even cast members from shooting behind-the-scenes photos and leaking them online (Longwell, 2015).

One of the most important parts of the unit publicist's job is to supply the studio/distributor with all of the written material necessary for an effective **media kit** and successful overall campaign. For the press kit, the main press release contains all the cast information and a summary of the story. The kit also includes: bios of the cast and other main participants; production notes that might suggest news stories; and backgrounders and fact sheets. Media kits are now distributed securely online to credentialed media, rather than as physical press kits. The **electronic press kit (EPK)** material is now available to press digitally, rather than on DVDs. To prepare the media kit and EPK, the Unit schedules and sets up photo and video shoots, interviews the cast and director, and drafts all of the written material.

Other aspects of the Unit's job are to work with the local press and the community. The Unit soothes irritations about the invasion of movie people and inevitable street closures; tries to control any potential negative stories; escorts, facilitates, and supervises any visiting journalists; and finally tries to prevent too much news getting out too soon. To motivate audiences to buy tickets, publicity should peak right before the premiere, not months earlier during production.

During production, the studio wants some exciting scenes shot early in the schedule to be leaked four or more months ahead of release. Together with the teaser trailer that announced the date more than a year ahead of time, the early leaks make up what Tad Friend calls the first act of the marketing campaign (2009).

Comic-Con and VidCon publicity

For blockbuster action and comic-book movies destined for summertime release, San Diego's **Comic-Con International** the prior July has become the showcase of choice. Movie distributors debut trailers and show sneak peeks. Multiple news stories and social media mentions generate advance awareness. In July 2015, for example, Comic-Con attendees got the first look at footage from *Star Wars: The Force Awakens* (Lucasfilm); *Suicide Squad* (Warner Bros.); *Batman v Superman: Dawn of Justice* (Warner Bros.); and *Deadpool* (21st Century Fox), among other exclusives: (Batcha, 2015, July 13). In addition to a panel and sneak peek for *The Hunger Games: Mockingjay—Part II*, Lionsgate featured a booth that let people have photos taken with digital Mockingjay facial tattoos, which were sent to their email ready to share on social media (Barnes & Cieply, 2015). The purpose of the photo-booth tactic was to spread awareness beyond convention attendees.

A couple of weeks later, studios court YouTube celebrities and vlogers at **VidCon** in Anaheim. Because "VidCon isn't just for shrieking YouTube fangirls anymore" (Spangler, 2015), studio publicity departments offer exclusive advance footage of upcoming films to stimulate social media commentary among the mostly young attendees.

Comic-Con and VidCon mean that production needs to commence more than a year ahead of time so that a trailer or sneak scenes can be cut, and so that the studio publicity staff can create excitement (and manage) the hoopla.

During production, the media targets and their audiences broaden to include the consumer media and moviegoers to create awareness that the film is coming to a theater near them sometime in the future. As discussed in Chapter 1, **consumer media** are any and all the places potential audience members read, see, or hear information about upcoming releases.

Post-production publicity

Post-production is the period after all the scenes are shot and before the pre-release crescendo to the premiere. The stars are off on other projects, the film is being edited, the special effects continue to be created, and the musical score and sound editing take place. There may also be one or more test screenings. The crucial fact for the PR staff is that the stars are **not** available to do interviews or attend events during post-production.

The unavailability of the stars is the reason that the Unit publicist has created and stockpiled the media kit, interviews, and website material that can be parceled out to maintain interest and excitement. During post-production, **trans-media storytelling** tactics can invigorate an existing fan base or establish a passionate new fan community. Energized fans voluntarily evangelize the film before, during, and after its premiere. Such avid fan communities can eventually fuel the demand for sequel after sequel. In one kind of trans-media storytelling, some creative PR practitioners make the website seem to be an extension of the world of the movie. For example, for Mockingjay—Part II, it appeared that members of the Capitol were using the website to communicate (McFarlane, 2015). Another trans-media possibility is to start a quest online and then take it into the real world for a scavenger hunt or experiential reward to be found by using GPS technology. In 2014, Paramount partnered with Google to create "an immersive experience called the Interstellar Space Hub." Users could create "their own 'space hunt' by clicking around the galaxy" in order to "unlock new movie-related factoids" about Intersteller (Hamedy, 2014).

During post-production, another tactic is to offer trips and tickets to the premiere as prizes for a contest online or on radio. Mentions during drive time on popular stations with the right target demographics remind the audience of the film's title and opening date.

According to Tad Friend, the second and third acts of the marketing plan take place during post-production: "five weeks before the film opens, you start saturating with a 'flight' of thirty-second TV spots; and at the end, you remind with fifteen-second spots, newspaper ads, and billboards" (2009). Publicity works in parallel with advertising during **pre-release**. Every media break and every ad becomes a further reminder to create awareness and turn awareness into purchase intention.

A month before its opening, Furious 7 created excitement on the USA cable channel, by offering a sneak peek during the premiere of a new series, DIG. The series premiere was preceded by a 10-hour Fast and Furious marathon that included pre-recorded exclusive cast commentary (Zal, 2015). The male audience is a target for the USA show and for the Fast and Furious franchise. Having a USA marathon reminds previous fans how much they like the franchise. It also allows new viewers to catch up all at once and become part of the fan community excitedly anticipating the premiere.

Pre-release publicity

The stars are back! By the terms of their contracts, almost all stars are obligated to be available to participate in publicity activities for about 10 days to two weeks around the release of the film. The publicist arranges for interviews with print media that will break Thursday or Friday of premiere week. The stars begin an intensive round of morning, afternoon, and late-night talk-show appearances, during which they talk about the film and show a clip.

Premiere publicity

The job of the premiere, according to Friend is "to 'eventize' a film, to move it to the top of the nation's to-do list" (2009). Studios spend from $150,000 to $500,000 to create a flashy event that will generate media coverage. As discussed in Chapter 4, premieres are usually scheduled for Monday or Tuesday evening, or Monday in Los Angeles and another event Tuesday in New York. The evening is scheduled so that red-carpet arrivals are covered live by the local early evening news. Then the movie is screened, followed by a glitzy party, which is in full swing to be covered by the local late-night news shows from 10:00–11:30. Media coverage will continue the next day with recaps on shows such as *Access Hollywood* and then later at night with star appearances on talk shows.

For many moviegoers, Thursday night is decision night. People plan their weekend activities. Ahead of Thursday night, PR pitches broadcast news outlets about the long lines of fans in crazy costumes waiting for mid-night screenings. Also on Thursday night, commercials flood the TV airwaves, and the most important stars appear on the talk shows that cater to the film's core audience segments.

Is It a Hit or a Flop?

First week of release

If the publicity and marketing people have done their jobs right, their efforts will **open the picture**. This means that the film will meet or beat box-office expectations, as discussed in the section above on the PR goal. If a film does well, PR trumpets the box-office number.

If the film misses the goal and does not meet or beat expectations, it will probably be considered a flop, or at least a "disappointment." Most likely the studio will cut off further PR efforts and media buys. Why throw good money after bad?

Second weekend of release

After a successful opening, media stories that appear during the second week of release include follow-up stories and human-interest stories. For example, there may be stories about how the film echoes a personal experience of the star or the director. The film was written by a screenwriter, whose screenplay may have been based on someone else's true story or on a novel; the participants' emotional connection to the story, however, helps readers relate to the film. During this week, the secondary stars and the director make the talk-show rounds offering their anecdotes and a clip from a scene that audiences loved.

Unless the second weekend is extended by a three- or four-day holiday, the box-office results for a blockbuster fall off for the second weekend. Nevertheless, the box-office total for the second weekend renders the final verdict on success or failure, but not taken in isolation. Instead, the industry follows a **40 percent rule of thumb**: if the second weekend's total *falls off less* than 40 percent, the blockbuster is considered a hit. If it *falls off more* than 40 percent, the industry considers it a flop.

Observers can do the calculations for themselves, although many news reports now publish the percentage decrease right along with news of the totals. For example, if weekend one earns $100 million and weekend two earns $65 million (only a 35 percent drop off), the film is a hit. In contrast, if weekend two for the same film only earns $50 million (a 50 percent drop), the film is considered a flop.

Conclusion

The status of hit versus flop has implications not just for the bottom line of the distributor that needs to pay off the hefty cost of production and marketing, or take a loss. It also has implications for all of the other participants. A star, studio executive, and even a publicist may be able to weather a flop or even two. A series of high-profile flops, however, means less bankability or employability in the future. Remember the industry saying attributed to Johnny Weissmuller, the Olympic swimmer who played Tarzan: "You're only as good as your last picture."

While the box-office results of a franchise tend to go down from film to film, too huge a drop kills off the possibility of future sequels. A franchise film flopping does serious damage to the studio copyright holder for years into the future. The PR team may feel that the producers gave them a weak film to sell. The producers may say that marketing and publicity did poor jobs. But in the end, everyone shares in the disappointment and in some of the taint of being involved with a flop.

That is another reason it is so important to create an excellent public relations plan with a realistic goal based on a solid grasp of the background and situation analysis. Set the box-office goal too high, and the industry sees disappointing results for week one. On the other hand, if PR acknowledges weaknesses and threats in the plan, more can be done to mitigate them. The plan can propose tactics that focus attention on strengths and opportunities in order to frame media attention on positive story angles.

For blockbuster films, the PR cycle begins when a script or even a pitch is put into development. Blockbuster PR is a marathon through the stages of development, green-lighting, pre-production, production, post-production, pre-release, the premiere and on through the second weekend. Some block-busters that have complex stories and nuanced characters may run for many weeks. Some develop Oscar buzz that keeps them in the public's awareness into the winter Academy Award season, as happened with *Titanic*, which eventually won 11 Academy Awards. The Oscar PR cycle is covered in the next chapter.

Key Terms—In bold in the text

Sample two-sentence definition and example

40 Percent Rule of Thumb: This is a short-hand way of judging whether a film is a hit, and it means that if a film's second week box office falls more than 40 percent, the film is considered a flop. For example, if a film made $100 million the first weekend, but only $50 million the second weekend, it would be considered a flop, and the distributor would cut off expensive TV commercials and public relations efforts such as scheduling talk show appearances.

Above-the-Line Talent
Audience Questionnaire
B-Roll
Background
Bankable
Below-the-Line Personnel
Blockbuster
Blockbuster PR Cycle
Box-Office Gross
Box-Office Potential
Box-Office Split
Buyer Persona
CinemaScore

Comic-Con International
Consumer Media
Crisis Management
Cross-Brand Tie-In
Demographics
Development
Directors Guild of America (DGA)
Electronic Press Kit (EPK)
Focus Group
Four-Quadrant Films
Franchise Films
Green-Lighting
Intellectual Property (IP)
International Alliance of Theatrical Stage Employees (IATSE)
Legs (or having legs)
Long-Lead Magazine
Media Buy
Media Kit
Merchandise Licensing
Movie Website
Opening the Picture
Planting the Flag
Playbook
Post-Production
Pre-Production
Pre-Release
Pre-Sold Title
Product Placement
Production
Psychographics
Public Relations Plan (See RFP)
Publicists Guild of America
Q Score
Quadrants
Qualitative Research
Quantitative Research
RFP or Request for Proposal (Public Relations Plan)
Screen Actors Guild (SAG)

Script Consultant
Situation Analysis
Spec Script
Start-of-Production Media Release
Studio Films
SWOT (Strengths, Weaknesses, Opportunities, Threats)
Talent, or Above the Line
Tent-Pole Films
Tracking Survey
Trans-Media Storytelling
Unit Publicist
VidCon
Writers Guild of America (WGA)

Suggested reading and resources

Friend, T. (2016, January 11). The mogul of the middle: As the movie business founders, Adam Fogelson tries to reinvent the system. *The New Yorker*, 36–49.
Lieberman, A., & Esgate, P. (2014). The definitive guide to entertainment marketing: Bringing the moguls, the media, and the magic to the world (2nd ed.). *Upper Saddle River*, NJ: Pearson.

· 8 ·

THE INDEPENDENT FILM PR CYCLE
AND THE FILM FESTIVAL CIRCUIT

Chapter Overview: When you finish this chapter, you should be able to answer the following questions:

- How are independent films different from blockbusters?
- How are independent films financed?
- What is the independent film PR cycle?
- What are the roles of film festivals in the Indie cycle?
- What is the typical distribution pattern of an independent film?
- SIDEBAR: The Entertainment PR Toolbox—PR Proposals (RFPs)
- SIDEBAR: The Entertainment PR Toolbox—Prepping the Client for Media Interviews
- SIDEBAR: The Entertainment PR Toolbox—Guerilla Marketing Stunts
- SIDEBAR: The Biz Markets Itself—The Oscar PR Cycle

Introduction

This chapter explains the ways that the development, production, post-production, and distribution of independent films differ from the process for blockbusters. Because of those differences, the PR cycle for independent films differs from the blockbuster cycle just covered in Chapter 7. Hundreds of new screenplays circulate around Hollywood each year, joining the stacks and stacks of unmade projects from previous years. Screenwriters use a new screenplay to try to gain access to the studio development apparatus, because, as discussed in Chapter 7, the studios are their own banks and distribute their own films, thus giving their films access to audiences in theaters.

A studio's distribution and marketing system, however, is geared to getting the mass audience into thousands of theaters—a costly process. By one estimate, Paramount would need to spend $20 million on the kind of marketing campaign it understands how to deploy. It doesn't make fiscal sense to risk that much money on a film with a budget of less than $1 million. In 2015, for example, Paramount acquired distribution rights to a low-budget film, *Drunk Wedding*, but eventually released it on video on demand, instead of in theaters (Barnes, 2015b, p. B2). In most cases, the studios will reject a film project without: a strong (and flashy) central role for a bankable star; a **high-concept**, a hook that can be conveyed in a phrase (Legos come to life); and bankable or pre-sold elements that presage a profit on investment. Therefore, a script that doesn't attract studio backing by default becomes an independent film … or dies.

Independent films are typically developed and produced outside of the studio system. After raising money to complete production and post-production, an independent film needs to find its audience. The first step is usually winning a place on a film festival's schedule. Festival success may lead to a distribution deal with an independent distributor. Next is a limited release in a few theaters. A small number of independent films have eventually gained enough critical and audience acclaim that they could be shepherded through the Oscar PR cycle (covered in a SIDEBAR in this chapter). This chapter will explain how creative publicity can raise the profile of a low-budget film by an unknown screenwriter and little-known director, and with a young, mostly unknown ensemble cast and make it into a serious contender for industry awards including Oscars.

Independent Films Differ from Blockbusters

Independent films are also referred to as little films, offbeat films, passion projects, specialty films, and prestige films. What these terms mean within the industry is that at the onset, the film has no established financing, because it does not have bankable elements, such as a big star. Since it does not have a studio home, it starts with no distributor in the US or abroad to get it in front of audiences. Therefore, even a project made for a miniscule budget is risky for investors.

Because it has no bankable elements, an indie needs a passionate (even obsessive) advocate. That person will likely be the screenwriter, who may also want to direct. By default, the writer-director becomes the executive producer. On the film side of the business (as opposed to television, discussed in Chapters 5 and 6), the title of **executive producer** usually indicates the person who raises the money to make the film, or the person who had the connections to the money (such as a deal at a studio). Only after the executive producer has raised money to cover the cost of production does a publicist become involved.

With no bankable elements and a small budget, PR has to be creative and agile to create public awareness, credibility, want-to-see sentiment, and perhaps even Oscar buzz. However, it is a long road from a screenwriter finishing a charming or moving screenplay about a girl coming of age among an ensemble of relatives; to shooting and editing the film; to winning slots in film festivals; to gaining a distribution deal; to reaching the break-even point, even with a small budget of $2 million, as reported on IMDb.com for *Winter's Bone*. That 2010 release won the 2010 Sundance Grand Jury Award and numerous other awards on the way to four 2011 Academy Award nominations, including for Best Picture and Best Actress, for a very young Jennifer Lawrence.

Some of the films that have made the trip to prestige, possibly profit, and the Oscar cycle include *Silver Linings Playbook*, *The Artist*, *The King's Speech*, *Little Miss Sunshine*, and *There Will Be Blood*.

Finding the Money to Make an Independent Film

Development

The minimum needed to start raising money is a completed, compelling 90- to 120-page original screenplay. The script should be written to minimize production costs: no special effects; few locations; mostly interior scenes; and roles that can be cast with attractive unknowns just dying to get some feature film footage to add to their own promo reels.

With the screenplay in hand, the executive producer-writer-director makes the rounds of likely financers. He probably starts with mini-major companies, such as Lionsgate and The Weinstein Company, which have established lines of financing. The next choice might be to sell distribution rights for various foreign territories in advance. At this point, an international partner might insist on attaching an actor with a high local Q Score (see Chapter 7).

The next choice might be creating a legal prospectus for **accredited investors** (meaning individuals of some financial means, who meet the legal definition of being able to afford to lose their entire investment on a risky undertaking). The Coen brothers (*There Will Be Blood*) have spoken about the challenge of raising small amounts from several dozen entrepreneurs and business people in Minneapolis, Texas, and New York for their first movie, the thriller, *Blood Simple*. They were able to entice people to listen to their pitch by having 10 minutes of footage that demonstrated their talent (Lowenstein, 2002).

On the next level of desperation, some obsessed screenwriters go to the bank of Mom and Dad or even put micro-budget production costs on their own credit cards—practices not advocated by experienced Hollywood producers. How many doting parents have mortgaged and lost their homes? How many would-be filmmakers have had to declare bankruptcy because of high-interest credit card debt? Hollywood professionals make a practice of never investing their own money in a film. The risk is too high, and they are already risking their time and reputation.

Through obsessive effort by a dedicated writer-director-executive producer, some independents raise money from a combination of **equity partners**, who gain partial ownership; foreign distribution pre-sales in individual global markets, such as Germany and Japan; **debt financing**, which means a loan that must be repaid starting immediately, like a car loan or mortgage; and location-shooting tax credits from local or state film commissions. Nevertheless, "indie films without stars will have to keep reinventing ways to line up financing," according to *Variety* (Goldstein, 2015, p. 52).

Green-lighting

When enough money has been raised to cover the cost of production, the independent film can go into production, i.e., the filmmakers give themselves the green light, usually with no firm U.S. distribution deal. An exception to this might be when the specialty arm of a distributor, such as Sony Classics, makes a distribution offer pending completion of production and post-production, as a way to avoid the production falling under costly Hollywood union contracts.

When a film goes into production, smart producers will allocate money for a PR Plan, so that materials can be assembled for later use on the film festival circuit and during the hoped-for distribution process. Green-lighting is when the independent film PR cycle should begin in earnest with a plan created and implemented by a publicist, rather than by an executive producer-director-writer who has other priorities.

The Independent Film Publicity Cycle

Producers of independent films and their publicists should remember that a studio does not green-light production on a film unless they know how to sell it. Indies shouldn't either. The first sales goal is a sale into distribution. After that the distributor needs to sell it to an audience, so the filmmakers need to know from the get-go who that eventual audience will be. Excellent public relations preparation is a key to these later sales.

A PR proposal or plan should include all of the elements discussed so far in earlier chapters. An in-depth situation analysis should identify: similarities to other films; which companies made distribution deals on those films, for how much money; and how those films performed in the indie marketplace. The next steps are: a SWOT analysis of the film's strengths, weaknesses, opportunities, and threats; target audience segmentation by quadrant and niches (Chapter 7); a defined PR goal; and objectives, strategies, and tactics for each stage of the independent film cycle going forward.

The Entertainment PR Toolbox— PR Proposals (RFPs)

The goal of writing a PR plan or proposal is to convince the client to hire your team, or convince upper management to allocate budget for the plan. To do so, the plan has to show in-depth understanding of the client's situation, leading to a definition of the PR goal and a roadmap for reaching that goal. A PR Plan/Proposal/RFP usually includes:

- Client background
- Client's current situation
- SWOT
- A statement of the main communications problem **or** main opportunity
- A PR goal aligned with organizational goals, usually dollars, or something that easily equates to dollars (Chapter 5)
- A logical target audience segmentation using industry-specific categories (Chapters 5 and 7)

- Buyer personas specifying media usage (Chapter 7)
- Objectives stated in terms of each target segment (Chapter 5)
- The PR tactics to be used for achieving each objective, depending on the client's budget, the timeline, and the specific project and its challenges, such as:
  - Website content (this chapter)
  - Press releases
  - Pitches of story angles and media targets (See the SIDEBAR in Chapter 12)
  - Print (target publications, how and when do you approach them?)
  - TV (interviewed by whom or featured how?)
  - Radio (news, talk, music, or a promotion on which appropriate stations in which markets?)
  - Social media (which, and how do you make the client stand out?)
  - Innovative digital tactics such as ones using augmented reality or global positioning
  - Cross-brand tie-ins (Chapter 7)
  - Guerilla marketing stunt (this chapter)
  - Event tie-in, charity tie-in, or issue tie-in
  - Other original creative elements that make the plan stand out from competitors
- Budget: This is highly variable, depending on the kind of project. For example, for independent films, one industry insider, Robert Marich, allocates an overall marketing budget of $800,000, which includes $580,000 for advertising (with no expensive monthly magazine ads or TV commercials). Of the remaining $220,000 Marich allocates about $10,000 to website development, other funds for trailers and advertising fliers, $30,000 for "festival support," and $125,000 for screenings and publicity, including developing website content (which doubles as press kit material) and for the other PR tactics and activities (Marich, 2013). While $800,000 may seem like a lot of money, remember that a studio distributor would spend millions more.

As with any project, public relations for an independent film should start with an accepted proposal or plan including a budget that the client and the publicist agree on.

Since most indie films are non-union productions, an independent production is a chance to gain experience as a unit publicist.

Caution #1 for aspiring film publicists

Many more films are shot than ever get accepted in film festivals or find a distributor. Therefore, don't agree to work completely for free, unless you get a written, **back-end deal** that guarantees a specific payment out of the filmmaker's gross proceeds from any distribution deal. Do not accept a percentage of box-office net, which is what the qualified investors usually agree to. They seldom recoup their initial investments. There may never be a net profit, even on a film that receives a lot of media coverage. A written agreement is also necessary, because any distributor that buys U.S. distribution rights will most likely have its own public relations team to see the film through distribution. So the filmmaker may try to promise a young publicist that if he works for free during production, he will receive a salary once a distribution deal is in place. The filmmaker can't guarantee that, because the deal will put later decisions in the hands of the distributor.

Caution #2

As a young PR person, before agreeing to spend any low-paid time, or especially before taking a back-end deal, read the completed, full-length screenplay. If there's no screenplay, just thank the filmmakers for the opportunity and wish them the best of luck!

You've watched lots of movies. Would you spend your own time and money to watch this completed movie? If you wouldn't, is there some other demographic that makes a well-defined audience segment for this film—at least one of the quadrants? In your judgment, does this script have interesting characters, a compelling story, and an adequate budget already in the bank for production and post-production expenses? Does the intended cast have the talent and ability to carry a film?

Don't agree to work on a "film" for a would-be director who only has a sketchy outline and is taking his pals out to improvise and shoot footage. Only work with talented people who clearly have the drive, internal fortitude, filmmaking knowledge, and financial and emotional resources to see the long, arduous process of feature film production through to the end and get it sold into distribution.

PR goal

The PR Goal for an independent film just going into production cannot be put in terms of box-office dollars, because there is not yet a distributor. Therefore, the PR goal is to get a distribution deal, which equals money. The strategy is to create and build brand awareness. And the tactics early on are to get any possible kind of media coverage, especially print clips that can be added to the press kit and linked to the website to bolster credibility.

Website and social media

Every film needs a professionally designed website, typically with a web address of www.thetitlemovie.com. The website should feature a compelling graphic treatment of the film's title and accommodate: video clips; photographs and galleries; a "front page" story; a prominent area for links to media coverage; a news tab that posts press releases in reverse chronological order; a press kit area for materials from the printed press kit after they have been individually featured on the front page; the video news kit (electronic press kit or EPK); and a statement about the availability to media of high-quality photographs. The website should also include links to popular social media sites such as Instagram, Facebook, Twitter, and LinkedIn. Likewise, every post on social media should include a link back to the movie website to drive traffic and help the site become and stay at the top of search rankings.

Website as a publication

The website functions as controlled PR (see Chapter 3), and as the film's own publication, with the publicist as editor. Every time the publicist creates a piece of publicity material such as a media release or an actor bio, it should be posted first as a "front page" story. When the next item is added, the first moves to a less prominent position and then is archived behind one of the tabs, such as the press kit tab.

Search engine optimization (SEO)

The more often new material is posted, the higher the website will move in the search rankings, so the publicist should post as often as practical.

Production unit publicity

Just as with a blockbuster, the first step is to write a start-of-production media release. With no big stars, the news release is unlikely to get any play in the Hollywood trades. Nevertheless, the release may be the first step in creating awareness with Hollywood film beat reporters.

Local coverage

The start-of-production release, however, is news mostly in the local area where the shoot is taking place. Local papers have news reporters. Some even have an entertainment critic/reporter who may jump at the chance to cover a Hollywood story with local angles. For example, way back in 1992, standing in for Punxsutawney, Pennsylvania, the town of Woodstock, Illinois, was the location of the shoot for *Groundhog Day*, directed by Harold Ramis, and starring Bill Murray and Andie MacDowell, released in February 1993. The local newspapers extensively covered the doings of the Hollywood people, including profiling local people who were cast as extras (personal knowledge of the author). The unit publicist for *Groundhog Day* created great local media relations that eased possible community tensions or resentment that their charming town square, main street that wraps around the square, surrounding local shops, and picturesque neighborhoods were transformed into limited-access movie sets for hours and days at a time.

Since then, Woodstock, Illinois, holds a yearly, multi-day Groundhog Day celebration, often graced with at least one guest connected to the original filming. By creating positive community relations through local media outreach back in 1992, the unit publicist helped pave the way for an enduring local tourist event and community celebration.

The local press and community may be less interested and less accommodating in locations near Los Angeles, New York, or Toronto, cities that are regularly used for location shoots. The unit publicist should nevertheless make every effort to pitch local angles to broadcast and print media, especially free neighborhood newspapers. Some of these may print the start-of-production release in its entirety as a news story. Any possible coverage is a clip for the press kit and starts building awareness for the title.

Press kit

Just as on a studio film, an important duty of the unit publicist is to prepare all of the press kit materials (See Chapter 7). Besides the start-of-production release, these include: a longer film synopsis; talent credits and bios; interviews with the talent; a fact sheet; and production notes and anecdotes that might spark future feature articles. Assemble these materials in an attractive two-pocket folder with a sticker on the cover showing a title treatment. The kit should be ready to give to interested media during production and at future film festivals. Print clips in the kit demonstrate media interest in the film and make it easier to get future stories.

Behind-the-scenes photography

Most productions will not want to pay for a professional still photographer to document every scene. The director, however, will surely understand the future publicity needs for high-quality photos of himself or herself on set with the actors and behind the camera. Hiring a professional photographer for a couple of days to get those shots and shots of the cast behind the scenes will pay off in column inches in film festival programs and future media coverage. On other days, the publicist can take candid snapshots and record short interview videos that can be posted on Instagram or Twitter with a link back to the website.

Photo releases

These days, people are used to candid photos taken almost anywhere being posted on social media. Just to be sure, however, the publicist should have a blanket photo release signed by each person on the production that allows for commercial and non-commercial use of photos taken during production.

Behind-the-scenes video

The location shoot of an indie will probably not be of interest to the entertainment news shows such as *Access Hollywood*. Therefore, as with photography, the budget should accommodate a couple of days of video interviews with the director and the cast, as well as behind-the-scenes footage. These interviews can be edited as needed and used first on the website. The video shoots can also function as media training for inexperienced talent to prepare them to handle the media that accompanies visibility at a film festival.

The Entertainment PR Toolbox—Prepping the Client for Media Interviews

Public relations practitioners in every field need to prepare clients, executives, and other spokespeople for their media interactions. Publicists of independent films have a special challenge.

Independent films debuting at film festivals often have directors and cast members who are less experienced and less media-savvy than those publicizing blockbusters. Therefore, this SIDEBAR gives guidance on how to prepare clients (celebs, executives, breakout stars, newly signed athletes) for media questioning. Situations may range from red carpets to talk show appearances, to being waylaid by TMZ in a coffee shop or outside a club at 3 a.m.

Even questions that seem benign can trip up those who are naïve or unprepared. For example, "What is your film about?" The client should be able to make her project sound fascinating in a short **sound bite** of one sentence or an **elevator pitch** of two to five sentences. Nobody wants to listen to a rambling line-by-line and scene-by-scene retelling of the movie's plot, and no journalist will quote it. Journalists are often unprepared for an interview. Therefore, the interviewee needs to know the basic facts about the film, and also be prepared with quotable quotes and charming anecdotes.

One guide for indie producers suggests that potential interviewees be prepared to answer these questions: "1. What is your film about? 2. What attracted you to the material? 3. What's the hook? 4. Who is in it?" (Free & Domingue, 2007, p. 43).

No matter how practiced they are with the media, almost all potential interviewees should be prepped for each interview with at least:

- the journalist's name and media outlet
- a reminder of any previous encounters or personal information that the interviewee should remember
- a brief summary of the kinds of stories that particular journalist writes
- and reminders to keep the focus on the title being publicized, or the day's talking points, not the interviewee's personal life

"Rehearse with your strategists," veteran *Variety* Editor and Columnist, Tim Gray, advises talent. Journalists hoping for a juicy quote may ask "about racism, gender equality, the folly of awards competition. … Anticipate these questions and figure out a response. (If you want to wing it, feel free. But be prepared to be tweeted and analyzed for weeks)," which is a strong recommendation for rehearsing talking points ahead of time (Gray, 2015b). For a cautionary tale about the outcome of an over-confident and under-prepared client interview, read Anna Peele's *Esquire* cover story about Miles Teller, which is listed in Suggested Reading (Peele, 2015). *The New York Times* described the profile, which damages the actor by quoting his own crass words, as "part of a long, if infrequent, journalistic tradition" (Kurutz, 2015). *Esquire* received a lot of media coverage about the profile, but it reflects badly on both the actor and his publicist.

Client preparation and media training are always important parts of a publicist's job. If an actor on a talk show forgets to mention the name of the film he's supposed to be publicizing, the public relations representative is to blame.

During production, the public relations objective is to begin creating awareness for the film. The tactics and tools are a combination of frequent website postings of each piece of publicity material as it is prepared; fun social media photos and videos linked to the website; and any possible print coverage, even if only a few lines, that can be added to the press kit to bolster credibility. A major responsibility is to prepare all of the press kit and EPK materials, as well as photos that will be needed to publicize the film later and to make it stand out on the crowded schedules of any film festivals that accept it.

Film Festivals Play Two Roles in the Indie Cycle

Film festivals such as the Sundance Film Festival and the Toronto Film Festival are contests that independent filmmakers pay to enter in order to win a coveted place on a festival schedule, along with the wide publicity and reviews that come with festival participation. The minimum a filmmaker needs to enter a festival is a completed, edited, ready-to-screen film on DVD … and the money for the entry fee, which is often around $50. Because the first rounds of judging take place before the festival schedules are announced, the deadlines are often months in advance. For example, Sundance Film Festival has a mid-August deadline for its January festival.

While filmmakers may enter numerous festivals, the entry process is time intensive, the entry fees add up, and the rules are complex. The most prestigious festivals hope to excite local audiences and a large press corps by showing world or U.S. premieres. Some festivals, however, have a separate category called "out of competition" for films that have already been viewed by even a limited paying audience or at other, rival festivals. These tend to be films that have respected distributors and will soon be in theaters.

Festival acceptance as a path to a distribution deal

So what can a filmmaker hope to win by entering a festival? 1. Publicity that begins with the festival's announcement of its schedule. 2. The awareness of potential distributors that the film has risen to the top of a rigorous selection process; for example, Sundance typically selects only 16 feature films out of hundreds of entries. 3. Access to an audience of film buffs and critics, who create an excited buzz around a film they like. 4. Reviews and other media coverage; for example, *Variety* and *The Hollywood Reporter* typically review every film on the schedule of major festivals. Also, their business reporters and those at *The New York Times* and the *Los Angeles Times* also typically write festival stories about the audience buzz and about bidding wars among distributors for favorite films. 5. The prestige of winning a festival Grand Prize, a critic's choice award, or an audience favorite award. 6. Finally, best of all, securing a U.S. distribution deal, which, you remember, is the goal of the PR plan initiated months ago.

Festival press coverage

Gaining wide press coverage is a strategic objective for the film festivals themselves in order to maintain their momentum and prestige from year to year. Media coverage is also an objective of the filmmaker. After a festival announces its schedule, a film's publicist should also immediately distribute an individual **festival participation press release** targeted to industry media in Hollywood and New York and to other press that has traditionally covered the festival. This important media release should include all of the credits and information from the start-of-production release. The release builds title awareness and helps separate the film from the festival crowd as one that has professional PR representation. Don't forget to service any media that covered the film during its location shoot.

While inexperienced talent may see a festival as an opportunity to party and spend a fun time in an exciting destination, such as snowboarding during Sundance, one industry guide recommends that filmmakers and publicists "make it your mission to sell out your screenings" (Foggia & Neal, 2007). Working hard to get media coverage is vital, because, "Even a one-sentence, enthusiastic quote can give you unbelievable yardage in your pursuit of deals down the road" (Foggia & Neal, 2007). As with other high-profile events, such as award ceremonies, the filmmakers, stars, and publicists need to remember that they are at a film festival primarily to work—which includes socializing and interacting with the media.

Guerilla marketing

Because the festival environment is so competitive, everyone promoting an indie film is thinking outside the box. Innovative tactics, sometimes known as **guerilla marketing** or a **PR stunt**, can make a film stand out, at least enough to get people into its screening.

The Entertainment PR Toolbox—Guerilla Marketing Stunts

Formerly known as PR stunts and disdained by some mainstream public relations practitioners, creative guerilla marketing is highly valued by the industry for its entertainment value; its ability to generate local (and sometimes national) TV news coverage; now for the possibility of becoming a viral sensation; and especially for its cost effectiveness. A good **PR stunt** or **guerilla marketing tactic** should be low cost (in comparison to buying TV ad time) and be so original and creative that it generates free broadcast coverage and social media hits.

As an example of a viral PR stunt, in the summer of 2014, the non-profit ALS Association, the organization that raises money for research to find a cure for Lou Gehrig's disease, became the beneficiary of the "ice-bucket" challenge, which some sports stars had sporadically been using to raise money for their various favorite charities. The challenge was either to donate $100 or post a video showing that you dumped a bucket of ice over your head. Each dumper also issued a challenge to three other high-profile celebs to donate or dump (but preferably both) within 24 hours. Challenging three others generated the exponential momentum to go viral. Athlete and celebrity ice-dumping incidents soon focused on Lou Gehrig's disease, which has destroyed the bodies of well-known athletes, among many others.

Videos of ice-dumping and challenges went out to Twitter followers and were featured in Facebook timelines. They were also featured in numerous traditional media outlets. The business channel CNBC featured its anchors meeting the challenge and then challenging three others, the more high profile the better. With such extensive free broadcast coverage and with the topic trending on social media, ALSA raised many times their usual summer campaign results.

Another stunt campaign had the goal of reviving the value of the "Lassie" franchise, by making Lassie a spokes-dog for product endorsements. This PR stunt resulted in a front-page story in the Sunday New York Times (Barnes, 2014a).

Examples of kinds of stunts used for movies include: flash mobs; unannounced performances; T-shirted brigades advertising screenings; rigged environments, such as a telekinetic café rigged to publicize Carrie, which has received more than 65 million views on YouTube ("Telekinetic Coffee Shop Surprise," 2013); projections on the sides of buildings; wild postings of posters on poles, which has been done since P. T. Barnum's day in the mid-nineteenth century; postings on construction fences, which can be paid for or illegal; and chalking or stenciling on sidewalks or elsewhere, depending on the local authorities and the permanence of the image.

New York public relations veteran Howard J. Rubenstein said, "Stunts still get attention because great fun is timeless. Done well, they create publicity that cannot be stunted" (Rubenstein, 2014, p. A18). Guerilla marketing tactics in a PR proposal help the plan stand out by demonstrating the team's creativity, initiative, and understanding of budgetary constraints.

Announcing a distribution deal

The New York Times has said, "Sundance first hit its stride in the 1980s partly because independent-film executives, split between New York and Los Angeles, came together in the middle to wheel and deal. The festival's heat has always come from the money changing hands" (Barnes, 2015a, p. B2). A flashy distribution deal gives the festival, the filmmaker, and the distributor credibility and visibility with the attending international entertainment media.

On the other hand, a deal is a partnership, with the buyer being the lead partner, so probably the distributor will want to make its own announcement about the acquisition. The film's publicist can work with the new distributor by providing access to the press kit and other materials, and by working on the filmmaker quotation to be included.

The publicist can caution members of the media who are tracking rumors that the filmmakers can't confirm or deny a distribution rumor; they would, however, be happy to do an interview to talk about the film itself. Then let the distributor know about the interview request. Most likely the distributor will want to be part of any such festival "buzz" stories too. Ahead of the film-maker's interview, a reminder about your previous media training is in order. Coach the filmmaker to talk about the enthusiastic response of festival audiences and how exciting it is to be a part of a festival that has "lots of industry people and distributors."

Being involved with a festival film that receives media coverage and achieves a distribution deal—the PR goal—also demonstrates the publicist's professional expertise to other festival filmmakers for possible future projects. A festival is a unique opportunity for a publicist to network for future work, because the business card for the film has the publicist's own cell phone number as the media contact number.

Festivals to generate pre-opening and Oscar buzz

Distributors are looking for independent films that have potential eventually to generate Oscar buzz, when the Oscar PR cycle begins late in the year.

The Biz Markets Itself—The Oscar PR Cycle

The Oscar PR cycle kicks in months after most blockbuster release dates, which are mainly in the early summer (see Chapter 7). Nevertheless, the nominations and awards play an important role in maintaining the global prestige of films, stars, and studios in terms of "Hollywood politics, bragging rights and brand image" (Follows, 2015). Academy of Motion Picture Arts and Sciences President Cheryl Boone Isaacs is quoted as saying that "'30 years ago, there was no such thing as an awards season. … But today, the awards race has a major influence on studio distribution patterns and is a driving force for marketing campaigns'" (Blair, 2015).

Figure 8.1: Cheryl Boone Isaacs started in motion picture publicity in the late 1970s and rose to the highest levels at Paramount, New Line, and other companies. After representing the Public Relations Branch on the Board of Governors of the Academy of Motion Picture Arts and Sciences for more than 20 years, she was elected President of the Academy in 2013. Photo credit: ©A.M.P.A.S./Todd Wawrychuk.

In recent years, major Best Picture campaigns for big studio films cost from $10 million (Follows, 2015) to $15 million (Abramowitz, Horn, & Welkos,

2005, p. A24), depending on how much is spent on expensive trade magazine advertising. During the nomination and voting seasons, the weekly glossy print editions of *Variety* and *The Hollywood Reporter* are thick with expensive, full-page ads that say, "For your consideration," along with compelling color images from hopeful films. Before the announcement of the nominations in phase one of the campaign, the trade ads are meant to raise awareness among Academy voters and spur them to view the film at special industry screenings or on screener DVDs mailed to their homes by the various PR campaigns. In phase two before the voting, "'you're trying to remind them why they love the movie, instead,'" one industry strategist is quoted as saying (Galloway, 2015, p. 48). Because of the limited advertising budgets of independent films, the media attention surrounding the nomination process, the industry screenings, and Oscar week press events are even more important than they are to blockbusters.

A film does not need to have been shown on 4,000 or more screens or make over $100 million in box-office grosses to be eligible for the Oscar process. **Oscar nomination eligibility** requires only *distribution* availability to the paying public on *one* screen for *one* week in *both* New York and Los Angeles *before* December 31. Films opening on Christmas Day therefore can be eligible for nominations. To hook their movie to the Oscar media train, many smaller and independent films open late in the year, after premiering at fall film festivals. When a film begins to generate Oscar buzz at a festival, the distributor may even push the release to later in the year, as Warner Bros. did in 2012 when it pushed back *Argo*, directed by and starring Ben Affleck, from September 14 to October 12 (McClintock, 2012).

Phase one from the release of the film until the nominations are announced, "'is more like a political campaign. But there's more legwork in Phase Two. Every appearance is vital,'" a veteran was quoted as saying (Lee, 2015, p. 16). Prime appearance opportunities include being nominated and/or being a presenter at a number of other awards events during the voting period, including the Golden Globes, the Screen Actors Guild (SAG) Awards, and the Directors Guild of America (DGA) Awards.

An Oscar campaign can be grueling, but also financially rewarding for everyone involved. For example, *Argo* had earned $110 million domestically before the Oscar nominations. During the voting process (with its non-stop publicity), *Argo* earned $19 million more, and then an additional $6 million after winning (Gray, 2015a, p. 8). Academy Award – winning actors and actresses usually get a bump in salary on their next projects. Public relations consultants are paid $10,000 to $15,000 per film with bonuses of from $5,000 to $20,000 for each nomination and each win (Follows, 2015, p. 10). Aside from the cold, hard cash value—which is never to be discounted in Hollywood—the five-month Oscar PR cycle from October through the awards broadcast raises the global profile of films in an era of many entertainment options, making the value of the Oscar and the Oscar PR cycle priceless.

Even the controversies in recent years about the lack of diversity among nominees in major categories might "boost TV ratings by heightening interest" (James, 2016, p. C1). People may tune in to the live broadcast to follow the controversy on social media and to be part of the conversation.

Because it can take from several weeks to several months for a distributor to sell a film into theaters, "The industry increasingly uses early-year film festivals to find those elusive gems and later-year festivals to position their most likely award candidates for success" (Dawn, 2011). Among the important fall festivals for launching Oscar contenders are Venice (late August), Telluride (early September), Toronto (mid-September) and New York (late September).

For independents, "exposure through awards is seen as a crucial, or perhaps the only means of survival. Small- and medium-size films enter the marketplace facing steep odds, and festival word-of-mouth is one way they try to gain a competitive edge" (A. O. Scott, 2014, p. C6). In the past, some films, such as *Argo* and *Juno* in 2013 and *Gravity* and *12 Years a Slave* in 2014, have pulled off splashy "premieres" at more than one fall festival (A. O. Scott, 2014, p. C6). Of late, however, the festivals are more careful to announce their slates close to their festival dates and not to give prominent slots and the best media exposure to a film that a competing festival has "sneaked" a couple of weeks earlier.

The Typical Distribution Pattern for an Independent Film

A festival premiere, great reviews, and audience buzz create awareness and excitement about the title in the film community. The film still, however, needs to reach a wider audience. That means opening to the public in movie theaters and getting audiences into those theaters. The distributors of independents have limited marketing budgets—not the $30 to $50 million typical of blockbusters—so they can't mount massive television advertising campaigns. They know that with no stars, special effects, big action sequences, or pre-sold elements, they are not able to fill 4,000 theaters on opening weekend.

The most effective and cost-effective advertising for an independent film is the movie trailer playing for several weeks in specific targeted theaters known for showing specialty or so-called art-house films, where the film will open. Trailers are seen by an audience of paying moviegoers, who are much more likely to see another film than are members of the general public who might see television advertising.

Platform release

Typically, an independent film opens small on a total of 2–10 screens in at least New York and Los Angeles and perhaps two or three other cities. If the film fills the 2–10 theaters and if it earns great reviews, the distributor sells it to more theaters and expands to additional cities and screens as buzz grows, in a release pattern called **platform release**.

For example, *The King's Speech* debuted September 4, 2010, at the Telluride Film Festival; screened at the Toronto Film Festival; opened Thanksgiving on four screens (two in NY, two in LA); and had box office of $355,000 on opening weekend, earning the year's record per screen average. The Weinstein Company widened the release to 700 screens Christmas Day and then to 1,543 on January 14, 2011, to a high of 2,584 screens the first week of February.

The King's Speech received 12 nominations and eight Academy Awards, including Best Picture. Eventually it earned almost $139 million in worldwide box-office grosses (according to its listing in IMDb.com), which is more than 19 times its $15 million budget. Although it had a higher production budget than most non-studio films, its release pattern nevertheless reflects the platform release pattern typical of independent films.

In 2014–2015, *Birdman* followed a similar pattern. Fox Searchlight opened it on four screens on October 17, 2014, and widened it to 857 screens on November 14. At its widest, it appeared on 1,213 screens. *Birdman* received nine Oscar nominations and won four, including Best picture, earning $103 million worldwide (boxofficemojo.com, n.d.) on an estimated budget of $22 million (IMDb.com, n.d.).

Independent Spirit Awards

The independent film industry has its own Independent Spirit Awards. The ceremony takes place just ahead of the Oscars to piggyback on the Oscar excitement—and to find the nominated stars and the film media in town for the pre-Oscar parties and events. This awards event offers an opportunity for media coverage and public awareness to smaller independent films, in addition to those nominated for Oscars.

Conclusion

An independent film with no big stars, no action or special effects sequences, and no pre-paid elements needs different public relations handling than a blockbuster. With a prospective indie film, often the writer-director-executive producer is one person, who first needs to raise the money to shoot and edit the film. Subsidiary rights may be sold upfront to raise money for production, and/or the exec producer may raise the funds strictly from private sources.

The actual PR cycle should start at green-lighting. To begin building awareness, every film should send out the important start-of-production media release. Because no distribution deal is in place to get the film in front of audiences, the PR goal for the film is to find a distribution agreement with a credible distributor. The quality of the finished film "earns" the distribution agreement, often by first winning inclusion in one or more film festivals.

Small films use festivals for two purposes: They use festivals early in the year for finding a distributor. Good audience response, positive reviews, and festival "buzz" induce the circling distributors to make offers, hopefully causing a bidding war for U.S. distribution rights. Indie distributors use fall festivals as opportunities for cost-effective premieres covered by the international film media in attendance.

After splashy festival premieres, most indies use the platform release pattern, opening small and expanding wider as word of mouth grows. Fall and late-year openings are common, for two reasons. First, there are no blockbusters in the marketplace, because the younger audience members (the under 25 men and women quadrants) are back in school. Second, films that build buzz about Oscar nominations can benefit from the Oscar PR cycle described in the SIDEBAR. From the announcement of nominations in mid-January through a few weeks after the Academy Awards ceremony, nominated films receive free, non-stop media coverage. This publicity is "priceless," because no distributor, not even a major studio, could afford to pay for it.

Key Terms—In bold in the text

Sample two-sentence definition and example

Accredited Investor: An Accredited Investor is one who meets that legal standard of having enough money to be able to afford to lose the entire investment in a risky venture such as an independent film. For example, a public relations practitioner should not be involved in an independent film that is illegally raising money by convincing low-income neighbors to take out a second mortgage or a title loan on a car.

Back-End Deal
Debt Financing
Elevator Pitch
Equity Partners
Executive Producer (film)
Festival Participation Press Release
Guerilla Marketing
High-Concept Film
Independent Film
Oscar Nomination Eligibility
Platform Release
PR Stunt
Sound Bite

Suggested reading and resources

Follows, S. (2015, January 12). How much does a Hollywood Oscar campaign cost? [Blog post]. Retrieved from http://stephenfollows.com/how-much-does-a-hollywood-oscar-campaign-cost/

Peele, A. (2015, August 5). Miles Teller is young, talented, and doesn't give a rat's ass what you think. Retrieved from http://www.esquire.com/entertainment/movies/interviews/a36894/miles-teller-interview-0915/

· 9 ·

SPORTS PR CYCLES, CELEBRITY ENDORSEMENTS, AND PSAS

Chapter Overview: When you finish this chapter, you should be able to answer the following questions:

- What are the PR jobs in sports?
- What is the sports PR cycle?
- Who are the key publics?
- What are the media outlets for sports PR stories?
- How do sports use social media and innovative technology to engage fans?
- Why do marketers pay high fees for sports celebrities to endorse products?
- How do teams and leagues demonstrate Corporate Social Responsibility (CSR)?
- What are PR problems or crises in sports?
- Are fantasy sports games of skill or gambling?
- SIDEBAR: The Biz Markets Itself—The Super Bowl
- SIDEBAR: The Entertainment PR Toolbox—Public Service Announcements (PSAs)

Introduction

The sports PR cycle is a yearly pattern determined by the individual sport's seasonal calendar. The big business of attracting fans to most sports and therefore the **sports PR cycle** includes: the off-season; the pre-season and exhibition games; the opener; big games, such as cross-town rivalries or a rematch of a hard-fought loss last season; the playoffs; the finals; the post-season; and the draft, which has recently become a huge production and a multi-day media event in its own right. The prototype final is the Super Bowl, which a SIDE-BAR will analyze for its prowess in marketing the sport of American football, as well as marketing products and the communal cultural experience of viewing live television.

The **goal of a sports PR plan** is to increase total revenue including ticket sales, merchandise, concessions, parking, and other revenue streams for the year, including for an individual game, a series, the season, and hopefully the post-season. This chapter's discussion of each part of the sports cycle covers typical objectives, strategies, tools, and activities, as well as stories and issues that support achieving that PR goal.

Finally, the chapter looks at CSR (corporate social responsibility) in sports, particularly the benefits to the leagues and to teams of non-profit initiatives and of athletes' participation in public service announcements (PSAs) and charity events. Likewise, a non-profit's partnership with a sports team or athlete can raise awareness of an issue or cause and can increase donations by harnessing the passion of fans.

Public Relations Jobs in the Sports World

If sports are your life, there is good news. The thriving field of **Sports Public Relations**, also known as **Sports Marketing** and at colleges and universities **Sports Information**, could also be your career.

Entering the field

The earlier an aspiring practitioner enters the field, the better. Many people working in communications positions for major-league professional teams and college teams got their starts as college students working for their college athletic departments. Perhaps they started as part of a work-study program or as a game-day volunteer or part-timer. Another chance for getting a foot in the door is an internship for college credit working for the college athletic department or for a local minor-league or major-league team. Skills needed for a sports information career include excellent writing, interpersonal and oral communication skills, the ability to multi-task and work well under pressure, and in-depth and ever-growing knowledge about the sport, the team, and individual athletes. Being a fan enables the sports PR person to understand the kinds of information, accurate statistics, stories, and angles fans feed on and that the media want to provide them. These days, the team's website is its own controlled publication, so writing, editing, and understanding the fan community are crucial.

Sports PR responsibilities

On game day, the main responsibility of the PR staff is to service the credentialed press and the television and radio producers and commentators. PR provides accurate and timely information, rosters, stats, quotes, and game notes. PR also controls pre- and post-game access to players and coaches, often on schedules and terms mandated by league rules and collective bargaining agreements. Teams at all levels including those in smaller major-league markets may also hire part-timers on game days "to do stats, run the clock and scoreboard, run stats and take and transcribe quotes" (NBA: Bobcats, n.d., para. 9, 13). In addition to college jobs and part-time jobs, entry-level opportunities may exist working for one of the more than 600 minor-league teams in the US. Since these teams often have the goal of developing players for their major-league owners, one minor-league public relations director has said, "'Instead of marketing the players [who may be called up to a higher league level at any time], we market the … [game] experience'" (Conn, 2006).

Most of the jobs in sports require multiple communications skills to prepare and convey information clearly for television, the Internet, and print (Billings, Butterworth, & Turman, 2012, p. 33). In the future, sports marketing will likely use more data mining techniques such as **collaborative filtering** to suggest, for example, merchandise choices based on others' choices (Chen & Lin, 2006, Proposed Techniques section, para. 6), as people have become used to on Amazon; and market basket analysis to decide which item would be popular for a promotion aimed at a specific market segment (para. 7). Thus, those in sports public relations should become familiar with current trends in research and data analysis—including statistics. After all, sports today are all about the stats.

Online

The bulk of sports information has moved from print to online formats. Online is easier for journalists, because they can avoid the tyranny of writing ahead of game results to meet hard-and-fast print deadlines (Billings et al., 2012, pp. 299–300). Now they can file the story when all the facts are in, and make it accessible to readers immediately. For public relations practitioners, the change to online may require ever-faster responses to requests by journalists, who now may try to scoop their colleagues by minutes or even seconds.

Audience development

Audience development and cultivating the next generation of fans are important objectives for achieving the revenue goal in the present and ensuring ongoing fan support into the future. To develop future fans, each team and each league has PR strategies such as "make family memories at the ballpark," supported by ticketing initiatives including family four-packs; in-park activities, such as autograph days; and giveaways such as team banners, bobble heads, baseballs or child-sized baseball caps to the first 50 kids.

Media training

During the season, a major responsibility of the public relations staff is media relations, which includes arranging interviews. Therefore, it is also important to do media briefings and training for all of the players and coaches, as discussed in the SIDEBAR in Chapter 8. Athletes should be prepared to answer basic questions, for example, "Why is today's game important?" and "What is your strategy for today's game?" Regarding any past or present injury, recent illness, or media criticism or controversy, "How are you feeling?"

Athletes should also be rehearsed on how to sidestep making personal comments about opponents or responding to gossip or to questions that are others' prerogative to answer, such as, "What is your plan for dealing with your feud with so and so?" or, "How is the coach going to use you today?"

The Sports PR Cycle

Most sports have a season when matches are played, and an off-season, such as spring and summer for American football. During the actual season much public relations work falls into the category of sports information—providing rosters, statistics, injury updates, and accurate game summaries and recaps. During the off-season, public relations needs to keep its fans interested and loyal, so they come back the following season to spend even more money on season tickets, concessions, and logo merchandise. Therefore, for the public relations staff, the work is ongoing and year around, although the nature of the stories and the media coverage change during the sports PR cycle.

Pre-season and training

The pre-season is all about hope and rising expectations. Ask Chicago Cubs fans. How is it possible that each year their fans hope anew? Ask Boston Red Sox fans. How did they stay loyal for 86 years until the team's unlikely World Series victory in 2004? Each pre-season, fans study player trades, profiles, and histories; crunch statistics; watch videos of spring training; listen to experts on sports talk radio, and … hope.

The power of public relations to find and tell compelling stories helps renew fans' hope year after year. PR stories told to and through the media feature the new players, the new lineup, the new coaches, and the new ways the old players used the off-season to come into training as better athletes than ever, despite encroaching age.

The team is new, it's a new season, and this time it will be different. We all hope. And we all love positive sports stories about the team's great potential for the new season. The new season brings such stories as, "Five Bold Predictions for the 2015 Chicago Cubs" (Spector, 2015), which predicted a 2015 World Series victory and referred to a guerilla marketing stunt that found a goat grazing on the Wrigley Field grass, supposedly bringing the end to a long and storied curse! In fact, the 2015 Cubs won a post-season wildcard game, but lost the National League Championship, so they didn't make it to the World Series. Maybe next year!

The 2015 football training season saw numerous stories pitched by college and professional teams' PR representatives to local and national media about the quarterback using virtual reality headsets to run and rerun plays without the usual physical wear and tear of "actual" reality. These stories promote the hope that a new training method will lead to a positive season outcome.

A PR stunt during the 2015 pre-season teamed MLB with HBO to have comedian Will Ferrell attempt to play 10 positions for one inning each on 10 teams in one day during spring training exhibition games. The stunt was filmed for an HBO special. It raised a million dollars to fight cancer (Axisa, 2015), and the hashtag #FerrellTakesTheField created a frenzy on social media (Arellano, 2015). By late summer, the HBO trailer (Ferrell, 2015, July 27) and other clips garnered over a million views on YouTube to publicize the September premiere, which would come as the long season pushed toward the playoffs.

Public relations activities such as these help fans forget that in team sports with playoffs and championship series such as the Super Bowl, every team except one—the champions—ended the last season as losers! Instead, fans want to hear about their team's intensive workouts and each player's great times on position drills, stories that support the perennial pre-season mindset—hope, which springs eternal during baseball's spring training and football's summer training camps. Hope sells tickets.

Season opener

The leagues set the schedule to maximize home team fan interest, but especially television viewership. Typically, the NFL opening game jump-starts the season in prime-time television on Thursday night with a hometown matchup between the Super Bowl champions and a strong competitor. The lone Thursday game enables PR to get the traditional media and social media conversations in full swing for the other season openers on Sunday.

Teams use many creative tactics to publicize the opener. For example, in 2015, the PR team for the Los Angeles Lakers posted a 30-day countdown on Facebook and Instagram. With #LakersTipOff, a new photograph showed a basketball hoop at iconic LA locations, each day closer to the Staples Center: (Salcido, 2015).

Big-game(s)

Cross-town rivalries such as UCLA vs. USC, the Los Angeles Dodgers vs. the Los Angeles Angels of Anaheim, and the Lakers vs. the Clippers can spark frenzies of local media coverage and ticket sales. The main publicity strategy is to make fans want to experience the excitement first hand of winning bragging rights for victory over their friends.

On the other hand, television executives hate a sports championship that is a matchup between teams in the same region. The network or cable channel paid huge sums to buy the rights; it's hard, however, to get the mass, nationwide audience (and therefore big advertisers) interested in a series that seems like local news.

Playoffs

Playoff games make extra money in ticket and beer sales for the strongest teams and in television licensing revenue for the league. To fans of losing teams, to most fantasy sports players whose leagues end before playoffs, and to less-than-avid fans of the playoff teams, the post-season seems to go on and on. Are we there yet?

The finals

In the US, the World Series of Major League Baseball, the National Basketball Association Finals, and the National Football League's Super Bowl are the big events. They determine the one winning team of each sporting season.

Figure 9.1: Phillies Citizen Bank Park, World Series Game 5, October 27, 2008.
Photo credit: 2008 Andi Stein.

As an event strategy, the Super Bowl has become the biggest of all, probably because it actually occurs on one specific pre-ordained day. Therefore, it is tailor-made for television, social media, and advertisers that want to reach a massive audience, as discussed in the SIDEBAR. In basketball and baseball, on the other hand, the finals are series of games played until one team wins four out of seven possible games. The win could come any day from Day Four through Day Seven. Especially after a grueling season and a long stretch of playoff games, it is a challenge for public relations to keep the excitement building, the fans coming, and the TV viewers watching.

The Biz Markets Itself—The Super Bowl

The Super Bowl is the most-watched television show in America year after year. This SIDEBAR looks at the championship game as a marketing machine for the NFL, the network broadcaster, the individual teams, and individual athletes. Because of the weight the event has taken on in popular culture, people who never attend or watch another football game all season—even vocal non-fans—will attend viewing parties, participate in betting pools, dance in their friends' TV room to the half-time show, and watch and argue passionately about the commercials.

The price of a 30-second Super Bowl ad was $5 million in 2016, and it goes up every year. Why? There's nowhere else that an advertiser can reach as large an audience all at once.

Because of the astronomical cost, entire PR initiatives are undertaken to publicize the ad purchase, the ad content (and what the network rejected as too risqué), the social media shares and comments about the ad, and the ad's place in the rankings of various online voting platforms. The public relations-generated visibility gives advertisers extra credibility, awareness, and cross-platform value. For a number of years, Doritos has generated enormous pre- and post-game media coverage for its online contest for aspiring filmmakers (and ad agency teams) to create the brand's Super Bowl ad or ads, with the chosen filmmaker receiving a big cash prize and national viewership.

Often the advertisers' PR team develops their own event strategies surrounding the Super Bowl. Budweiser, which makes the Super Bowl each year its major advertising initiative, also creates live, week-of events. For example, in 2014 in New York, the brand crated a "Bud Light Hotel" by taking over and completely rebranding the Norwegian Gateway cruise ship inside and out. On the nearby dock of the Intrepid, a WWII aircraft carrier, Bud erected a tent for four nightly rock concerts, all of which received media coverage, for example, in *The New York Times* (Barron, 2014).

In 2015, Pepsi, which has been the named sponsor for the half-time show for a number of years, also leveraged its spend in 40 promotional activities over a number of weeks. Beginning on Thanksgiving with a concert for veterans, the activities included a crop circle in the form of a Pepsi logo near the stadium (Steel, 2015b).

The NFL network contract always reserves airtime for the NFL to self-advertise or to promote its own CSR initiatives, such as its long-running campaign with the United Way, NFL Play 60, to promote exercise and combat childhood obesity. In 2015 in the wake of several domestic violence controversies, it used the high-profile timeslot right at the beginning of the half-time show when the viewing audience is always at its peak for a gripping PSA showing an abused woman pretending to be ordering a pizza, while actually calling 911 for help. This is an example of using the power of advertising, and the power of the most-watched TV show of the year for what one television critic called, "the single most important thing to air on television this year" (McNamara, 2015, p. A1).

Post-season/off-season

During the 2014–2015 off-season, the Angels and the Dodgers shared a joint billboard, which they announced via a press release, to honor American League MVP Mike Trout and National League MVP Clayton Kershaw. The billboard introduced a social media campaign with the hashtags #MVPTrout and #MVPKersh leading up to the annual exhibition Freeway Series scheduled between spring training and opening day ("Angels and Dodgers," 2015). The campaign had three objectives: to keep the fans engaged during the long off-season; to sell tickets to the matchup between long-time rivals; and to lock in ticket sales for regular games of each franchise. While the fans are at the ballpark for the Freeway Series, expectations for the new season are high, so they are likely to buy advance tickets.

The off-season is also when the public relations team can involve players in some strategies such as charitable and community initiatives that they don't have time for during the season, as discussed in the section on CSR below.

The draft/trades/free agent signings

Off-season, the draft, trades, and free agent signings are all big news for sports franchises and for fans. They are all about hope and renewal. PR works to frame each story in the most positive way and gets the player information and coaches' commentary to the media and fans as soon as possible.

The NFL Draft has become a major television and media event in itself, especially because of the popularity of fantasy football, whose players want to jump-start their knowledge about new players before their personal fantasy drafts. Before, during, and after the draft, it receives major coverage by sports talk radio, newspapers, and ESPN on the TV and radio and in its monthly magazine. The NFL also saturates Twitter and Facebook with news about the upcoming draft (Heurta, 2015). Such efforts reach fans, but also generate traditional media coverage. Many journalists use Twitter for finding and interacting with sources and readers, as well as for promoting links to their own stories.

The PR cycle in year-round sports

Some sports such as professional golf and tennis are virtually year around, but even these have their own PR cycles and typical stories. In such sports the PR cycle is determined by the importance of the various tournaments. To generate ticket sales, tournament PR highlights each commitment from a star athlete. Pitches and stories focus on individual players' fitness, rising players to watch, the likelihood of the strongest rivals meeting in the final, and the chances that this tournament's outcome will change player rankings. For tournaments that come right before a major or Grand Slam event, stories focus on the chance to see major stars up close, and how these matches presage those to come.

Key Publics

Key publics for sports public relations include media and fans, as discussed above; business partners including sponsors; community members, both potential ticket buyers and residents of the neighborhoods surrounding the arena; young athletes; and future international audiences.

Sponsorships and naming rights

Sponsorships in sports range from equipment, clothing, and shoe brands that sponsor individual athletes, such as Roxy's deal with Winter X Games star Torah Bright (Higgins, 2011) to naming rights for stadiums and arenas. The price of **naming rights** ranges up to a reported $10 million per year through the year 2032 for the Houston Texans NRG Stadium (ESPN Sports Business, 2013; Stadiums of Pro Football, 2015). Sponsors also buy naming rights to tournaments, races, and meets, sometimes sponsoring (and naming) a series of matches or an entire tour.

The large dollar investments in naming rights mean that the public relations practitioner representing various entities must be aware of the contractual terms for publicity. For example, for a named stadium, the contract probably requires the company's name in all public relations uses, rather than saying the "team's stadium" or "the stadium" and perhaps also including the named company in a separate boiler-plate summary in releases related to the stadium experience, the stadium facilities, or the stadium itself.

Neighborhood residents

Residents of the neighborhoods around a sports facility are of special concern to teams. As with film studios, theme parks, fair grounds, and clubs, arenas cause traffic congestion. Fans can cause late-night noise, littering, and public nuisances such as late-night carousing and property damage. Vandalism and fan misbehavior can lead to neighborhood protests, complaints to the city council, and attempts to change local laws to impose additional restrictions on parking, noise, and liquor sales in and around the sports arena.

A multi-pronged PR approach is needed to promote good community relations, and as always, it is best to act in advance of trouble. This means being aware of community sentiment by remembering that the term public relations implies reciprocity, and that the gold standard for PR is symmetrical two-way communication, as discussed in Chapter 1.

Efforts to understand the community can range from informal conversations, to tracking sentiment on social media, to doing formal surveys. For example, for many years the Charlotte NBA team had been the Charlotte Hornets, until the team relocated to New Orleans and eventually changed its name to the Pelicans. Meanwhile, many Charlotte residents resented their team abandoning them, even after they got a new team. When the Hornet name was again available, the team had Harris Interactive, which is now part of Nielsen, conduct a local poll, which revealed that 82 percent would support a change back to the name Hornets (Newman, 2014). With the decision made, the team did an intensive local awareness campaign, including having the Hornet mascot knock on the doors of homes with basketball hoops out front to give them a Hornet branded net, which would advertise the Hornet's colors to the entire neighborhood. The results of the rebranding campaign included 30 additional corporate sponsors and an increase of 77 percent in merchandise sales. Even more importantly, "sales of new season tickets were second in the N.B.A. only to the Cleveland Cavaliers, where LeBron James is making his return" (Newman, 2014). It's clear that this research-based PR initiative contributed to achieving the overall organizational and PR revenue goal for the newly re-dubbed Charlotte Hornets.

Good-neighbor strategies

There are a number of strategies for promoting good neighborly relations. For example, sports teams and other kinds of venues can actively remind fans and customers to be considerate of neighbors via jumbotron announcements and exit signage at gates and parking lots. Teams can create special behind-the-scenes experiences for neighbors, either for free, or in connection with special lower ticket prices or ticket packages for those within a certain radius of the park. The section below on CSR talks about the value of creating goodwill in advance of any difficulty or trouble.

Media Targets for Sports Stories

Where do you get your sports information? If you are a sports fan, you proba-bly realize that many sports stories, such as the latest scores and high-profile injuries, are available almost everywhere from online to social media feeds to print and broadcast outlets. The only question is, which can be trusted? So much sports information in the mass media is superficial, repetitive, or third-hand.

If you work in sports information for a league or team, you want fans to go directly to the official websites, where you control the information (and your client benefits from the advertising dollars). But fans also want to read in-depth analysis and informed opinions from outside the organization. Such articles may be found in publications not working to instantaneous deadlines. These include such consumer publications as *Sports Illustrated* and consumer and trade magazines and websites dedicated to sports niches. *Backpacker* or *Bicycle Retailer and Industry News* are just two of the more than 200 examples ("Trade Publications List," n.d.) of smaller trade publications looking for fresh angles to interest discerning readers of stories about their favorite sports.

Public relations practitioners in sports may choose outlets on this long list of trades to pitch for profiles of individual athletes, or stories about team initiatives, or product and sponsor partnerships. Those who work in other fields, such as film and television publicity, may find a publication hungry for a cover story about a Hollywood celebrity's love of its niche sport to add some pizzazz to its newsstand presence.

Using Social Media and Innovative Technology to Engage Fans

Sports teams have found a number of ways to harness the power of social media. Many fans rely on Twitter for frequent updates on games, for example. A number of athletes have huge fan bases on Facebook and Twitter. According to **Hootsuite**, a social media dashboard that allows pre-scheduling and cross-platform social postings, among the most followed athletes are Cristiano Ronaldo, the Real Madrid soccer star; Los Angeles Laker, Kobe Bryant; and Rafael Nadal, the Spanish tennis star (Kritsch, 2013). Their social media strength comes from authenticity, thanking fans for their support, sharing photos, sharing news headlines, being honest and emotional, and re-tweeting and responding directly to some fans' comments. Used the right way, which often requires the PR person to do some training of younger athletes, social media create the sense of a direct relationship with fans by showing a more rounded, unfiltered picture of the athletes in their daily lives.

The downsides of social media are the negative comments and **trolls**, anonymous users whose nasty, profane, and sometimes threatening comments have caused a few athletes to quit using social media, or at least to take a break.

Sports Celebrity Endorsements for Products

When an athlete endorses a product, or a brand develops a product line under the athlete's name, both the athlete and the brand gain a power boost from the cross-brand promotion. In Michael Jordan's NBA career, did shoes make the man, or did the man make the shoes? Nike Air Jordans are still avidly collected cultural icons, but the cross-brand partnership wasn't inevitable. Jordan revealed in an interview with Darren Rovell that his first choice would have been Adidas, which as a smaller European brand couldn't match the Nike offer ("Michael Jordan," 2009). The rest is history—and a lot of money for both the athlete and the brand. Both a brand and an athlete gain by the advertising, broadcast coverage, and other media exposure they give one another.

Risks of celebrity endorsements and naming rights

If your client is a consumer product company, of course, there are risks in making an athlete the face of the brand, including: sagging athletic performance; bad sportsmanship; offensive behavior off the field or on social media; and breaking the law. When dubious or serious issues arise, numerous athletes such as golfer Tiger Woods have lost sponsorships or have agreed not to wear the sponsor's clothing until a media storm dies down. The organization or brand needs to act quickly: "Organizations can retain the trust of donors by acting quickly when blindsided [according to USC marketing professor Jeetendr Sehdev], as UCLA did by returning an initial payment on a $3 million gift for kidney research from [former L.A. Clippers owner Donald] Sterling" (Gose, 2015). Sterling was publicly disgraced and forced to sell his ownership interest when a recording of him making racist remarks became public, and the NBA wanted him gone as an owner.

For the public relations person who works for a sports organization or represents an athlete, research and due diligence are essential for vetting a company, product, or non-profit organization to make sure that an intended partner company is legitimate; that a product to be endorsed meets federal regulations; that an investment opportunity is not a scam or Ponzi scheme; and that a charity is rated as using a high percentage of all donations to benefit its stated cause or beneficiaries directly, not just for staff pay and perquisites.

Corporate Social Responsibility (CSR) in the Sports World

To some the business of a business is business, i.e., to make money for its owners/stockholders. A broader view of a business, for example, a sports franchise, perceives it as part of the interwoven fabric of a complex community of stakeholders, including owners, fans, employees, families, neighbors, the community, and the wider world. The enthusiasm—even fanaticism—of sports fans makes it clear that teams hold a special place in the local community, one that often results in special privileges such as tax breaks and community bonds sold to raise money for a new stadium. **Corporate Social Responsibility (CSR)** describes the moral obligation that a company (or team) has to participate in the life of the community. The team should reciprocate on its privileges and uses of community resources as basic as paved streets by participating in improving life for everyone in the layers of human existence from the local to national to global.

CSR initiatives for sports teams can include philanthropy and charitable giving, sponsoring events, and making grants such as equipment grants to local schools. Besides money, teams can donate signed memorabilia and logo merchandise to charity auctions, as well as arrange for appearances of athletes at local fund-raising and athletic events. Sports organizations can recruit general employees and fans as volunteers for time-intensive activities such as beach cleanup. They can encourage athletes to coach free skills camps to inspire youngsters. Sharing facilities, such as practice ice rinks, may be especially needed and appreciated by local community teams. Ice time at 3 a.m. is better than no ice time at all to 15-year-old aspiring National Hockey League players, though perhaps not to the bleary-eyed parent who schleps them to practice.

Sometimes sports organizations are able to include partners in their CSR efforts. For example, the NFL partnered with Kellogg as a sponsor of the NFL Play 60 program to promote youth fitness. Athletes can appear in public service announcements for local and national causes, and generate attention and donations that a non-profit would otherwise be unable to achieve. Taken together, Corporate Social Responsibility (CSR) initiatives strengthen community relations and create positive images of the sport and the team as good corporate citizens.

The Entertainment PR Toolbox—Public Service Announcements (PSAs)

When the license of a local broadcast station is up for renewal, the owners have to prove that they have been working in the public interest, in exchange for their use of the public airwaves. One kind of evidence is a schedule of the **public service announcements (PSAs)** that they have run for free for non-profit organizations or for government entities. As mentioned in the section on CSR, sports PR specialists will often be involved with charities and fund-raising campaigns. Sports stars can make compelling appearances in PSAs, because so many people look up to them as heroes and role models.

One challenge with PSAs has been getting them shown. When queried by a non-profit organization, most local TV and radio stations may ask that they be sent a ready spot and their scheduler will decide if they use it and when. "When" is often in the middle of the night when few people are watching or listening.

Now public relations people have additional, inexpensive digital options. The PSA can be posted on Facebook or on YouTube with links to it from social media mentions on other platforms such as Twitter. These days a well-conceived PSA, particularly one with a popular celebrity such as a sports star, can become a viral sensation, and sometimes even generate news media coverage as well.

Research has shown that organizations that participate in CSR initiatives increase the engagement of employees (Glavas & Piderit, 2009) and other stakeholders. Such initiatives are especially important for teams that are not attracting positive media coverage in other areas, such as coming off a losing season (Stoldt, Dittmore, & Branvold, 2012, p. 16). In fact, a strong CSR program that generates frequent positive media coverage increases goodwill and acts as a buffer, a kind of insurance, when difficulties arise.

PR Problems or Crises in Sports

In recent years the NFL has faced an endless series of PR problems and crises. To name just a few: the Ray Rice domestic abuse scandal and criticism that the league penalty was just a slap on the wrist (Rhoden, 2014); the Tom Brady deflate-gate controversy and criticism that the penalty was too harsh and violated the collective bargaining agreement; and the ongoing controversy about the permanent damage to players caused by in-game concussions. The concussion issue led to several years of negative media coverage about brain-damaged older players and early deaths; the league's callousness and stonewalling; the inadequacy of various proposed settlement funds; and a couple of high-profile young players deciding to quit the game to save their bodies and brains from potential irreversible damage. Fans, however, keep watching and ratings keep going up: One commentator said, "the NFL—that is, its billionaire owners and their front man, commissioner Roger Goodell—seems to grasp the sport's vicelike hold on U.S. consumers," and therefore the league runs out the clock on legal deadlines and on the public's attention span (Lowry, 2015).

In the past, professional baseball faced controversy about steroid use. Cycling was rocked by revelations that Lance Armstrong's Tour de France titles were tainted by doping. College teams are regularly rocked by accusations against unsavory booster behavior and entitled players blithely accepting illegal gifts and privileges. In these cases, the team and its parent organization need to activate crisis plans, make an immediate press statement, as discussed in Chapter 6, and take appropriate action immediately.

Fantasy Sports: Skill or Gambling?

To participate in **fantasy sports**, a player pays an entry fee to possibly win money by achieving the best statistical results for a hypothetical team "drafted" or chosen for a period of time, traditionally an entire season. Winning is determined by the actual on-field performance of the specific athletes drafted. Private, season-long fantasy sport competitions among fans existed for decades with little controversy.

Fantasy sports has grown from a niche pastime played among small groups of friends to a major cultural phenomenon with an estimated 32 million players spending more than $15 billion yearly. Adding in the value of the fantasy football participants' time spent, *Forbes* writer Brian Goff estimates a $70 billion market for fantasy football alone (2013). ESPN, SiriusXM radio, and Yahoo are just a few of the major media organizations that earn revenue from the passionate fantasy sports fan base.

Since the goal is to win money, how do fantasy sports not come afoul of laws in most states against sports gambling? Athletes and coaches betting on sports or any evidence of game fixing causes a crisis for the team and league and may end an athlete's career. In fall of 2015, two companies that were running competing daily fantasy games flooded the airwaves with commercials to attract more business. They unfortunately also attracted legal scrutiny. A number of state attorneys general began investigating the companies and the structure of the daily games to decide if daily games are actually games of skill. If instead, they are games of chance, they may violate an individual state's laws regulating gambling. The outcomes will play out in the courts, probably over a number of years.

Conclusion

New sports leagues are launched to harness player and fan interest and to create the potential for large profits, so there are many entrepreneurial opportunities in sports public relations. One way for a sport to gain legitimacy is for the PR person to pitch and place an in-depth story in a well-respected outlet. Such a story appeared a few years ago about the new seriousness and competitiveness of women's roller derby published by *The New York Times Magazine* (Wachter, 2009). **E-sports**, meaning competitive video game tournaments with growing audiences online and in arenas, are covered in Chapter 11. Other sports developing new leagues at this writing include **drone racing**. The "pilot" wears goggles with a video feed from the camera of the drone, which races at more than 70 mph on a pre-determined closed obstacle course.

Some new sports leagues struggle despite strong publicity, while others grow from niche interests to being followed by an ever-widening fan base. Developing sports offer a chance for future sports PR specialists to make a mark for their sport and for themselves.

Key Terms—In bold in the text

Sample two-sentence definition and example

Collaborative Filtering: This is a data mining technique used by sports leagues and other sellers that aggregates information collected about a customer's demographics and likes with the previous purchases by people with similar data points to provide suggestions and attractive promotions for further purchases. For example, public relations practitioners might use data, crowd sourcing, or social media metrics on the sales of various athletes' jerseys to choose which athlete to pitch for a major feature story.

Corporate Social Responsibility (CSR)
Drone Racing
E-Sports
Fantasy Sports
Goal of a Sports PR Cycle
Hootsuite
Naming Rights
Public Service Announcement (PSA)
Sports Information
Sports Marketing

Sports PR Cycle
Sports Public Relations
Troll

Suggested reading and resources

Favorito, J. (2013). *Sports publicity: A practical approach*. New York, NY: Routledge.
Michael Jordan: Adidas's biggest mistake! (2009, March 10). [YouTube interview with Darren
    Rovell]. Retrieved from https://www.youtube.com/watch?v=nWi_VZlIhP0

· 1 0 ·

THE MUSIC PR CYCLE

Singles, the Album, Awards Shows, the Tour, and Festivals

Chapter Overview: When you finish this chapter, you should be able to answer the following questions:

- Why is media relations work important in the music industry?
- How can digital media be used to create awareness?
- How are artists using social media and two-way communication?
- What is the music PR cycle?
- Which music awards are important and why?
- How are tours publicized?
- How are music festivals publicized?
- SIDEBAR: The Entertainment PR Toolbox—Breaking the Rules
- SIDEBAR: The Biz Markets Itself—The Grammy Awards

Introduction

This chapter looks at public relations work that supports the music industry, which is valued at $15 billion for 2014, with $4.3 billion having been invested in A&R and marketing in 2013 (International Federation, n.d.). **A&R** stands for **Artists and Repertoire**, the department that oversees the scouting, signing, and development of artists. Before the digital upheavals that changed music business models, major record companies would sign artists with potential and invest heavily in their development over a period of years. Usually the deal was a seven-year contract that required three or more albums. The record company's goal was to make the public aware of the artists and their albums, hopefully leading to breakout popularity after two or three albums. Profits from the label's more established artists supported the incubation period for new artists.

In addition to producers and publicists, the A&R team included radio promoters to get songs airplay. The artist's manager scheduled gigs at small venues, while the record company would pair its newer artists as opening acts for its more established artists in larger venues.

Today, 46 percent of global music sales are through digital channels (International Federation, n.d.). Digital piracy is a multibillion-dollar problem. Listeners want music for free. They also want musical experiences that are personal and cannot be infinitely replicated. Artists want to be paid for their creativity and work. Therefore, live performances—gigs, concerts, tours, and festival appearances—are more important than ever to fans and artists.

The profit margins of record labels are squeezed, so they spend less on artist development. Also, some established artists have decided they don't need a record company's CD distribution apparatus, because they can sell their own music digitally.

As a result, record companies often restrict their signings to artists with a following developed locally, regionally, and even worldwide through a strong online presence. Bands have to hire their own PR representatives to gain the publicity that creates awareness and develops a base of fans who will purchase downloads and buy tickets.

This chapter discusses the various parts of the **music PR cycle**, which includes singles, albums, awards shows, and tours. It also covers the public relations for music festivals.

Music Industry Media Relations

The media have always been the gatekeepers between music and its potential audience. Exposure is the first step to creating awareness, which is a precursor to selling music and creating fans. Exposure can mean a gig at a local bar, a video on YouTube, or a song on a streaming service. These decisions are the purview of the artist's management. A music publicist, on the other hand, creates awareness through media relations by using the capabilities of traditional and digital media to generate unpaid media coverage.

Using traditional media means working through journalists to generate printed news stories about new albums or artist signings (hard news based on press releases); reviews of newly released music (to guide readers in their purchases); interviews and feature stories (soft news based on press kits and media pitches, to guide readers in their spending for music); calendar listings so the public knows where, when, and how much (to help readers make weekend entertainment decisions); and reviews of performances, which may encourage those who missed a performance to buy the record or to attend the next scheduled performance. All of these media placements, but especially reviews that expose readers to new music, are important in creating awareness for artists and their music.

One-sheet and press kit

A press kit provides journalists with the materials they need to write interesting stories for their readers, resulting in free media coverage for the artist. A press kit for an artist contains: an interesting bio; a professional photo(s); **clips**, which are copies of articles, reviews, and quotes from printed and respected online sources; and a CD complete with artwork and the publicist's contact information. These days, instead of a full press kit, a well-designed, nicely reproduced **one-sheet** with a photo, short bio, and short quotes may be sent with a CD (Hyatt, n.d.). The more information and details a publicist gives journalists and reviewers, however, the more likely they are to write at length about the artist.

When working with the media, advance time is crucial. Hyatt recommends two to three weeks at a minimum for an online campaign; four to six weeks lead time for a local campaign, which would include calendar listings; and three to four months lead time for a national campaign (Hyatt, n.d.). A journalist is not even going to listen to a CD or pitch that arrives too late to meet her deadline. As with all public relations efforts, advanced planning and a realistic timeline are essential for success.

Trade publications

The main industry trade journal of the music industry is *Billboard*. Its weekly charts for every category of music are the scorecards for the industry, just as the

Nielsen ratings are for television. In fact, Nielsen owns *Billboard*, which also has an app for the charts. The **Billboard charts** (*Billboard* Charts, n.d.) rank the week's music consumption through a formula that combines album and download sales with streaming plays. Because streaming services currently pay a royalty of less than ¾ of one cent ($.007) per stream, the formula requires "1500 song streams to equal the value of one album sale" (Sisario, 2015b). At this point, strong streaming, which can be more than 50 million, on services such as Apple Music and Spotify often determines the differences in rankings. This is an indication of how far the music industry has moved from CD sales only as a measure of when a record goes "platinum."

Another important publication is *Spin*. An outstanding placement would be a great photo (submitted by the publicist) and write up in "Best New Artists" (*Spin* Lists, n.d.).

Consumer publications

Consumer music publications include *Rolling Stone*, where a cover photo and interview can mark a high point in an artist's career, or *Vibe*. It would be a mistake, however, for artists or their publicists to think that these high-profile publications are the only media to approach. A company call Music Outfitters has an online, 16-page list of music publications and websites (Music Outfitters, n.d.). Many of them, such as *Saxophone Journal* may seem too specialized or niche ... unless the band you represent has a dynamite saxophonist, for example. In that case, if you investigated, you would see that the every-other-month publication includes reviews of new releases and a calendar of performances.

Third-party endorsement

For an emerging artist, it is crucial to accumulate clips to include with press kit material. The third-party endorsement implied by previous media coverage influences other journalists. If they see that an artist has been reviewed, profiled, or interviewed previously, even by a publication with less circulation, they are more likely to look at the submission positively themselves. The prior clips also help them pitch doing a story to their own editor.

Local coverage

As with independent films (Chapter 8), local angles are a good starting point. Consider among others: the free newspaper for the neighborhood where one of the band members grew up or now lives; a musician's college newspaper; or the local website for the neighborhood of a coffeehouse where the band will be playing. A well-written news release or bio and a CD to review may help the band find their first "professional" fan. One industry commentator said, "Don't worry about generating tons of press. Concentrate on appropriate media contacts within your geographic and budgeting limits. Then WORK those contacts with constant, but polite communications that will provide your contacts with useful information to do THEIR job" (Knab, 2011). Like avid music fans everywhere, music journalists love to discover and champion a new artist. To support the burgeoning career of artists they believe in, reviewers may write reviews that border on love notes. Such relationships are golden and should be carefully nurtured by the public relations representative and the artists themselves.

Digital Media—Effective and Mostly Free

Now that many of the music media have moved online, media relations work extends beyond the websites of the traditional music publications. The digital revolution has upended the entire music business and its public relations practices.

Email marketing and CRM

Email allows direct delivery to fans of information such as performance dates and album release dates. Digital communication allows automation of relationships with fans and fan clubs. Digital tools also greatly enhance PR's ability to get the word out and increase awareness among those who were already interested in an artist. Fan club communications such as email blasts and online newsletters came early in the business revolution toward digital **customer relationship management (CRM)**. To facilitate easy customer (and fan) interaction, many public relations practitioners now use tools such as those provided for a fee by ConstantContact.com and Salesforce.com. These and other cloud-based services automate much of the tedious work of the PR past, such as addressing, stuffing, and stamping envelopes to send expensive controlled materials to long mailing lists. The time can now be spent on strategizing and creating compelling content to be distributed digitally that will motivate fans to pre-order music and purchase new merchandise.

Fans especially value access to upgraded ticket packages. In recent years, Ticketmaster/Live Nation allocated 8 percent of tickets to the artist, which "has been prized by musicians as a way to interact directly with their audiences and make extra money through deals that include backstage meetings with the artists or special merchandise" (Sisario, 2015c). It was also a way for a band's management and PR strategist to have direct access to the online data and metrics. In 2015, Ticketmaster was trying to take back the allocation (Sisario, 2015c). Artists were complaining that the company was stripping them of the extra money, the data, and the direct relationship with fans.

The promotional power of music videos

MTV was created in 1981 as music television to play music videos and other music-related programming without much cost for creating TV content. The record companies footed the bill for creating the music videos, because TV play supported album sales. MTV's weekly Top 10 countdowns had previously been mostly the territory of local Top 40 radio. Now on TV, viewers could experience the excitement of a visually experimental video or a live performance. When MTV transitioned from music to other formats such as reality, online platforms filled the void.

Social networking sites (SNSs)

Musicians were early adapters who recognized the potential of online social media. The early social networking site Myspace was popular with musicians, because they could load their music into their profile. Fans old and new could listen and find one another. From the earliest days of YouTube, music videos were popular content. Pasting a video's URL into email, fans could share their obsessions. Videos could go viral. This included videos of major acts and total unknowns. For example, Justin Bieber was 12 when his family posted his first home video in early 2007. Bieber's YouTube videos led to his discovery by fans and music business insiders.

These days streaming services such as Pandora, Spotify, and Apple Music allow listeners to discover new artists. Companies have sprung up to help artists widen their reach and make money from their digital footprints. One service called TuneCore will handle worldwide digital distribution for a year for $9.99 per song or $29.99 per album. They also administer publishing rights, collect money owed globally, and run a paid service that guarantees Internet radio play on channels of known artists with similar styles (Sisario, 2012; TuneCore, n.d.).

Musicians and music are popular on all mainstream digital media, including Facebook, Instagram, and Twitter, and on specialty sites such as Soundcloud; the video site Vevo; and Bandcamp, which encourages fans to pay more than the artist-established minimum rate per song "to support the artists they love," and "they do pay more, a whopping 50% of the time" (Bandcamp, n.d.).

Today, a lot of talent scouting and A&R activities have moved online. Finding new music before others have discovered it is a major preoccupation of both music fans and record labels, especially the hundreds of new digital labels. Three with great websites are Fearless Records, Rise Records, and Hopeless Records, a Van Nuys, California, label whose mission includes raising money for charity. Now even small labels need sophisticated websites where visitors can play featured videos; find information about the label's roster of artists, their albums, scheduled performances, and tour dates; and buy music and merchandise. Posting new website content for musician clients needs to be part of most public relations plans, so that the official website where the artists reap the biggest percentage of sales rises to the top of search results (SEO).

Masters of Social Media

Music artists have become the masters of social media. Twittercounter keeps moment-by-moment metrics of Twitter accounts. As of January 31, 2016, three of the top five most-followed Twitter accounts belonged to music artists. Katy Perry (82 million), Justin Bieber (74 million), and Taylor Swift (70 million) top President Obama (just over 69 million) and YouTube at No. 5 (a mere 59 million followers). Artists Rihanna, Lady Gaga, and Justin Timberlake, plus Ellen DeGeneres, and Twitter itself round out the top 10, meaning that six of the top accounts belong to music artists (Twittercounter, 2016).

According to *The New York Times*, in August 2014, when Taylor Swift began publicizing her *1989* album, she ranked fifth, and had fewer than 43 million followers (Sisario, 2014b), versus today's almost 70 million. This increase is an indication of how active Swift is on Twitter, and how important Twitter, Instagram, and Facebook have become. In fact, Twitter was central to the success of Swift's awareness campaign for *1989*. A case study of the public relations for *1989* (Bolduc, 2014) showed that Swift received a lot of print coverage, including articles that talked about her masterful use of social media (Saad, 2014;

Sisario, 2014b). Making news about what one does to make news is a time-honored reason for innovating and breaking the rules, whether with a guerilla marketing stunt, a surprise appearance, or another unexpected PR tactic.

The Entertainment PR Toolbox—Breaking the Rules

As always in entertainment, the most publicity comes to those who are the most creative—those who make news. Despite the recurring cycles, entertainment publicity should never be cookie-cutter or slavishly follow a pattern, because predictability soon becomes boring.

Creative thinking and rethinking "the way it's always been done" can be extremely effective—as long as it's clear that you actually **know** how it's usually done, which you're learning from this book. Then you can explain why a particular client or project will benefit from **breaking the rules**.

As with all PR initiatives, there should be a clear strategy and rationale for all creative efforts, and clear desired outcomes. For example, in 2013, Beyoncé broke the "rules" of the cycle and dropped a surprise album of 14 songs, complete with 17 videos, all slickly filmed and edited in secret with no leaks or even hints. The surprise generated reams of print and broadcast coverage. Weird Al Yankovic followed with a low-budget version of the same strategy. With no budget from his record company to make his videos, he partnered with different websites to release a video a day for eight days in July 2014. Yankovic had also made videos for his previous album in 2011, thereby claiming to have originated the strategy of surprise videos (Sisario, 2014a). Other similar "surprise" albums-with-videos will eventually receive a ho-hum response. The tactic will become the "rule" that cries out to be broken or creatively reinvented.

Music fans love the unexpected. In music, and in other areas of the entertainment business, surprise is part of the entertainment.

Besides interacting directly with fans on social media, a big surprise of Swift's 1989 campaign was that she and her team set up multiple opportunities for her most avid fans to interact with her in person. One opportunity was for a number of them to participate secretly in a video for "Shake It Off." They can be seen rocking out toward the end of the video, which has been viewed on YouTube more than 1.3 billion times—that's billion with a "b"!

Another fan thank you came in the form of secret listening sessions with Swift for special fans in several cities. The fans were contacted via Twitter. The tactic resulted in #1989secretsessions trending on Twitter (Bolduc, 2014), as well as coverage in *The New York Times* (Sisario, 2014b) and the *Los Angeles Times* (Saad, 2014) mentioned above (Bolduc, 2014).

As part of the launch of his 2014 album X, Chris Brown used Twitter to publicize a scavenger hunt. In Los Angeles he tweeted out the name of each location where he would autograph X CDs, as he was heading that way on a Starline Tours open-topped, double-decker bus (Burchett, 2014).

Because of its ease of photo sharing, Instagram is also popular with music artists. To publicize X, Chris Brown posted an Instagram photo of himself with an X over his eye. Fans globally followed suit. Brown's Instagram account gained 100,000 followers in the week ahead of the album's release (Burchett, 2014).

These are just a few examples of creative social media tactics musical artists and their public relations teams have been using to create awareness for their music and to communicate with their fans. As each new digital platform debuts and gains traction, it is up to the PR practitioner to figure out: if it can be used to communicate with the client's fans or customers; which of its features are unique or most useful; where it fits in the overall PR plan; and if using it is worth the effort.

Any new digital platform may offer a unique public relations opportunity. By using it creatively, a PR campaign can *earn* attention in news stories in traditional media, where *buying* attention (advertising) would be too expensive. Remember that to gain media coverage, PR must *have* news or must *make* news.

The Music PR Cycle

The life cycle of an album begins with individual songs and follows a predictable process through the stages of development, production, post-production, release, and the post-release tour that make up the **music PR cycle**. As with other areas of entertainment, there are predictable media targets and PR placements for each stage.

Development

During development there are two targets for publicity: music business insiders and passionate fans. For an established band, industry insiders can be reached

through the music trades discussed above. Typical story angles include reveal-
ing the names of the song producers and collaborators the band will be working with, as well as responding to rumors that the band is already in the studio,
about which the publicist may want to be coy.

Fans are most easily reached through digital media such as the band's website, Facebook, mailing lists, Instagram, and Twitter. An entertaining way to
create engagement is **transmedia storytelling**, inventive tactics that require fans
to use several digital platforms to figure out what is happening. A classic example was the record label Fueled by Ramen's teaser campaign for the March 2008
release of Panic at the Disco's album *Pretty.Odd*: "On Dec. 11 the Web site for
the band ... turned completely white, with no explanation. Before long, curious
fans noticed that the source code for the page contained a clue that hinted at
the release" (Levine, 2008). Later puzzles led to song samples, a blog, and "clues
scattered around various Web sites" (Levine, 2008). The transmedia story, which
had to be deciphered to be understood, caused discussion and excitement among
fans. Fueled by Ramen opened preorders for the "Panic" album successfully in
January, and earned respectable sales after the March 2008 release, during the
recession, when fans did not necessarily buy music. The teaser campaign did its
job—creating advance awareness that an album was coming soon.

Production—In the studio and dropping a single

Since albums begin with songs, stories about the artist "in the studio" create
awareness. For larger labels and big artists, production stories may interest the
business press, because eventual sales may influence the quarterly stock results
of the parent media company.

Other important story angles for the business press concern general industry trends and conditions. For example, in July 2015, a number of music organizations representing labels, artists, unions, and retailers announced "New
Music Fridays," a move to have all songs and albums drop on Fridays worldwide ("New Music Fridays," 2015). Conforming the release date globally
allows songs to compete on an equal footing for rankings on the *Billboard*
charts and streaming services. The change was also obviously an attempt to
prevent piracy in markets where the music hadn't yet been released for sale.

It remains to be seen if artists and their publicity teams will give up the
option of surprise drops early in the week when the competition for media
attention would be less intense. Wouldn't it be better to encourage simultaneous worldwide release, but to allow each campaign to decide the best day

of the week? That is likely to happen anyway, since publicity and marketing folks have always maneuvered to find an uncluttered date. No one wants a lot of head-on competition for media coverage and fan attention.

Consumer publicity during production aims to stir up anticipation. For example, band members themselves, collaborating artists, or visiting celebrities may post Instagram photos of the band at work or hanging out in the studio.

Next comes the exclusive release of the first single, often on a nationally syndicated radio show such as Ryan Seacrest's morning drive-time show. Typically, the exclusive includes an artist interview and an announcement or teaser about when the album will drop.

Post-production

Consumer awareness and the intention to purchase both increase as the release date nears. Taylor Swift's team used several Instagram photos to give hints about her new album. Then on August 18, 2014, she announced the release date of the album, along with a live stream of the first single, "Shake It Off." The astoundingly popular Vevo video (see above) was released the same day (Wood, 2014), as was a digital download of the song. Here the artist's team built excitement. The video was a free sample, and the download was available for instant gratification. Both functioned as publicity and generators of media coverage for the coming album, just as movie trailers do during production and post-production.

Usually at least one more single is released to build the excitement as the release date of the album approaches. For spring or summer albums, an ideal song would be one that becomes the anthem of that particular summer. To support the excitement about "this summer's song," the industry tracks the stats, "with charts and playlists that pop up as early as May" (Sisario, 2015a). There have long been songs that tried to capture the essence of summer, such as "By the Beautiful Sea" way back in 1914 and "Under the Boardwalk" in 1964. According to *The New York Times*, more recent ones include, "Rihanna's 'Umbrella' (2007), Beyoncé's 'Crazy in Love' (2003), and Nelly's 'Hot in Herre' (2002)—all of which blared out of radios, car stereos and bars seemingly everywhere all summer long" (Sisario, 2015a).

As with any area of public relations, a seasonal hook can be effective in gaining publicity and in the popularity of the product itself. Although it is obvious that the time to release an album of Christmas songs is just ahead of the holiday season, music artists often need help from their publicists and their label to see less obvious marketing angles.

Release

When an album is released, media targets include all consumer media that cover music and popular culture. Television is still the most important way of reaching a mass audience. Publicists for established stars such as Taylor Swift can place them on many of the biggest talk shows, including *Good Morning America*, *The Today Show*, *The Ellen DeGeneres Show*, *Jimmy Kimmel Live*, *Late Night with Seth Meyers*, *The Tonight Show with Jimmy Fallon*, and others. Appearances on these shows can include an interview segment, a skit with the host, and/or a live performance of one or more songs. These shows deliver to a mass audience the news that a new album is available that "everyone" will be talking about. The live TV performance is a free sample that excites viewers and makes them feel in the know, even if they don't listen to Top 40 radio or read newspapers.

Another important television venue is *Saturday Night Live*. A well-known artist can be booked as the host, who delivers a monologue, participates in skits, and performs a number of songs. The host can poke fun at himself in the monologue, which makes him seem accessible and human. Acting in the skits shows an artist's versatility and may lead to other opportunities as a guest star in situation comedies, dramas, or even feature films. For a less well-known artist or a musical group, a great placement is as the featured musical guest on *SNL*.

Radio has been important all through the PR cycle as the singles were released. For the release of the album, the publicist should book call-ins with popular drive-time shows in all of the major markets. Shows syndicated nationwide such as "On Air with Ryan Seacrest" are especially important.

If the artist is well known, the publicist should pitch long-lead print media several months in advance so that stories, and if possible magazine covers, will break when the album is released. CDs and press kits or one-sheets should be sent in advance to consumer media that have music reviewers, even for new artists, as discussed above.

The industry trades will add to the excitement about the album release by announcing the week's chart ranking. The trades also write about artists that have debuted near the top of a chart and those that have debuted higher than for previous albums. The publicist can use data from chart rankings in press releases and pitches to specific journalists offering, for example, an exclusive interview.

As can be seen, a well-planned and well-coordinated public relations program for an album puts the artist in the news for several months through the stages of the PR cycle from development through production and post-production, with a crescendo around the release.

Post-release—Awards shows

The post-release part of the cycle will depend on the success so far of the publicity, the quality of the reviews, and the sales of the CD, digital downloads, and streaming. Garnering nominations for awards, winning awards, and performing on awards shows are the first element of the post-release phase of the PR cycle for a successful album with one or more hit singles. Although some of the awards are more prestigious than others, all of the shows focus the public's attention on music. Scattered as they are throughout the nine-month television season, televised music award shows keep making news and reminding the music-buying public to listen to and buy music, so they can hear their new favorite songs again and again.

The **MTV Video Music Awards (VMAs)** show presents the least serious of the music awards. It kicks off the music awards season with a bang at the end of August. MTV no longer relies on music videos for much of their programming, so instead of taking a serious approach to the topic, the network cultivates and encourages controversy.

The VMA show tries to make news and usually succeeds. Nominees and attendees strive to outdo each other in the outrageousness of their clothes (Lady Gaga's meat dress in 2010); performances (Miley Cyrus and Robin Thicke in 2013 and Miley Cyrus as host in 2015); artist interactions (Madonna kissing Britney Spears in 2003); and acceptance speeches (Kanye West interrupting Taylor Swift's acceptance speech to say that Beyoncé should have won in 2009). The awards themselves may not mean much, but the artists' behavior keeps pop culture mavens and entertainment news shows talking for weeks—even years—afterwards. If you doubt that statement, do a search combining the name of a controversial artist and VMA, and you will see how often past VMA appearances have been cited through the intervening years.

The **American Music Awards (AMAs)** was created for ABC television as a competitor to the much more prestigious Grammy Awards. The AMAs are positioned strategically late in November, ahead of the competing announcement of Grammy nominations in early December. Artists participate, because appearances as performers, presenters, and winners help promote music sales for the Christmas season. If grandma and grandpa don't know what to buy as presents, the names mentioned during the show may trigger their memory of artists the kids have been talking about. The **Country Music Association Awards (CMAs)** are also on ABC, also in November, and also function as Christmas gift suggestions.

Award shows later in winter and spring publicize spring and summer tours, as well as festival appearances. In February, CBS presents the most prestigious music awards show, the **Grammy Awards (Grammys)**, which are discussed in the SIDEBAR.

The Biz Markets Itself—The Grammy Awards

Figure 10.1: GRAMMY and the gramophone statuette and logos are registered trademarks of The Recording Academy® and are used under license.

Because winners are determined by votes of a broad range of musicians and other industry members of **The Recording Academy**, the Grammy Awards, which are broadcast on CBS in February, are the most prestigious music awards. Therefore, managements, publicists, and especially the major record labels with large marketing budgets all try to position their artists to garner nominations. Nominations are announced in December, just in time to give the albums a boost in sales as holiday presents. Randall Roberts, the music critic for the *Los Angeles Times*, said, "Tacitly, we should all be clapping for the skills of the marketers, radio men, booking agents and publicists who funnel the artists through screens, airwaves and stages and into the ears of the voters" (2014, p. D1). Because there are relatively few nominations compared to the sheer volume of new music each year, major record companies that put a lot of marketing dollars behind gaining nominations continue to garner the majority of the nominations for their artists. "You can't vote on what you haven't heard, and those who understand the game of campaigns know how many man-hours and strategy sessions are required to earn a Grammy nod" (Roberts, 2014, p. D1).

The Grammy Awards are the most important showcase of the year for music artists, because the show crosses genres and has the largest mass audience. Advance speculation focuses on who will perform, and most importantly, which artist will get the opening performance slot. Winning is nice, but performing is a better way to connect with the broad television audience. Viewers receive a free sample, not just of the music, but also of what it would be like to see the artist live on tour or at a music festival. Recent opening performances include, ACDC's "Highway to Hell" medley, 2015; Jay Z and Beyoncé's "Drunk in Love," 2014; and Taylor Swift's "We Are Never Ever Getting Back Together," 2013. To make news, to encourage viewers to watch live, rather than recording and time shifting, and to increase Twitter and social media engagement, many Grammy performances are first-time duets. Collaborations across musical generations, genres, and political points of view make news by being one-time-only events. Duets have included Eminem and Elton John in 2001, Beyoncé and Tina Turner in 2008, and Lady Gaga and Elton John in 2010.

The music publicist helps strategically position a client to perform on the Grammys and be seen by one of the largest television audiences of the year. Grammy performances and awards function as advance publicity for announcements throughout the spring of tours and festival appearances.

Since the live musical performances are the big draw, who hosts seems to affect the ratings less than for the Oscars and Emmys. LL Cool J, a rapper who won Grammys in the 1990s, has been a pretty consistent host in recent years. As a CBS star of the long-running series, *CSI: Los Angeles*, his genial, low-keyed hosting gig is a three-hour promotion for his prime-time series for a young mass audience that is not CBS's regular demographic.

As presenters and on the red carpet, artists parade their unique rock and hip-hop styles, many of which are candidates for "worst-dressed lists." The fashion risks provide fodder for shows such as *Fashion Police*. The glamor angle provides amplification of the Grammy event for days and weeks afterwards, as images are published in magazines such as *People* and *Us Weekly*. Some outfits become iconic and are talked about years later. These include Jennifer Lopez's deep-below-the-navel V-neck in 2000 and Bjork's swan dress in 2001, a copy of which Ellen DeGeneres donned for a joke while hosting the 2013 Emmy Awards.

The Grammys use a full array of social and online media to augment the broadcast, enhance second screen viewing, and stimulate conversation and engagement before, during, and after the show. The 56th Grammy Awards in 2014 resulted in a record number of social media interactions of 34 million (The Recording Academy Today, n.d., p. 10). The 2015 Grammy show was the TV season's most tweeted special event with "13.3 million people viewing 13.4 million tweets" (Jarvey, 2015), topping the Oscars and second only to the Super Bowl. Such engagement on social media amplifies the conversation and drives music and ticket sales.

Chapter 4 talks about the philanthropic efforts of The Recording Academy, which are supported by ticket sales, charity fundraising efforts, and global television licensing fees earned by the Grammy broadcast. For the music business, however, the main reason for the existence, continued participation of headliners, and the monumental effort to produce and publicize the Grammy Awards broadcast is to sell music to the mass audience.

Country music has another awards show in April that publicizes tours for artists in its genre, the **Academy of Country Music Awards (ACM Awards)**, also on CBS.

Post-release—Tours and music festivals

After gaining television visibility on award shows, the second element of the post-release phase of the music PR cycle is a tour of cities across the country and sometimes globally. Tour publicity is discussed in the next section.

Launching a Tour Nationally and Publicizing It Locally

Publicity for tours is challenging, because there are two components. First, the national campaign includes the announcement of the tour itself, the date tickets will go on sale for the entire tour, and media releases touting how fast the tickets are selling. Second, publicity during the tour concentrates on each local and regional media market in succession, so that awareness peaks in the days leading up to the local shows. Ariel Hyatt recommends that a national campaign start three to four months ahead (Hyatt, n.d.), which is why Grammy appearances and wins in February are so important for selling tickets to summer tours. Hyatt also recommends four to six weeks' advance work for the individual local tour stops (Hyatt, n.d.).

According to one British tour promoter, in order to be successful, a debut regional tour for a new band takes about six months' planning. Successful planning means recording an EP and a video beforehand, and doing a lot of pre-tour publicity, as discussed above. A strong social media presence, the debut of the EP and the video, and the tour itself, when handled well, can gain interest from bigger venues, festivals, and even record companies (Williamson, 2015). "Indie acts are expected to come with fans," (Frere-Jones, 2010, p. 93), according to The New Yorker, which quotes the head of the British record label XL as saying, "'I encourage people to make their music absolutely as great as possible and then build the start of an audience themselves, which should be possible if the music really is as good as it could be'" (Frere-Jones, 2010, p. 93).

For emerging artists with one or two albums and a national profile, touring usually means being signed as the opening act for a more major artist. In that case, the artistic goal (and the publicity goal) is to win over the fans of the headline act, so that they buy downloads and albums. Publicity should help gain awareness and add to the excitement and ticket sales. An excellent example was outlined in a student case study of Christina Perri's fall 2014 North American tour with the better-known artist, Demi Lavato. Concurrent with the announcement of opening for Lavato, Perri dropped a new single, performed it on *The Today Show,* and appeared on *The Late Show with Seth Meyers.* These are big gigs for an artist on her second album, and Perri and her publicity team used social media to full advantage to promote both the appearances and her future live performances opening for Lavato, a strategy which she continued into the tour (De Castro, 2014). In this case, Perri and her publicity team were working to prove their value as an opening act, not just by the quality of the performances, but also by their work helping to generate media coverage and audience excitement.

In spite of, or because of how readily available digital downloads are these days, fans crave the one-time-only immersive experience of a live performance. They want to be able to say, "I was there when. ..." To feed this desire for the unique experience, even on an extensive tour, in 2015 Taylor Swift, for example, had special guests from various generations and genres perform with her on different nights on her *1989* tour. Guests included Nelly, Steven Tyler, Nick Jonas, Avril Lavigne, Mick Jagger, Lorde, and Justin Timberlake, among many other surprise performers (*Billboard* Staff, 2015). Surprise guests are great for publicity and social media conversation afterwards, which drives excitement for the next show the next night or in the next city. Fans can say afterwards, "It was one-time only. You had to be there."

To sum up, the success of the album sells tickets to the tour. The tour in turn sells more albums and merchandise. In turn, the memorabilia remind fans of how great the live show was. This primes the pump for what the artist does next. This multi-year music PR cycle keeps the artist's career rolling.

Music Festivals

Music festivals are other opportunities for artists to perform live. Since there are hundreds of festivals, most with multiple stages, and some over multiple days and even multiple weekends, there are opportunities for artists to perform, almost no matter what stage they are in their careers.

Publicity to establish a new festival is beyond the scope of this book; however, after a festival's first year, the publicity becomes a full-year cycle. This year's festival promotes next year's festival by announcing the dates—and if possible—the name of at least one of this year's hit artists, who has already agreed to come back. The festival website can begin posting pictures of festivalgoers—a changing array that can last all year. Early-bird ticket sales should be announced while people still remember the fun they had. Announcements of new signings to the lineup should be spaced out for maximum coverage by the music trades and regional press. New batches of tickets and new entertainment packages and offers can also create ticket purchase intension. Successful festivals often sell out the first day sales open, despite the tickets costing hundreds of dollars for a weekend months away for which only a few performers have been announced.

As with any recurring event, each year's public relations plan forms the template for the next year's plans. Modifications can emphasize the most successful elements, as well as new avenues of outreach and surprises.

Conclusion

Digital technology may have changed music production and distribution. Randall Roberts, music critic for the *Los Angeles Times*, however, has said that music promotion still follows this pattern: "release track, push to radio, drop video and get streams, create social media buzz, market your nominees, snag nods, broadcast the hoopla on network television, hope for solid ratings and one or two breakouts, repeat" (2014, p. D10). Roberts oversimplifies. This chapter shows that the actual PR cycle starts earlier during development, and lasts longer from production and dropping the first single through post-production of the full album, release, post-release award shows, and post-release festival appearances and a tour.

This chapter also acknowledges that with endless downloads and streams of exactly identical digital replicas of music, fans value more than ever their own unique, personal encounters with the artists and their music, requiring creative PR tactics to satisfy avid fans. Music artists can become adept users of social media that allow them to interact with all their fans and, at times, with specific fans.

Public relations activities can help create unique experiences that fans value including such things as cross-generational parings like those for duets on the Grammys, as well as surprise shows in small or unusual venues, and backstage passes or other meet-the-artist opportunities. More than ever, fans want to experience artists up close in small venues and at music festivals that put together unique lineups. PR opportunities that feed fans' desire for close contact include surprise, one-time-only opportunities. Taylor Swift feeds her fans' desires, not just with her listening sessions, but also by inviting a variety of artists to join her for one-night-only on her tour, so that each tour date will be unique, prompting attendees to say, "You should have been there!"

For emerging artists, publicists need to build media relationships from the ground up, aiming for print and online listings, clips, and reviews in local and alternative media. It is especially important to cultivate social media interactions with local fans and ongoing relationships with all members of the media who mention, cover, or review an artist. This PR legwork early in an artist's career lays the foundation for a long, successful career made up of many PR cycles.

Key terms—In bold in the text

Sample two-sentence definition and example

Academy of Country Music Awards (ACMs): The Academy of Country Music Awards broadcast is on CBS strategically scheduled in April to enhance artists' public profiles for the spring and summer. For example, the public relations teams for country artists such as Blake Shelton can leverage a nomination, a win, and especially an on-air performance to create excitement for ticket sales for an upcoming summer tour.

American Music Awards (AMAs)
Artists and Repertoire (A&R)
***Billboard* Charts**
Breaking the Rules
Clips
Country Music Association Awards (CMAs)
Customer Relationship Management (CRM)
Grammy Awards (Grammys)
MTV Video Music Awards (VMAs)
Music PR Cycle
One-Sheet (music)
The Recording Academy
Transmedia Storytelling

Suggested reading and resources

Baskerville, D., & Baskerville, T. (2012). *Music business handbook and career guide* (10th ed.). Thousand Oaks, CA: Sage.

Music Outfitters. (n.d.). Music journals, music magazines, music newspapers and music periodicals. [16-page list of publications relevant to music PR.] Retrieved from http://www.musicoutfitters.com/musicpublications.htm

· 1 1 ·

THE VIDEO GAME PR CYCLE

Mobilizing Fan Communities

Chapter Overview: When you finish this chapter, you should be able to answer the following questions:

- What are the different types of games and platforms?
- What is the video game PR cycle?
- How are blockbuster games publicized?
- How are indie games publicized?
- How are casual games and apps publicized?
- How do indie game and app creators use crowd funding and early access funding?
- How are eSports publicized?
- SIDEBAR: The Entertainment PR Toolbox—Navigating GamerGate and Other Controversies

Introduction

In 2015, "The biggest weekend blockbuster of the year was a video game," *Call of Duty: Black Ops III*, which earned more than twice as much as the opening weekend box office of feature film, *Jurassic World* (Pierson, 2015). In

2013, *Grand Theft Auto* V reached $1 billion in sales in three days, faster than any previous video game or feature film. We know that because Take-Two Interactive sent out a press release (Take-Two Interactive, 2013). Just as with blockbuster films, sales figures for games can make news. Take-Two's media release was picked up immediately by mainstream and video news outlets. It was commented on extensively in video blogs and became part of the cultural conversation for months afterwards. National Public Radio's *Planet Money*, however, pointed out that despite the fast pace and jaw-dropping numbers of video revenues, Americans still spend more money in total on movies, because of the downstream value from streaming, on-demand viewing, and DVD rentals (Maxon, 2013). Even five years previously, the mainstream entertainment press would not have predicted the ascendancy of video games sales. Previously, video games were thought to be a niche product targeted almost exclusively to males in their teens and twenties who hung out alone or in small, odd cohorts in parents' basements.

Changing demographics

Sales figures demonstrate that the stereotype is outdated. The demographic of video game players has broadened. In 2014, according to the Entertainment Software Association (ESA), 155 million Americans played video and computer games; 42 percent of Americans played more than three hours a week (ESA, 2015, p. 2). Women represent 44 percent of players and there are more than twice as many women over 18 who play as men under 18 (ESA, 2015, p. 3). Despite these statistics, an outbreak of vicious misogyny and threats against prominent women gamers made mainstream news in 2013. Dubbed GamerGate, the uproar exposed a cultural divide. GamerGaters were males who launched forum and social media tirades of name-calling and death threats against female gamers. There was pushback from the broader audience of gamers who believe that informed criticism can co-exist with passion for games. (See the SIDEBAR later in this chapter.) The controversy is another indication that the audience of video gamers is diverse and can no longer be described as a niche.

Video games have grown into a flourishing entertainment industry, since the first computer games were created in academic and commercial computer laboratories in the 1950s and '60s. Though negatively reviewed by *The New York Times* (Catsoulis, 2014), the feature-length documentary, *Video Games: The Movie* (Braff & Snead, 2014), gives an overview of the industry's history. The film, however, mostly steers clear of industry controversies.

Game devices

Gaming now encompasses diverse demographics of people who enjoy a wide range of game genres on a number of different devices and in a variety of circumstances. These include individual play on smartphones, hand-held devices, computers, or consoles; in-person play with a few friends or family members; massively multiplayer online games (MMOG or MMO) and social games; and more recently, team and individual competitions, called **eSports**. Competitions may have spectators viewing on line, live in a sports arena, and/ or at closed-circuit showings in movie theaters. Public relations professionals need to understand the needs of this diverse audience and find effective ways to communicate with them.

Websites that sell downloadable games and offer periods of free play prior to purchase are moving the distribution model away from retail outlets such as GameStop and Best Buy. In 2014, digital format sales including "subscriptions, digital full games, digital add-on content, mobile apps and social network gaming" dominated physical sales for the first time, growing to 52 percent (ESA, 2015, p. 13). Developments in recent years that have affected PR include the increase of social and competitive game play and especially the emergence of eSports; **Twitch** (a subscription video game viewing site); and gamer YouTube channels that make video games into a spectator activity.

For marketing purposes, games fall into the general categories of blockbuster or franchise games, independent games, casual games, and apps. The life span of a video game, which determines the public relations cycles, can be divided into development, production, beta testing, the build up to launch, and the release. Except for beta testing, these stages are familiar from the chapters on television, movies, and music.

Game testing

When a game is nearing completion, it is **alpha tested** internally. Developers hire game testers to play the game and to discover intermittent bugs. When a game is later **beta tested**, the video producer gives access to the unreleased game to a number of actual gamers. If the players discover bugs during hundreds of hours of play, the producers can make further fixes before the release. The beta-testers also let the company know their feelings about how the game plays. For PR purposes, the beta-testing stage is similar to test-screenings for films or to a musician's unannounced performance of unreleased songs in a small venue. Creators want to understand audience responses in order to make necessary modifications.

As an added benefit, beta-testers' sense of exclusivity and insider knowledge can generate word-of-mouth excitement, because the gamers feel that they are part of the process of game creation. The passion of engaged communities both online and off is familiar from the *Star Trek* and *Star Wars* phenomena in television and film. Gamers seem to be even more enthusiastic about proselytizing for their favorite game and discovering and sharing secret information about an upcoming release.

This chapter will look at using the video game PR cycle to launch a title, and the ways that the energy and passion of gamers and fan communities can pre-sell sequels and spread the word about new games.

Gaming Platforms and Games

Game play, which started on computers, has broadened to include a variety of other game hardware. In addition to PCs, the perennial top competitors are the latest iterations of Sony's PlayStation, Microsoft's Xbox, and Nintendo's Wii and 3DS. As of early 2015, "the Wii U remains behind Xbox One and PS4 lifetime sales, despite the fact that the Wii U had a head start on its competitors" (Macy, 2015). Public relations planning for the game devices is beyond the scope of this book, because they are consumer electronic products that deliver entertainment, not entertainment in and of themselves. However, keep in mind that the **PR cycle for devices** breaks down into the stages of new-model development, production, pre-release, and release. Devices that will be released during the first half of the year tend to be announced at one of the many dedicated press events at the **Consumer Electronics Show (CES)**, a gigantic trade show, in Las Vegas in early January. Devices for late-year release are announced at various international and domestic events from mid-year onwards.

Each new game for a device supports the ongoing sales of that device, so each company wants to create or license exclusive games that become top sellers. For example, in late October 2015, Microsoft debuted *Halo V: Guardians*, resulting in news stories about gamers lined up to buy the game and about sales records. Reportedly costing more than $100 million to produce and exclusive to Xbox, *Halo V* was meant to drive holiday sales for Microsoft's Xbox One (Krantz, 2015).

Figure 11.1: Consumer Electronics Show, Las Vegas, January 6, 2016.
Photo credit: 2016 Carol Ames.

On the other hand, each device gives a game publisher access to less than a third of the market. Therefore, most major unaffiliated game publishers such as Activision Blizzard, Electronic Arts, and Take-Two Interactive now release their leading titles simultaneously for multiple devices including for Android and iOS smartphones and tablets.

A flood of games

Almost 900 new games are released in the United States each year, and many of them are released simultaneously for multiple devices (Futter, 2015). In this highly competitive environment, to boost device sales, the device makers try to develop their own exclusive games. In addition, they seek exclusive long-term or even short-term licensing windows from major publishers for highly anticipated franchise games.

Meanwhile, the game developers, game publishers, and device makers are all looking for the next breakout original game that can become a new franchise. As in the film industry, **franchise** refers to a product for which fans will be eagerly awaiting a sequel or subsequent chapter. To feed gamers' desire for the next and the new and, of course, to increase sales figures, some publishers now sell additional **downloadable content (DLC)**. Some even publish and sell certain games in chapters, just as in the 19th century Charles Dickens's novels often appeared as serialized weekly chapters in newspapers, before being published in book form.

Top-selling games tend to be the latest installment of franchise or blockbuster games from major gaming companies that can release on multiple devices. The five top selling games in the first half of 2015 and their publishers were *Mortal Kombat X* (Warner Bros.); *Grand Theft Auto V* (Take-Two Interactive Software); *Battlefield Hardline* (Electronic Arts); *Call of Duty: Advanced Warfare* (Activision); and *Minecraft* (Microsoft), according to the financial publication *Fortune* (Morris, 2015).

ESRB ratings

Just as in the film and television industries, controversies about the levels of sex and violence have forced the industry to self-regulate in order to head off political and legislative efforts to regulate what is acceptable. To self-regulate, the industry joined together to form an industry lobbying organization, the **Entertainment Software Association (ESA)**, which created the **Entertainment Software Ratings Board (ESRB)**.

All video games and apps must now have an **ESRB rating** before being sold in physical retail outlets or online in the United States. Rating letter and age designations range from eC for Early Childhood to M for Mature 17+ and A for Adult 18+. Each rating can include several content descriptions from a list of more than 30 categories. These range from Cartoon Violence and Comic Mischief to Crude Humor, Sexual Violence, and Use of Drugs, among others. A third ratings designation describes the interactive elements: Shares Info; Shares Location; Users Interact; Digital Purchases; and Unrestricted Internet (ESRB, "About ESRB Ratings," n.d.). All of the ratings are meant to aid parents and other purchasers in their decisions about which games are appropriate for which users.

Rules for advertisers

Advertising materials released prior to the game being rated should include this designation: RP Rating Pending. Advertisers must follow the Entertainment

Software Ratings Board's **Advertising Review Council (ARC)** "Principles and Guidelines for Responsible Advertising Practices." Among other tenets, the principles forbid misleading "the consumer as to the product's true character" and forbid targeting ads to groups such as teens for whom the game is not rated, for example if it is rated Adult 18+ (ESRB, "Principles," n.d.). These restrictions concern advertising, paid content, and promotional materials such as demos that are directed to general consumers—not to the trade media.

Rules for public relations

For public relations purposes, "Editorial content is not subject to review." This exempts most public relations generated coverage: "Editorial content is considered to include, but not be limited to, game reviews, news stories, TV series/specials, etc. that a company did not produce, underwrite, sponsor, or pay a third party to produce" (ESRB, "Principles," n.d.). This is an important exclusion, because free editorial media coverage is "uncontrolled PR," as discussed in Chapter 3. The editors and journalists control the context and content, not the public relations person who sent out the press release or pitched the story.

The Video Game PR Cycle

The first step for a public relations practitioner is always to create a plan, as discussed in Chapter 8. The next is to have it approved by the company or present it to the prospective client in order to be hired to do the job. Video game publicity is no exception.

As mentioned above, the **video game PR cycle** covers the stages of development, production, beta testing, the buildup to launch, and the release. Video games are released throughout the calendar year (Futter, 2015). As with all product releases, the PR cycle should be adjusted to peak at the time of release. The biggest buying period for video games is the holiday season. Blockbuster and franchise games with recognizable titles that can cut through the holiday advertising clutter are often scheduled for release from August through early November.

Public relations should be planned as early as possible. Just as with films and television, the audience for information during the development process is mostly within the trade media. Because of the avidness of game fans of pre-existing franchise games, however, there is always a core community of users looking for "secrets" and insider information about upcoming versions.

Early, adept PR involvement can provide a positive frame and guide online commentary to feed fans' anticipation.

To tantalize fans, the PR team should begin to assemble assets to be parceled out over time to the media to tease interest and excitement. Assets might include high-quality photographs of character and background sketches, as well as video interviews with artists and developers. The duration of the actual campaign, however, is usually about a year for a blockbuster title, but six months or less for a **casual game**. A casual game targets less committed players, typically is easier to learn to play than hardcore games, and is often played on smartphones or tablets rather than PCs or gaming consoles. First-look footage debuted at industry events, teaser clips, and teaser trailers keep excitement high. As with blockbuster films, the danger is too much information and sample content getting out too soon, resulting in unrealistic expectations and disappointment or over-familiarity when the game is finally released.

Background and situation analysis

The introductory section of the PR plan on client background includes the company's history, especially its record of game releases; its typical game genres; ratings; reviews; and online presence, such as its website, forums, and game communities. The background and reputations of the lead producers and artists are also important. Another important part of the background is to list and evaluate major media coverage the company, the game's developers, and the company's games have received in the recent past. Background requires in-depth research and helps guide every element of the plan from the goal to choices of which publications and journalists to target for the media tactics.

Describing the current situation helps everyone in the company and on the PR team to understand what is going on in the wider world of entertainment, what the upcoming video game is, and how it can be sold. In an article on game PR in *Gamasutra*, Tammy Schachter of Electronic Arts Games was quoted as saying, "Long before the game is even playable, we work together to find the language that properly communicates the features of the game and build a timeline that maps to their development schedule'" (Thomsen, 2009). The development status—where the game is in the development and production process, and where it falls versus other company games and competitors' games—helps focus the timeline of the public relations plan.

Inexperienced and lazy publicists try to gloss over or fake these two important sections and skip straight to the SWOT analysis. Steve Cross of the marketing company CO2 is quoted as saying, "'You have to be aware of what is going on at the same time, not just in gaming, look at the big picture and make sure that your campaign is true to the product'" (Batchelor, 2013).

The Entertainment PR Toolbox—Navigating GamerGate and Other Controversies

In late 2015, **SXSW Interactive,** the portion of the South by Southwest Music Festival focused on games, announced two gaming panels for its spring 2016 conference related to online threats of violence directed mainly at female gamers. A week later, the trendy, supposedly progressive festival issued a press statement saying it had canceled the panels … due to threats of violence. The cancellation triggered protests that the festival had allowed itself to be bullied (Martens, 2015a; Wingfield, 2015a). This was just another incident in a long-running controversy dating back to at least 2013, when the flip side of "community" in the game world has boiled over into the "real world."

Analyzed from a PR standpoint, the announcement and cancellation were a PR crisis that damaged the reputation of SXSW. The crisis could have been avoided, if the festival had prepared a more thorough PR plan.

If SXSW's 2016 conference actually had a PR plan, the background and situation analysis sections were faulty. The event producers should have: known that the controversy was super-heated; anticipated the vitriolic response if they decided to program panels related to the controversy; and stuck by their programming decision, rather than caving to threats. Or alternatively, they should have decided from the start not to program the panels.

How could they have known? By reading the newspapers. By talking to people in the industry. In other words: by research and more research. One journalist had previously described the ongoing, roiling controversy as so ugly that the FBI had gotten involved because of extreme social media posts "threatening rape and crippling injury, [which] have been so violent that some of the intended targets have gone into hiding" (Martens, 2014, pp. D1, D7). An industry petition signed by more than 2,400 members of the industry appealed for a sense of decency. The online petition by game developer Andreas Zecher advocated that, "everyone, no matter what gender, sexual orientation, ethnicity, religion or disability, has the right to play games, criticize games and make games without getting harassed or threatened. It is the diversity of our community that allows games to flourish." The petition also asked those who saw threats online to report them to the sites where they appeared (Zecher, 2014). Unfortunately, even that massive online show of industry support for tolerance of diverse points of view did not stop the harassment.

Posting under #Gamergate, opponents of the petition spoke out. They attacked the women and others who claim to feel threatened and blamed them for trying to censor and suppress the **GamerGate** proponents' right to freedom of speech. In an opinion piece, the video game critic for *The New York Times* despaired at the anti-intellectualism of the GamerGaters who wanted to return to the days before gaming included a few indie games about topics such as depression, transgender issues, and, oh yes, bullying (Suellentrop, 2014).

In an OpEd piece in *The New York Times* that same week, Anita Sarkeesian had written about having canceled a speaking engagement at Utah State University, because of threats of "'the deadliest school shooting in American history' if I was allowed to speak. When the Utah campus police said they could not search attendees for firearms, citing the state's concealed carry laws, I felt forced to cancel" (Sarkeesian, 2014). According to the opposing side (the GamerGaters), these threats shouldn't frighten their targets, because trash talk and threats are authentic ingredients of gaming culture!

In the wake of the SXSW cancellation, "a London-based, right-wing social media celebrity who has become a darling among hyper-masculine gamers" (Ng, 2015, p. E1), Milo Yiannopoulous, declared that SXSW's scheduling of the panel discussions was "a thinly veiled attempt to censor pro-gamergaters like himself" (Ng, 2015, p. E6), who support anything-goes gaming commentary. To this contingent, women who want to be gamers should just suck it up. They should not try to change macho-posturing adolescent gaming culture by acting as if they are really in danger.

The public relations plan for SXSW should have anticipated and planned for the passion of the responses from both sides. Then the controversy, which would have been expected, could have been used to support the intellectual credibility of the SXSW Interactive Festival. Instead, the controversy led to the embarrassing cancellation that damaged the festival's progressive reputation.

A couple of days after the cancellation, SXSW reversed course again. It announced a full day's program called "The Online Harassment Summit."

It also issued a press statement, an apology: "By canceling two sessions we sent an unintended message that SXSW not only tolerates online harassment but condones it, and for that we are truly sorry" (Martens, 2015b). The damage to their reputation was already done, however. With a solid PR plan in place, they would not have been taken by surprise, either by the response to scheduling the panels, or by the response to canceling them. With a solid PR plan in place, they would not send "unintended" messages.

The client background and current situation provide the historical and current competitive contexts. This allows the experienced PR practitioner to understand and go beyond what's been done in the past and to make the most of what's happening right now, while avoiding pitfalls.

SWOT analysis

As discussed in Chapter 7, the **SWOT** analysis is divided into strengths, weaknesses, opportunities, and threats. The focus in the SWOT is on the specifics of the particular game that is to be publicized. Each game is unique.

Strengths are internal to the client, in this case the game itself. Strengths might include: being part of a franchise with an excellent sales record for previous installments; the reputation of the lead developers; the artists; falling into a popular genre; the demographics of that genre; the potential to broaden the reach of the game; the storyline; the characters; and the music, among many other elements, including the game's special elements and in-game challenges. Buying a new game is not just about what genre the player typically likes, but also about what skills the gamer already has or would like to acquire (Raczkowski, 2012, pp. 66–67). Entertainment value is important, but so is the gratification of actually being successful.

Weaknesses are also internal. Being a new or unknown game is a weakness. Being in a genre that hasn't had a recent best-selling title is also a challenge, as is any extreme deviation from the pattern of previous games, if it is part of a franchise. Unresolved bugs and the failure to include promised or expected game elements because of deadline pressure or budget limitations are also weaknesses. Any change of lead personnel, such as a different developer or artist, is a weakness from a PR standpoint, because fans are likely to perceive the change as negative. Weaknesses also include deficiencies in any of the categories listed above under strengths.

Opportunities are circumstances external to the client that offer possibilities for positive exposure, for example the Consumer Electronics Show (CES) for hardware or the **Electronic Entertainment Expo (E3)** for video game announcements and sneak peaks in mid-June in Los Angeles. The high consumer demand of the holiday season is an opportunity, especially for blockbuster titles debuting from August onward.

For any game that is well reviewed and well received by fans, various awards are opportunities for news coverage. The D.I.C.E. Awards, for example, are nominated and voted on by the 30 thousand industry peer members of the Academy of Interactive Arts & Sciences. Although these awards aren't yet as high profile as the Oscars or the Emmys, they receive extensive coverage in the gaming media as part of a yearly conference called the D.I.C.E. Summit. The term D.I.C.E. stands for "Design, Innovate, Communicate, Entertain," according to the Academy.

Another award opportunity is the Game Awards. These are a streaming-only event with nominees and winners chosen by a group of game journalists and publications. Geared for an audience that doesn't watch much television, the show includes "ways for viewers to click on ads and download games in real time" (Wingfield, 2015b). According to *The New York Times*, the early December event "reflects the hunger among game publishers for the critical recognition that can spark sales of their products during the all-important shopping season" (Wingfield, 2015b).

Threats are negative elements outside of the client. Like earthquakes, they exist in the environment or the industry and cannot be controlled by the client or the PR team; they must, however, be anticipated and response to them must be managed intelligently. A competitor's title is a threat, especially if it is in the same genre or if it is launching at around the same time. Even the most avid gamers have limitations of money and game-playing time. Negative reviews are threats, as are negative hashtags, viral memes, or nasty online comments.

Statement of the main communications opportunity or problem

Different people can look at the same information and interpret it differently. The statement of the main communications opportunity or problem is your chance to get everyone to agree on a central strategy for the proposed campaign. Tammy Schachter of Electronic Arts was quoted as saying, "'We're always looking for the 'big idea' that is going to help the game break through the noise and get gamers and press to take notice'" (Thomsen, 2009). For *Need for Speed: Shift*, that meant a focus on how true to life the experience of the game is. Since the strategy was "It's real," the primary media relations tactic was a press event to give journalists rides at a real racetrack in real race cars driven by the game developers, who are really race drivers (Thomsen, 2009). In this case, the statement of the main communications opportunity for this Electronic Arts game was to convey that the game delivers the thrills and excitement of driving real racecars, or as the website states: "A true driver's experience" that includes: "Roaring engines, squealing tires, crunching collisions. And above all … speed, speed, and more speed! Nothing was overlooked to deliver the most realistic racing experience possible" (Need for Speed, 2015). Both the PR plan and the game delivered on that promise.

Goal statement

The goal statement should be in terms that everyone in the company can understand. As with most entertainment business public relations plans, the overall goal should not be put in squishy terms like awareness, as measured by before and after surveys, or even increased engagement, which social media analytics put into figures and graphs. Many people in the organization won't understand the terms and will wonder why they are wasting money and time, when what's important is getting the game out. It's hard to prove a direct correlation between those concepts and the success of a game. Awareness and online chatter, for example, can be orgies of ridicule and hate. Therefore, for video games, as with other entertainment clients, the goal should be specified in terms of money (total sales/revenue) or something that easily equates to money (numbers of units sold or digital downloads). Instead of being the goal, awareness and social media engagement should be used in objective statements related to specific target segments.

Target audience and buyer personas

A lot of the information for these preliminary sections of the plan should be available internally. The developers and artists have been involved with the game from concept on. If they don't know, the game may already be in trouble. Game consultant Scott Steinberg said, "Not only do most game makers say that they don't know how to drive public awareness to their titles. Many can't even identify their core audience, beginning [*sic*] the question, 'If you don't know who you're making a product for, why build it in the first place'" (Steinberg, 2011). If internal research shows confusion about the target audience, external research such as focus groups will help define the audience.

For doing research, Katie Rawlings, head of marketing for Gem Creative, is quoted as saying, "'Anyone can research the target market through surveys, polls, and focus groups via online media'" (Batchelor, 2013, Rule 4 sec.). Research results should be embodied in the buyer personas and guide the PR plan's strategies and tactics. Unless you know who your target customers are and what media they typically consume, there's no way to know how to reach potential buyers and make them aware that your game is coming out soon.

Applying your audience research, first choose one category, depending on the game: either hardcore gamers or casual gamers. Gender and age: Research to discover the proportion of males and females and their age distribution in your target category. Next, specify the rating category. Media targets must be different if the game is meant for teens versus adults, for example. Next look at the genre and the sales history of the genre, looking at the statistics for males versus females and for younger versus older. This process should produce a core target audience segment and one or two secondary segments, ranking from most important to least important.

Creating a **buyer persona** or imaginary bio that represents each target segment achieves two things. First, it personalizes the category, so that everyone working on the project knows that "Joe" is a 21-year-old hardcore gamer, who spends 20 hours a week playing role-playing games. The most crucial details in the buyer persona or imaginary bio are the result of research into the target audience's media use. Their media usage determines the traditional and digital media channels to focus the plan's tactics on, so that the client's messages reach and persuade them. For example, perhaps your research shows that the target segment learns about new games from specific print and online magazines, such as *Game Informer* and *GamePro*, two of the top game publications (Cision, 2011). Therefore, the PR plan's tactics should include specific, exclusive pitches to these publications. If Joe does not use Pinterest, for example, there is no point posting there, unless it is a favorite of one of the secondary target buyer personas.

Objectives and tactics

Specify objectives for each target segment, as outlined in Chapter 5. An objective for the "Joe" segment might read: To achieve awareness of the release date among 75 percent of young male hardcore gamers by two weeks before the release. To achieve this objective, the plan might include specific media pitches, as well as posting developer diaries and blogs, among many other options.

Work the plan

Practitioners need to be flexible enough to take advantage of current events and unanticipated opportunities. It is nevertheless important to work from the plan. If the opening sections of the plan are done seriously and in sufficient depth, it will be fairly easy to decide which tactics to include and which to exclude. An activity may sound "cool," but don't go off on a tangent that doesn't help achieve a specified objective and contribute to the goal.

Publicizing Blockbuster Games

Blockbuster games are sometimes called **AAA titles**. They are usually follow-up installments of game franchises, although they may be based on pre-sold concepts from other arenas such as the Star Wars films or the Lego toys. Campaign timelines for AAA titles are typically a year or longer, with the title promoted from announcement through release. Often the company announces the game at E3 at the Los Angeles Convention Center in mid-June and begins accepting pre-orders six months in advance of release.

As with blockbuster films, blockbuster games have an already established audience eagerly awaiting the release. For example, *Call of Duty: Black Ops III* "set a record for 'engagement.' Fans spent more than 75 million hours playing the game online the first three days" (Pierson, 2015).

Continuous two-way communication with fans/community refines the understanding of the target market. With pre-existing fans avid for information and tidbits, creative puzzles and transmedia storytelling can keep fans in touch with the world of the game between releases. For example, ahead of the announcement of *Grand Theft Auto V*, Take-Two updated a website connected with a Scientology-like religious cult within the franchise and launched a related Twitter account (Bennett, 2012).

Content marketing

Content marketing involves the PR/marketing/production team creating original, game-related content and distributing it either on the company website or elsewhere on the Internet. For example, ahead of *Halo 4*, Microsoft produced, "the popular Forward Until Dawn webseries, which racked up 5m views per episode. That show exists largely to promote the new Halo, and yet few consumers would identify it as an ad" (Batchelor, 2013, Rule 3 sec.). Microsoft debuted one 15-minute episode per week during the five weeks leading up to the release. The series reminded Halo fans of what they love about the long-running game series; it also introduced the complex Halo world to those who hadn't played the first three games. Interviews within the episodes were versions of developer diaries and blogs that often appear on gamer-targeted websites. Viewers didn't consider the Halo webseries an ad, because it was entertaining and informative in its own right.

Effective content marketing gives people information they want when they want it, not information a company forces on them by interrupting what they are doing, as most traditional advertising does. Any gamer who reads or hears about a game will probably first check out the game's website. A robust website that is updated frequently with interesting information, visuals, and video clips is the most important content marketing initiative in an effective public relations plan. On the website, information is always available when people want it. When the game is nearing release, the website can include a pre-order button to turn awareness and purchase intention into advanced sales. For blockbusters, a large pre-order number is news that can be announced via a press release to stimulate even more pre-sales.

Post-release

Once a blockbuster is released, publicity can concentrate on sales figures, the numbers of online players, and the excitement of the fans. Post-release, a blockbuster game has a chance to grab gaming media coverage all over again by offering downloadable content. The new wave of publicity not only sells the DLC, but also the game itself, because it reminds those who haven't yet bought the game that they are missing out. These are the same gamers who may already be feeling left out when their online and offline friends talk about the game.

Another opportunity to remind the market about the game is by offering a high-priced boxed set that includes extras, commentary, and additional elements, much like the director's cut of a beloved film. The new game elements generate lots of discussion among a game's most devoted fans.

For a game franchise, the long-range publicity and release strategy should be to keep fans involved and passionate, so they will continue to want more of the game for years into the future. This keeps long-running franchises alive and creates fan pressure for a sequel to a new game that has become a hit.

Publicizing Independent Games

Like an independent movie, an **independent video game** or **indie game** is usually developed and created without a distribution deal or the financial backing of a major game publisher or console maker. Made with severe budget constraints, indie games rely on public relations to generate awareness and word-of-mouth excitement. Most advertising is too expensive. Because resources are limited, the PR timeline is closer to release than with blockbusters, with campaigns of six months or less.

The past credits and reputations of the developers are key to getting news items in gaming magazines and websites. Digital media will often post short developer interviews, diaries, and blogs, even about games from relatively unknown developers. Most of all, gamers and their preferred media outlets want visuals and samples: What does the game look like? What is the world of the game? How does the game play? In other words, why is the game interesting?

The **Game Developers Conference (GDC)** in San Francisco each spring and internationally at other times of the year is a place developers can go to learn, network, and promote their games. Part of the GDC is the Independent Games Festival, which is meant to be the Sundance of the game world. The conference provides a unique opportunity for a game to gain exposure to media and possible fans, because it offers a pavilion where the award finalists can actually be played. Games receiving various awards have gone on to win other accolades, to become best sellers, and to become favorites in their genres (Independent Games Festival, 2015).

If a developer is doing a subsequent game in the same genre, studio branding can be effective. Consumers already know what to expect from certain companies, lessening the need for intensive marketing. Position the game as coming "From the studio that brought you. …" Rami Ismail of the developer Vlambeer is quoted as saying, "'Whatever you do, figure out what you are,'" and communicate it, because, as Graft continued, "Marketing in many ways is an extension of your game" (2014). The push with an indie game, casual game, or app should be to get it in people's hands and let them tell others about it.

Reviews

Reviews are free editorial coverage. Reviews are essential to gain momentum for an independent game. This presupposes that the game is good. Reviews are uncontrolled PR. Neither the publicist nor the developer should attempt to pressure or influence a reviewer.

It is a major challenge for a small development company—or any game company—to have a finished, debugged game available early enough for PR to make it available to reviewers in time for reviews to appear right at the release date. A playable version is also crucial for pitching feature stories to gamer magazines and websites. Unlike with a franchise sequel, reporters can't know in advance what a new indie game is going to be like.

Publicizing Casual Games and Apps

Mobile gaming revenues were estimated to exceed revenue from console games for the first time in 2015. With Nintendo's latest console struggling versus PlayStation and Xbox, Nintendo announced its immanent entry into the market for smartphone games (Chang & Pierson, 2015). Because of Nintendo's size and industry prestige, its Tokyo announcement grabbed front-page headlines in Los Angeles and elsewhere worldwide.

Most publicists of a casual game, however, start with an unknown title and a small-to-nonexistent marketing budget. For a casual game or mobile app, the main strategy should be to convey how much fun it is. Again, this means creating awareness, getting reviews, and getting it into the hands of people who will talk about it on social media and show it off to their friends in person. Adam Saltsman, developer of *Hundreds*, is quoted as saying that the strategy "'is to make it easy for people to tell other people how cool your thing is'" (Graft, 2014). Players then become evangelists for your game, doing the selling for you. A common profit metric for downloadable games is **cost per install (CPI)**, with the majority of the costs attributable to buying online ads. Public relations resulting in unpaid mentions helps control CPI.

Retargeting

On the paid advertising side, tracking technology called **retargeting** allows for ads that are reminders. A marketer for a company that uses data for retargeting said, "you should be trying to drive increased engagement with your game … this could mean reminding users who have downloaded your app to come play, or encouraging users who have registered to make their first in-app purchase" (Kiladis, 2014, Dec. 17). Retargeted ads use cookies left on a computer identifying a product a user shopped for online, but did not purchase. The ads may show up in search results for weeks afterwards, even long after the consumer bought an alternative product, such as a competing game, through a different seller.

Reviews again

Reviews of apps—free editorial mentions—again are important for creating awareness. For iPhone apps, Apple gives the developer 50 individual promotional codes for free downloads of each version (iPhone Development 101, 2015). For the most important or most targeted reviewers, one marketer suggests providing a code in your original pitch email, even if a few codes may be wasted (Bernard, 2009). Reviewers who have to email back to request a code may not bother. Another Bernard suggestion is to include a great short video of less than two minutes that gives the reviewer a quick look at what the app does (2009). As with all media pitches, providing everything the journalist will need in the first pitch email makes it as easy as possible for the journalist to cover your client.

Kickstarter, Early Access, and Other Crowdsourcing Platforms

Digital and social media facilitate two-way conversations with audiences. Public relations practitioners use the capability to good advantage by having tactics that utilize the posting, networking, and forwarding power of Facebook, Twitter, Instagram, and other social media sites.

Kickstarter

Recently the crowd-funding site **Kickstarter** has become a node for publicity for independent games and smaller projects. Kickstarter's rules require that each project set a funding goal and reach that goal by a specified date in order to receive the money pledged, and not have it released back to the donors. Projects also must offer premiums for donors at various funding levels and give periodic Kickstarter updates to assure donors that their money is being used for its intended purpose.

To reach a Kickstarter goal, public relations should have a robust website in place for the game with additional content beyond what can be found in the Kickstarter pitch, such as full professional bios of the lead developers (content marketing). There should also be a strong social media presence, either already established by PR or ready to trigger through a service such as Thunderclap, discussed below. People have to be told about your Kickstarter campaign in order to participate by donating and/or telling their friends, so that the game project meets or exceeds its goal by the deadline.

Orchestrating a Kickstarter campaign by leveraging social media outreach may be one element of a publicity plan for an indie game or casual game. Reaching, and especially far surpassing, a Kickstarter goal is news for a press release, because it means that the developers can continue towards completion. In early 2012, inXile Entertainment raised almost $3 million, far exceeding its goal of $900,000, to make *Wasteland 2*, a new installment of a beloved 1988 game (Wasteland 2, 2012). The developers' pitch included promising funders they would have input on how the game was constructed. Access to the game at various stages of development was a Kickstarter premium to funders. Another was the chance to place a personal artifact in the game for donors of $2,500 or more, among many other premiums for various levels of support. As a known title with renowned developers, the *Wasteland 2* pitch succeeded on Kickstarter.

Unfortunately, many video game projects on Kickstarter have failed, therefore receiving no funds. For example, in late 2015, despite having a polished Kickstarter presentation including a video, a demonstration of game play, and a presence on four social media platforms plus YouTube, *Aberford: A Video Game of Zombies and 50's Housewives* failed. It received pledges totaling only $104,000 of the $657,000 goal (Aberford, 2015). The developers received no money.

Early Access funding

Customer funding for video games also occurs outside of Kickstarter, especially on the game website, **Steam**, run by Valve Corporation, where gamers can buy **Early Access** to a game. Gamers' feedback is used to improve and refine game play, and their payments are used to finish the game. At release, they receive the final version, also through Steam.

There have been some controversies about access that was too early, so that what the buyer received was unplayable, or the game was never finished. In late 2014, Valve/Steam updated their rules and guidelines for Early Access. As quoted on the subscription game site Giantbomb.com, guidelines include not selling access too early: "'If you have a tech demo, but not much gameplay yet, then it's probably too early to launch in Early Access'" (Klepek, 2014). On the other hand, the developers should be open to more than reports of bugs, because, "'Early Access is intended as a place where customers can have an impact on the game,'" according to the guidelines (Klepek, 2014). Launching in Early Access on Steam was one of the stages outlined in the *Wasteland 2* Kickstarter campaign, and Steam play was a Kickstarter premium.

Thunderclap

Thunderclap.it, which calls itself a "crowd-speaking platform" (Thunderclap, 2015), is a way to crowd source social media reach. **Thunderclap** follows the Kickstarter model. Instead of a money goal, however, Thunderclap has a supporter goal of people willing to share their social media contacts to spread the word about an idea or product. If the project reaches its supporter goal, all of the supporters automatically spread the message to their entire networks on that date. In October 2015, the director's cut of *Wasteland 2* reached 341% of its Thunderclap supporter goal, with a social media reach of 186 thousand. Video games can use Thunderclap to attempt to trend on social media on the day of release, or to spread word about Kickstarter crowd funding campaigns before the funding deadline.

Making Allies of the Gaming Community

As seen with Kickstarter, Steam, and Thunderclap, video game producers are finding more and more ways to let their end users participate in creating and marketing games. The importance of the fans to the publicity process was highlighted in June 2015. E3 admitted 5,000 fans chosen by various exhibitors for the first time, "with the hope that their followings on social media will amplify the expo's reach" (Pierson & Villarreal, 2015, p. C1). In fact, game publishers had already been inviting fans to their pre-conference press events, "to spur enthusiasm. Electronic Arts, for example, invited hundreds of high school and college students to its media briefing" (Pierson & Villarreal, 2015, p. C4).

eSports, Twitch, and YouTube

Competitive gaming began as small groups of friends playing in arcades or suburban basements and migrated online along with massively multi-player and role-playing games. Now major league gaming tournaments feature paid and sponsored professional gamers. They compete for thousands of dollars in prize money in events organized by leagues such as ESL (which stands for eSports League) in arenas as large as Madison Square Garden in New York City and Staples Center in Los Angeles. Many additional spectators watch in movie theaters or through online streaming services.

To the disdain of some football, basketball, and baseball fans, ESPN and other broadcasters are exploring how to participate in the growing phenomenon. In late 2015, according to the *Los Angeles Times*, Activision Blizzard hired Steve Bornstein, formerly of ESPN and NFL Network, to oversee new competition initiatives. Viewership of ESL's events more than doubled from 2012 to 2014, according to the company, "to more than 50 million hours, reaching 70 million individuals, mostly online" (Dave, 2015d, p. C3). Another company that organizes tournaments with qualifying rounds online and finals presented live and streamed is Major League Gaming (MLG).

A number of game publishers either already run tournaments for their games or are adapting their games to better support competitions. For example, Riot Games runs competitions called LOLesports for its League of Legends game.

The eSports industry is so new and in flux that PR efforts currently seem ad hoc and hit-or-miss. With the leagues being modeled after professional major league sports, however, public relations seems mostly to follow the sports PR cycle discussed in Chapter 9. Since some of the leagues are owned or controlled by game companies, such as Activision Blizzard, however, it's already pretty clear that league play will be used to publicize new versions of a game, and that a new version of a game will publicize the league in which it is played competitively.

Local eSports

Local and amateur initiatives are also growing. Super League Gaming organizes afternoon tournaments for Little League-aged children in movie theaters, which are underused during the daytime (Vodnala, 2015). There are a number of other localized, amateur efforts. Just as athletic sports have local leagues and practice gyms, gamers in some places now have local arenas to practice, compete, and improve their knowledge and competitive skills. New ones, such as eSports Arena in Santa Ana, California (Dave, 2015a), are small businesses that need to publicize themselves locally. Since they offer practice, fun matches, and local competition leagues, logical marketing models could be gyms, billiard parlors, and bowling alleys.

Twitch

Twitch is an eSports subscription streaming service for competitions and recreational viewing. Twitch probably first came into the consciousness of non-gamers via August 2014 front-page articles in *The New York Times* (Wingfield, 2014) and in other papers announcing that the company had been acquired by Amazon for around a billion dollars. As the *Los Angeles Times* business section pointed out, "The long-term ad revenue from a Twitch acquisition could also be massive. Twitch caters to an attractive demographic, typically young, tech-savvy men who have time on their hands and money to spend" (Chang & Rodriguez, 2014, p. B5). Twitch, which shares ad revenue with gamers who run popular video feeds, had an estimated $1.6 billion in ad revenue in 2015. It also created a TwitchCon convention in San Francisco for fans and online stars to mingle in person. There it announced that it would offer the ability to upload recorded content starting in 2016—a move to better compete with YouTube's efforts to gain gamer loyalty (Dave, 2015b).

YouTube

YouTube is awash with uploaded, game-related content: "Video game enthusiasts worldwide spend 2.4 billion hours each month on YouTube watching fellow gamers compete and discuss tactics and strategy" (Dave, 2015c, p. C4). YouTube shares ad revenue with popular content creators. In addition, in late 2015, YouTube moved toward charging subscriptions called sponsorships of $3.99 a month per channel, which undercuts Twitch's $4.99 fee, as the competition for gamers' eyeballs and dollars heats up.

Conclusion

The video game industry now targets a broad demographic. It is also rife with competition, innovation to bring gaming into mainstream culture, and controversy about who "owns" and defines gaming culture. As with every kind of client, PR practitioners for video games need to create clear, well-thought-out PR plans that lay out a roadmap to success.

Blockbuster games now sometimes have bigger opening sales than major films. Blockbuster games tend to be franchise installments of previously successful titles. Their PR cycle includes activities during development with its alpha and beta testing; the buildup to launch; the release; and often later releases of additional downloadable content. With blockbuster titles, publicity can focus on familiar or "pre-sold" elements and leak tidbits and secrets to an avid fan community.

The PR cycle for independent games is shorter, and the budgets are more constrained. Since the title and the game are unfamiliar, the PR cycle focuses on getting the word out about what makes this game interesting and distinctive. Whenever possible, the PR team and developers need to get a playable version of the game in people's hands, so they can experience it and talk about it. The same is true with casual games and apps, which have exploded in popularity with the spread of smartphones. All kinds of games, of course, benefit from media mentions and good reviews—the more the better. Crowd funding on Kickstarter and early access funding on Steam have been successful PR tactics for indie and casual games. Some PR plans also crowdsource social media awareness though Thunderclap.it.

The rise of eSports has added an extra dimension to gaming PR, as companies move to develop professional and amateur leagues for their games. The subscription service Twitch and numerous free and subscription channels on YouTube now allow a number of gamers to share subscription and ad revenue, further professionalizing the world of gaming. League gaming, as well as virtual reality and 360-degree video, were in the forefront of the CES 2016 trade show, and foretell future areas of work for public relations.

Many areas of the industry are in flux. Innovative public relations practitioners are needed to create solid PR plans that communicate company messages to their target publics and harness the passion and energy of fan communities.

Key Terms—In bold in the text

Sample two-sentence definition and example

AAA Title: For video games, AAA Title, another name for blockbuster games, refers to big-budget games that are usually part of a popular franchise and are expected to achieve high sales. For example, the "Call of Duty" franchise has broken records in the past, and therefore the public relations team can use leaks that remind people of what they've liked about past games in the series to create excitement for the latest release.

Advertising Review Council (ARC)
Alpha Testing
Beta Testing
Blockbuster game
Buyer Persona
Casual Game
Consumer Electronics Show (CES)
Content Marketing
Cost Per Install (CPI)
Downloadable Content (DLC)
Early Access
Electronics Entertainment Expo (E3)
Entertainment Software Association (ESA)
Entertainment Software Ratings Board (ESRB)
eSports
ESRB Rating
Franchise
Game Developers Conference (GDC)
GamerGate
Independent Video Game (Indie Game)
Kickstarter
PR cycle for devices
Retargeting
Steam
SWOT (Strengths, Weaknesses, Opportunities, and Threats)
SXSW Interactive
Thunderclap
Twitch
Video Game PR Cycle

Suggested reading and resources

Braff, Z. (Producer), & Snead, J. (Director). (2014). *Video games: The movie* [Motion Picture]. USA: Mediajuice Studios. (Available for streaming on Netflix).

McGrath, B. (2014, November 24). Good game: The rise of the professional cyber athlete. *The New Yorker*, 86–97.

TOURISM, ATTRACTIONS, TRAVEL, AND HOSPITALITY

Seasonal PR Cycles

Chapter Overview: When you finish this chapter, you should be able to answer the following questions:

- What is the public relations goal for attractions and tourism-related businesses?
- How can tourism publicity "sell the dream," and what is the selling moment?
- What are the seven seasons related to PR cycles in travel and tourism?
- What is news for a year-round tourist attraction that has a high season and a low season?
- What is the PR cycle for tourism and attractions that have a long open season, followed by a closed season?
- How can publicity help develop a one-season business into a multi-season attraction?
- What is the PR cycle for once-a-year attractions?
- How can tourism public relations convert one-time customers into regulars?
- SIDEBAR: The Entertainment PR Toolbox—Pitching
- SIDEBAR: The Entertainment PR Toolbox—Responding to Unusual Press Queries

Introduction

Tourism and travel are multibillion-dollar industries comprising everything from local, seasonal micro-businesses, such as a farmer's front-yard vegetable stand, to global enterprises, such as airlines. Local repeat visitors mean business for restaurants, museums, attractions, and historical sites. The economic downturn of 2008 made even large tourism destinations aware of the need to attract locals for multiple visits. Wide media coverage (generated by skillful public relations) touted the benefits of **staycations**, a recent coinage meaning economical outings and day trips that don't require overnight stays or costly transportation.

More distant tourists stay at hotels and short-term rentals for multi-day visits to sites and attractions. Many may enjoy themselves so much they become repeat visitors and go beyond the obvious tourist attractions to discover hidden gems and locals' favorites. Visitors of all kinds attract development of additional recreational activities, arts options such as film and art festivals, and other niche entertainment options, such as ghost tours and chili cook-offs. Regular visitors may rent for more extended periods, especially with the ease and ubiquity of Airbnb and HomeAway. They may buy vacation homes and become part-year residents. Some eventually buy a home, or open their own business or become full-time resident retirees, who volunteer for civic and cultural organizations and become part of the fabric of the community.

Civic and business organizations often support local and regional development and tourism bureaus, not just for the current economic benefit, but also to encourage future development. For example, state funding of the Phoenix Convention Center, a light rail connection to the airport, and a subsidized downtown hotel is credited with being the catalyst for transforming downtown Phoenix into a walkable, sustainable city core attractive to millennials (Oates, 2015). Developing the tourist capacity to host major televised sporting events such as the 2015 Super Bowl in nearby Glendale allowed Phoenix to showcase its transformation for the world.

There are hundreds of different kinds of entertainment business that haven't been covered so far in this book. Many of them are related to travel and tourism. *Attracting Attention: Promotion and Marketing for Tourism Attractions* by Andi Stein (2015) covers all aspects of attraction management including corporate and HR. This chapter takes an in-depth look at public relations.

Most tourism businesses could probably benefit from developing and executing a well-thought-out public relations plan. As a public relations professional, you may be invited to submit a proposal for a tourism business or organization that is somewhat outside your core expertise. This chapter will show how to create an effective PR proposal based on careful thought and research.

The first step is to look for a PR cycle. By discerning a repeating pattern of times or events that might benefit from intensified effort, you can marshal the public relations strategies, tactics, and tools discussed throughout this book to prepare an effective plan, no matter the potential client's business.

This chapter also demonstrates how a PR-created story can engage the imaginations, first of the media and then of readers or viewers. For an audience of individual journalists, the public relation practitioner's story idea is called a **pitch**. Possible pitches for tourism clients are discussed throughout this chapter, and the art of pitching is covered in the SIDEBAR.

The Entertainment PR Toolbox—Pitching

Successful media pitches are like successful matchmaking. They depend on the matchmaker (the PR practitioner) finding the right fit (interests, personality, background, and chemistry) between a target journalist and a story idea (the happy couple). In other words, pitching is challenging. It requires research and in-depth knowledge about both the journalist and the story idea. Like a good match, a story pitch must be a special, specific story idea and angle offered exclusively to a particular member of the media. Hospitality expert, Jon Boroshok, said to "identify the right reporter at the right publication" (2005). He suggested tying a pitch to the season; the editorial calendar of the publication; a bigger story in the news; or a trend (Boroshok, 2005).

Per David Meerman Scott in *The New Rules of Marketing & PR*, pitches must stand out as targeted, not spam. For an email pitch, which many journalists prefer, Scott published a suggestion from Peter Howe that an effective subject line is: "PR pitch for *Boston Globe* reporter Peter Howe" (Scott, 2011, p. 294). Gayle Goodman quoted another journalist as urging "'a crisp clear message' in the subject line, to compel him to read it" (Goodman, 2012).

A pitch is different from a press release, which is a complete news story written by the public relations practitioner and distributed widely to an entire media list. Multiple news outlets may choose to cover a story based on a media release, even though similar articles will appear elsewhere.

A pitch is different. The story angle must be exclusive, not just spam that's being sent to dozens of publications with a changed subject line. A pitch is spam if:

- it is not strictly exclusive
- it doesn't apply to that journalist's beat
- it doesn't apply to the journalist's readers
- it isn't new to those readers
- it doesn't help that journalist do her job

No matter how many hours you worked to research and write your pitch, if you want to make a match, your pitch email has only a few seconds, the length of a wandering glance, of a Tinder swipe, to catch the eye and hold the interest of the target journalist.

Destination identity

The first step in preparing a public relations plan for a new client is always to research to prepare the background and do a situation analysis. A tourism business at a fixed location, such as a theme park or a museum, should have a **destination identity**, unique focus, or image that makes it different from other similar places (competitors). If it has an identity already, how would you describe it? If it doesn't have an identity, how can your plan help differentiate it to create a unique and memorable one?

Tourism consortia often strive to create a local or regional identity that resonates with tourists. Examples include Orange County, California, which has the slogan "Forever Summer"; Las Vegas has "What Happens Here Stays Here"; and New York has the "Big Apple." In the SWOT analysis, these external campaigns represent opportunities. Can you propose a way to ride on the coattails of your area's bigger-budget tourism campaign, particularly if it has a large spend for television advertising?

What do tourists want?

Entertainment in general provides a diversion or break from people's day-to-day lives. Tourists also seek a change from their regular lives. People travel to some place different to see something different—even if they eventually decide, "There's no place like home." How would they know, if they hadn't experienced some place different? Country people visit the city to see their future or their children's futures. City people visit the country to see their pasts or to feel close to the natural world.

Successful destination cities or regions should have: a variety of food choices including unique regional cuisine; shopping, including local food specialties or cultural items; accommodation choices at a range of prices; and a variety of activities for all ages. How does your client help the region satisfy these needs for visitors?

Iconic images of a place differentiate marketing in advance of travel and trigger place memories afterwards. Examples include distinctive buildings (the Empire State Building, Disney Hall, and the Sidney Opera House); monuments (the Washington Monument and Mount Rushmore); and natural scenery (the Grand Canyon, Niagara Falls, Mt. Etna). In a SWOT analysis, local icons represent opportunities for greater visibility and possibly cross-promotions.

What tourists do you want?

What are the demographics, psychographics, and geographics of your target customers? You have to know who they are, where they are, and what media they use to be able to reach them. Creating buyer personas helps everyone understand the target audience segments.

Customer expectations

Most businesses realize that customer expectations are key to customer satisfaction. Meeting or beating expectations means customer satisfaction and positive word of mouth. People love to talk to friends in person and online about wonderful travel experiences. Missing expectations, however, means dissatisfied customers and bad word of mouth, which online platforms such as TripAdvisor and Yelp amplify.

Some businesses don't realize the important role of marketing in creating expectations. While clients want to put out the best, most positive stories possible, hype is a dangerous prelude to disappointed expectations. Best practices, for example, include, "Make sure any photographs of guest rooms are 'typical' of the property, rather than the one-of-a-kind 'best room.' An accurate representation is imperative, under penalty of negative media backlash" (Boroshok, 2005).

Negative media backlash, sometimes called **blowback**, destroys the effectiveness of a public relations strategy. Sometimes it even causes public ridicule. For example, in 2007, Disney created a video titled, "Welcome: Portraits of America," for the U.S. Department of Homeland Security and the Department of State to be played in customs areas of domestic airports and in embassies abroad. Among its positive, diverse images of people and landmarks were beautiful images of Niagara Falls. The problem was, "Disney's filmmakers … chose the Horseshoe Falls, the only one of Niagara's three waterfalls that is almost entirely on the Canadian side of the border," and a view accessible only to visitors of Canada ("Falls PR," 2007). The lead of the *Los Angeles Times* article asserted: "The Bush administration appears to have annexed a major Canadian landmark" as part a promotional campaign ("Falls PR," 2007). The video is available on YouTube, with images of the "stolen" falls around 1:40 and 4:00 ("Welcome," 2007). The moral of the story for PR practitioners? Public relations materials should tell the truth in words and images.

The Goal of a Tourism Plan

Excellent research for the background and situation analysis will allow you to set a realistic, achievable goal for the PR plan, which again should be in dollars or figures that easily translate into dollars. To define a tourism goal, gather data from state, regional, and local sources, such as the tourism bureau and the Chamber of Commerce. How much did visitors spend during the most recent year versus the previous two years? Are hotel occupancy rates increasing or decreasing? What about airport statistics on the comparative number of domestic and international arrivals each year? It would be unrealistic for a tourism business to increase sales by 20 percent, if regional data shows tourism activity to be down 20 percent year over year with no signs of recovery.

Customer perceptions

The goal should also reflect external threats, particularly the competition. What are customer perceptions of price, quality, benefits, features, and service, not just in a vacuum, but also versus the competition? For example, in Southern California, Disneyland always charges higher prices than its nearby theme park competition, Knott's Berry Farm, as well as Universal Studios Hollywood, and Magic Mountain. Plan goals for each company reflect their strengths in the marketplace at any moment, and may shift, for example, when one of them opens a new ride or attraction. To understand customers' perceptions, you have to ask them via surveys and focus groups.

From this research and from discussions within the client organization, you can arrive at a realistic goal figure in dollars (total sales, or revenue from ticket and merchandise sales) or something that translates into dollars (hotel occupancy rate and average rate per room).

Selling the Dream

The term **selling the dream** refers to a strategy for creating awareness and purchase intention in travel and tourism clients by engaging their imaginations and helping them picture themselves relaxing in an exotic, new place. "Picture" and "new" are key terms here. Compelling photographs and video images as well as evocative visual descriptions convey a destination's unique identity. What makes this place different and exciting? What about the experience will make the traveler feel like a changed person? The story told by public relations materials should engage the imagination—even the fantasy life—to sell the dream of being there.

Selling the dream, of course, creates expectations. The actual experience of the traveler needs to deliver on the dream. The dream being sold should not be hype, as discussed below in the section titled, "Has the dream destroyed itself?"

The selling moment

One of the longest-running campaigns based on selling the dream is Southern California's oldest travel marketing effort. Its potential customer is anybody who doesn't live in Southern California. Its **selling moment**, the time period when the target customer is most susceptible to the sales pitch, is the dead of winter. In most of the country, it is below freezing outside. Snow is piled high. The short days with little sunshine are dank and depressing. People are looking ahead to many weeks more of the same.

The dream being sold? Images show a far-off land of flowers, orange groves, and sunshine. Fantastic visions of flowers float before winter-weary eyes.

The sales strategy? Pasadena's Rose Parade. In 1890, a local hunt club in the small, rural town of Pasadena decided to promote their area's great weather and year-round flowers as a beautiful place to buy or build a winter home. They invited friends from other parts of the country and produced a winter festival that included a sports tournament of competitions such as foot races and tug-of-war, as well as a parade of flower-bedecked carriages ("History of the Rose Parade," 2015). People who attended went home to the Midwest and spread the news: Some people have an orange tree or a palm tree in the yards of their bungalows. Southern California is paradise in winter.

Media coverage

Through the years, the festival's reputation grew, not just through word of mouth, but also through news coverage, i.e., unpaid media placements. News photos appeared in newspapers and photo magazines. Eventually, newsreels in movie theaters and radio and then television news broadcasts covered the parade and the yearly New Year's Day football game. Since many years ago, on the morning of January 1, while most of the country shivers, Southern California struts its stuff (flowers, palm trees, music, and mild temperatures) on

Figure 12.1: "Union of Hearts," Union Bank Float honoring the American Heart Association, 127th Tournament of Roses Parade post-parade display of floats, January 2, 2016.
Photo credit: 2016 Carol Ames.

nationwide telecasts of the Rose Parade. The participation of marching bands from across the country also guarantees plenty of hometown media coverage. Stories of the ways band members and the community were raising money for their wintertime trip to beautiful California probably started months earlier.

Does the dream deliver?

How well does the reality of a trip to the Tournament of Roses Parade and the Rose Bowl game meet or beat the expectations about Southern California created via yearly media coverage? These days, what is the experience of a typical tourist, let's say a midwestern supporter of the Big Ten team playing in the year's Rose Bowl game? Is the actual experience **delivering the dream**?

The weather is definitely better than at home in Wisconsin or Kansas— shorts and T-shirt weather for walking along the miles of beaches and board-walks on the oceanfront. No snow. It seldom even rains on the Rose Parade. There are stunning flowers, especially the cascades of gaudy, fuchsia-colored bougainvillea, a tropical plant that is unknown at home. Some rose bushes are in bloom, despite the page of the calendar. Orange trees in yards? Check. Palm trees? Check, including the otherworldly forty-foot-tall ones with just a tuft of fronds at the top that sway and bend erratically in the wind. Vistas? Check. The blue Pacific, instead of brown, snow-streaked fields.

Is there something for everybody? Venice Beach has skateboarders, roller-blading, and crazy-looking entertainers. (Visitors are definitely not in Kansas anymore.) Hollywood and downtown Los Angeles have clubs for partying into the night. Universal Studios gives a sense of the studio as a film factory, while offering themed rides for kids of all ages. There are thousands of restaurants ranging from taco stands to fine dining on California cuisine (the first U.S. cuisine to go fresh and local), and dozens of specialty food trucks that converge in popular pedestrian areas, announcing their current location via social media. Hotel choices abound, as do shopping areas ranging from garment district cheap chic to Rodeo Drive couture to Abbot Kinney Boulevard trendy.

Iconic images to photograph include the Hollywood sign, Disney Hall, the sweep of the bay from Santa Monica to Malibu, and the turbaned guy at Venice Beach who rollerblades while playing a battery-powered guitar—and posing for photographs. Of course, there is Disneyland, "The Happiest Place on Earth." In sum, Southern California's unique destination identity meets or beats tourists' expectations with varieties of experiences that visitors of different ages crave … mostly.

Has the dream destroyed itself?

Hollywood? Where do visitors find the glamour and romance of the movies? Not there. Despite decades of redevelopment and civic prodding, and despite volunteers who polish the star-shaped plaques dedicated to dozens of stars on Hollywood Boulevard, the center of Hollywood itself around the Chinese Theater and the exterior of the Hollywood and Highland retail mall is still "touristy" in the worst sense and always feels a little dirty. As a municipal street with free access for all, Hollywood Boulevard lacks the staff of privately run Disneyland. The happiest (and probably the cleanest) place on earth has squads of smiling cast members to pick up trash during the day and 600 elves on the night shift to pressure wash gray gobs of tossed chewing gum and to refresh painted surfaces (Martin, 2010). Public areas everywhere that draw crowds of tourists face the same challenges as Hollywood Boulevard. Globally only Singapore seems to have solved the problem of keeping public areas as clean as private malls ... by banning chewing gum and imposing stiff fines for a variety of public cleanliness infractions, ranging from littering to spitting (Metz, 2015). Meanwhile, the reality of Hollywood, at least on the sidewalks of Hollywood Boulevard, disappoints expectations.

But who wouldn't still want to move to California and buy a nice bungalow in the middle of an orange grove by the beach? The dream that sold California real estate unfortunately wiped out the scenic orange groves most of the way inland to Riverside. The weather and the Rose Bowl keep people coming in the winter. But the traffic, congestion, and million-dollar price tags for tiny bungalows may keep them from coming back, buying a vacation home here, and eventually becoming part of the local community. Public relations professionals in the tourism industry need to focus on selling the elements of a dream that deliver today, not those that belong to the past.

Updating the dream

Civic organizations, tourism bureaus, tourist-oriented businesses, and public relations practitioners need to evolve their offerings, slogans, icons, and activities to reflect current realities. What will the new icons be? In Los Angeles, the binocular-shaped building that houses Google? Or Google's soon-to-be new campus in the iconic WWII-era wooden hangar where Howard Hughes's wooden transport plane, the *Spruce Goose*, was built? In Southern California, as everywhere, innovations in tourism offerings and in their PR plans are essential for the next stage, whatever that may turn out to be. **Updating the dream** by promoting new iconic images, slogans, and stories in the media will help a destination continue to meet or beat the visitor expectations created by those stories.

Nature's Four Seasons Plus High, Low, and Closed

This book has shown how the public relations for various entertainment businesses follow a recurring pattern, which we have named the PR cycle. Business plans ask for an analysis of **seasonality**, meaning a discussion of when and why customer demand increases or decreases. Usually both demand for entertainment and audience availability are uneven throughout the year. Therefore, so are PR opportunities. If there is little customer interest in a kind of entertainment during a particular season, journalists and bloggers are not going to respond to a pitch about it.

The seasonality of demand and PR opportunities may depend on **nature's four seasons**. As an obvious example, skiing is a winter sport. Other sports have their own seasonal pattern. The baseball season starts in the spring and is at its height throughout the summer, when kids are out of school and many people have time off work. Baseball stretches into the fall by engaging fans in the excitement of the pennant races, playoffs, and World Series.

Sometimes seasonality is affected by human-created events connected to one or more of nature's seasons, such as the winter holidays. For another example, the U.S. school year was originally scheduled to allow rural children to work during the busy summer farm season. On the other hand, network television's cycle follows the school year with lulls during the winter holiday season and the summer. When urban kids are on vacation from school, families like to do things together, including staycation activities and more distant traveling vacations. The media's willingness to pick up story pitches varies depending on the varying seasonal interests of their audience.

High season and low season

Entertainment venues and attractions may be open year-round, but nevertheless have a **high season** (busy time) and a **low season** (less busy time). Tourist businesses, such as ski lifts, may have only two seasons: high season and **closed season**. Recognizing the seasonality of demand for a client's goods or services is one step in determining the PR cycle for that client.

Having News or Making News Year Around

The ongoing challenge for public relations is to have news or make news. This is especially challenging when a tourism business is open year-round. Such businesses usually have a high season and a low season. You don't, however, want to make news with headlines that read, "Business is slow." Nobody wants to go where nobody is going … unless you can pitch a story about someone setting for record for the most rides on the rollercoaster in one day. This story can draw locals for repeat visits, because it conveys the message that it's fun to go to the amusement park when lines are short.

News-making strategies

Possible PR strategies for year-round-tourism businesses include: encouraging repeat visits by creating seasonal markers and celebrations; extending the high season; opening a new attraction or exhibit, or re-theming an existing one; and developing and publicizing an alternate business to attract off-season guests.

Seasonal markers

Seasonal markers for the Christmas or winter holiday season are a long-running tradition, and may differentiate one stage of the PR cycle for your client. All across the country, municipalities decorate the streets. New York City, which tries to do things bigger than elsewhere, has made an annual event of lighting the Christmas tree at Rockefeller Center. Local and national media cover the event each year. Across the street from the tree lighting is the flagship Saks Fifth Avenue Department Store. Saks and its competitors such as Lord & Taylor, Macy's, Bloomingdales (Cross, 2015), and others have made a November tradition of unveiling extravagant, holiday-themed window displays that draw crowds of locals and tourists alike. Some of them are likely to enter the stores to shop, which is the purpose of the strategy of providing free window displays to the public.

Disneyland generates repeat visits for the holidays by lavishly redecorating the park and re-theming the daytime and nighttime parades, as well as the fireworks and several of the longest-running rides. For example, "The Jungle Cruise" becomes "The Jingle Cruise."

Halloween is another American tradition that has been increasingly important, because it allows tourist attractions and businesses to offer something new and therefore to make news during the low season. In Southern

California, Knott's Berry Farm becomes Knott's Scary Farm, complete with mazes, zombies, and ghouls. Started as a special, two-night event in 1973 (Galaviz, 2015, Aug. 25), this seasonal re-theming now generates crowds of 20,000 people a night from late September through Halloween. The mazes and screams are talked about on social media and covered extensively in print and broadcast. News media might be interested in a pitch about the monster auditions or doing a behind-the-scenes story about creating the scary looks.

Disneyland does a more kid-friendly Halloween Party from early September to early November. In fact, going from high season (summer) to Halloween to Christmas—each a trigger to re-visit the park—is a way that Disneyland scores multiple re-visits, particularly from locals. As a result, many locals now buy expensive yearly passes so as not to miss any of the special activities. Yearly pass holders, who need to receive good value to keep re-enrolling, also spend money at restaurants and gift shops during their frequent visits.

Las Vegas strategy to get guests in the door

In Las Vegas, the Bellagio Hotel makes news multiple times a year when it debuts a lavish seasonal flower display. Its atrium is a must-see, family-friendly, "free" sight for repeat visits from locals and from anyone visiting Sin City— and only a few steps away from its beckoning casino. The free seasonal flower display is part of an all-encompassing Las Vegas strategy: Get people in the door by offering them something different to see that is free, such as a theme (Paris; New York; Venice, Italy; ancient Rome). Once they're inside, keep them there looking, eating at the buffet and restaurants, and shopping until they lose money gambling, after a few too many "free" drinks offered during time spent at the blackjack tables and slot machines. But first, get them in the door. Caesar's Palace used to have a one-way moving sidewalk that carried guests the great distance from Las Vegas Boulevard (the Strip) to the casino. Once a person was inside, it was almost impossible to find a way back outside. Now Caesar's uses a long corridor of Forum Shops to transition people between the Strip and the casino. The shops offer winners many tempting ways to spend their money, before they can exit onto the sidewalk.

A voice in the C-suite

Some news-making strategies require changes in operations, such as staying open late and hiring more personnel, for example, Knott's Scary Farm's ghosts. Seasonal decorations and activities cost money. The need for companywide buy-in is one reason that the head of communications should be a valued counselor to the **Chief Executive Officer (CEO)** in what is called the **C-suite**, or executive council. A title such as **Chief Communications Officer (CCO)** signifies equivalent status and a voice at the table with the **Chief Financial Officer (CFO)** and the **Chief Operations Officer (COO)**.

Extending the high season

One strategy to make news is to create special events, thus **extending the high season** as long as possible, as Major League Baseball does with its long schedule of post-season competitions. Going from the high season (summer) to drawing crowds for Halloween to re-theming for the winter holidays means that Disneyland has, in effect, extended its high season into weeks that might more naturally be part of the low season. This leaves only January as slow. February has Valentine's Day, which can also be publicized as a seasonal celebration.

Not every outdoor attraction has the California and Florida Disney parks' warm winter weather that allows the busy season to be extended beyond Christmas. Many, however, can create a celebration themed to the fall foliage, the harvest, Halloween, or Thanksgiving. Print and broadcast news regularly cover stories about special events tied to the four seasons. Therefore, seasonal events are markers of the PR cycle for a number of year-round attractions.

Seasonal markers as customer traditions

Creating a seasonal celebration costs money. As with charity events discussed in Chapter 4, repeating an event in subsequent years amortizes the costs over time. It also increases the likelihood of media coverage. Repeated events also can become family traditions with revisits eagerly anticipated year after year. A winter festival with snowmen for the kids and an ice-fishing competition for adults could be an opportunity to generate news coverage, customer visits, and added revenue. Ice hotels attract adventuresome winter travelers to at least four northern cities globally, including Quebec City, Canada.

Openings

The media want something new—news. Customers also want something new. So an obvious public relations strategy is to have a **grand opening** of something new. For example, Disney will begin constructing "Star Wars" lands in

California and Florida in 2016 (Glusac, 2015). This high-profile, cost-intensive initiative generated media and fan excitement at the time of its announcement at the D23 fan expo in August 2015 (Miller, 2015). News interest will remain high through construction and throughout an entire grand opening year or longer. "Star Wars" fans from multiple generations will want to attend. More importantly, many people who have enjoyed Disneyland or Disney's Hollywood Studios in Orlando will have a reason for a return visit.

Meanwhile in November 2015, to publicize the upcoming "Star Wars" movie in December, Disneyland gained wide media coverage by taking the refresh-and-re-theme approach. It launched the Season of the Force, a temporary makeover of Tomorrowland that included Space Mountain becoming Hyperspace Mountain (Martens, 2015c) and a special exhibit of "Star Wars" props and memorabilia.

Special exhibits

Museums used to have the same-old, same-old exhibitions of their permanent collections—no news, no news coverage, and dwindling attendance. Museum directors discovered that **special exhibits** of themed groupings from the permanent collection, or exhibits that draw items from similar museums and collectors around the world bring crowds of visitors, when they are well publicized. The news coverage and word of mouth about special exhibits mean that many museumgoers now need advanced-sale tickets for a specific day and time.

The Guggenheim Museum Bilbao in Spain took the concept of the special exhibit to the extreme. In lieu of assembling its own local permanent collection, the museum instead constructed an iconic building by architect Frank Gehry, who a few years later created the Los Angeles icon, Disney Hall. The Bilbao museum makes news repeatedly by opening special exhibits mostly of art from the Guggenheim Foundation's collection. The iconic museum building makes Bilbao an international tourist destination and a cruise ship stop. Publicity about the special exhibits brings art lovers from throughout Europe for repeat visits. For venues with special exhibits or for theaters, the openings of new shows form the focal points of the PR cycle.

Anniversaries

Anniversary celebrations make something new—news—out of what has already existed for years. Angles for anniversary celebrations include stories about the founding, profiles of long-term employees, and celebrations of fans and repeat visitors. Photographs and film clips of the past make great angles for anniversary stories. Not to let go of a good news angle too soon, Disneyland's 50th Anniversary year stretched for 18 months from May 2005 through September 2006. Thus the anniversary included the highest season—summer—twice!

To gain media coverage and help sales, anniversaries need to be planned well in advance. For example, a special anniversary logo that is incorporated into advertising, signage, and packaging can be used all year, so the design and ancillary materials such as banners and stationery need to be ready by January 1. After the planning and preparations, the public part of the cycle begins late the previous fall with the announcement of the celebration, the debut of the logo, and the unveiling of the schedule of special events. The PR cycle for anniversaries includes the announcement, the build-up to the kickoff event, and the actual anniversary date, on which a commemorative event or party will again make news.

A story pitch might be about soliciting items or suggestions of items for a time capsule. Sealing the capsule makes a visually interesting broadcast clip for coverage of the anniversary itself.

When journalists need a new angle

PR opportunities and news stories tend to reoccur in predictable cycles—sometimes too predictable. Longtime journalists don't want to bore themselves or be boring to their readers, so they are always looking for a new angle. With a venerable, year-round tourist attraction such as Disneyland, reporters hope to dig up something new. Sometimes the ideas they come up with or hear rumors about border on the bizarre, as discussed in the SIDEBAR.

The Entertainment PR Toolbox—Responding to Unusual Press Queries

Responding to media questions and requests is a vital part of the job of public relations. A reporter calls, emails, or texts when she is working on a story. Perhaps she wants to include your client in an industry roundup story, or she offers the opportunity to comment on an industry issue. Both of these queries are fairly simple to deal with, even if they do interrupt your plans for the day. You can provide client information for the roundup; for the industry issue you can say you'd like to get her an executive quote, which you can do and get back to her by her deadline.

Those working in public relations have to continually reprioritize, and responding to a reporter's request by deadline should always be a PR person's top priority.

Some reporter queries are less standard, or even bizarre. When a reporter is working on breaking news or chasing a rumor he wants you to confirm or deny, the pressure is on. You don't have the context. The reporter catches you off guard. You have to think quickly.

Let's say you work in media relations at Disneyland, and you get a phone call from a reporter who says something like this: "I understand that somebody on one of your rides just scattered cremated human remains. Would you like to comment?"

Your response should be that you haven't heard about it. Can he tell you a little more, so you can figure out how to track it down? Try to get as much information as possible about the source of the rumor and what sort of actual verification, if any, the journalist has. Most reporters won't tell you much, but any hint may help you get to the right internal source for specifics to confirm, deny, or comment on the story. Promise you will look into it and get back to him. What is his deadline? Then keep your promise.

When you hang up, move quickly to contact sources within the company, for example the heads of security and operations.

Is this weird example made up? Is it unrealistic? No.

A few years ago, an article appeared in the *Los Angeles Times* about just this topic—whether or not someone had scattered human ashes at Disneyland. The article said, "'A witness described the substance as a baby powder that quickly dissipated,' Disneyland spokesman Rob Doughty said. 'We reopened the attraction after determining there was no hazard to our guests.'" An indirect quote in the article added, "Disney officials said they were unaware of any confirmed ash-scattering incidents in the park, and they didn't believe it to be a problem" (Yoshimo, 2007).

The printed story vividly demonstrates how an accomplished public relations practitioner handled an unexpected and potentially damaging press query. Doughty did internal research and confirmed details of the alleged incident, which he was able to categorize as unverified—a baby-powder-like substance. This press statement also specified the actions the company took to safeguard guests. Doughty also tamped down speculation by adding, according to the published article, "From time to time, guests do ask permission to disperse ashes on park premises. The answer, Doughty said, is always no" (Yoshimo, 2007). See the SIDEBAR in Chapter 6 for more details about crafting and issuing press statements.

Because you know your client better than most of the media does, your job as a PR practitioner is to help reporters keep their coverage fresh. You need to pitch interesting, new ideas for stories—stories that you want to have told and that deserve to be told because they will engage the audience in thinking positive thoughts about your client.

Developing split personalities

The occupancy rate of a hotel in a tourist area will go up in the high season. The question is how to survive the low season. Often the answer is to become a convention hotel during the low tourist season, perhaps aided by a municipality or Chamber of Commerce that recognizes the need to attract more business travelers by building a large exhibition area for trade shows.

Business meetings and conventions usually take place weekdays. Many hotels split off an additional personality and become a wedding and prom venue on weekends. A lavish Sunday brunch, an event unto itself that attracts families and locals not just on Mother's Day, also previews the kitchen's skill and creativity for future weddings. A story pitch for a feature on the chef shopping at the local farmer's market would convey the message that the restaurant's food uses locally sourced, fresh ingredients.

The PR cycles

There will be more than one PR cycle for businesses that have split personalities. For example, bridal venues with a high summer season often host or participate in bridal shows during the fall and winter when people are planning their weddings. Like any trade show or expo, such events recur regularly and involve an intensification of public relations activity.

Extending the high season, celebrating openings and anniversaries, and creating alternate businesses for slow seasons and slow days of the week are all ways to buttress the bottom line. They also mean news angles for media coverage.

Two Seasons: Open and Closed

Many tourist businesses are either open for the season or closed. Theme parks in many parts of the country and lakeshore and seashore amusements in climates with harsh winters are examples. For these, the PR cycle will include a build-up to opening day similar to the sports season model. That model encourages thinking of the closed season as the off-season and preparation. For pitching the media, story ideas might answer questions of a typical customer: What's going on behind closed gates to get ready for the opening? What will be new? What is the schedule of special events?

Stretching One Season to Multi-season, Multi-activity Attractions

Specialized resorts also face the challenge of attracting guests during the seasons that the main attraction—such as skiing—is closed. The Vail Cascade Resort and Spa in Colorado does so by publicizing split personalities: as a summer resort, a meeting venue, and for weddings. Its website touts 13 area championship golf courses, as well as 43 other kinds of summer activities, plus 26 events, including a Tough Mudder competition; music, dance, jazz, and art festivals; and a rodeo (Vail Cascade Resort & Spa, 2015). The wedding tab's photo gallery on the website has a summer bride lifting her dress to show off her cowboy boots. Another shot shows a couple still in their formal wedding attire sailing across the green mountain landscape on the ski lift. Any of the summer events presents opportunities to pitch stories along with stunning photography to national travel media. Stories executed on this additional PR cycle will inevitably also mention skiing and snowboarding.

When the season for winter sports approaches, the Vail Cascade website's main page runs a countdown to opening day and a pre-opening sale for pre-Christmas break stays, when snow conditions may be iffy. While the special offers may not be special enough to generate media coverage, the outlook for the coming snow season always makes news both locally and nationally in travel and winter sports media.

Closed for the season ... or not entirely

Baseball and football stadiums, which are also closed for much of the year, explore options for alternative business. In late fall of 2015, three MLB stadiums hosted the Cricket All-Stars Tour (Wharton, 2015) to draw expats and immigrants from countries that love the sport and to introduce it to American sports lovers. Similar past exhibitions have successfully introduced basketball to Europe and Asia, for example. The NFL has also benefited. After a number of exploratory years of exhibition games in England, Wembley Stadium, the home ground of the England national football team, meaning soccer, currently presents three NFL full-season matchups of American football.

Another alternative for a stadium property is a non-sports activity. For more than 45 years, the exterior grounds and parking lots of the Rose Bowl in Pasadena have been rented to the producer of a booming flea market with 2,500 vendors and 20,000 bargain hunters the second Sunday of every month. Many in the crowd probably never attended a UCLA football game there, much less a Rose Bowl Game on January 1. Two travel media pitch angles would be that the flea market is a great place to mingle with a local crowd or that it is a treasure trove of Americana, where a traveler can discover a one-of-a-kind souvenir.

Once-a-Year Events

The PR cycle for once-a-year attractions or events is based on the predictable pattern of development, production, pre-opening build-up, and the opening. Here the open period may be one day only, as we saw with the Grammy Awards; a weekend, which we saw with music festivals; or a number of days, such as a state fair. Public relations stories during development might be announcements of the names of producers (a big deal for the Academy Awards); announcements of talent signed (a headlining music artist for the opening weekend of a fair); and announcements of new attractions.

As the event draws closer, the public becomes interested in how the producers are going to pull off the challenges. Each year, for example, the media cover stories about decorating the Rose Parade floats, which the rules require to be covered completely with organic plant materials. Volunteers from civil organizations and church groups do much of the labor-intensive gluing of brown seeds and the delicate attaching of thousands of roses. Stories can be pitched about individual organizations or specific volunteers. An example might be a multi-generational family with a beloved family tradition of helping decorate a town's float and then going out for pie. The big media push, of course, is for opening day—even if it is also closing day.

As with lengthier high seasons, it is a good idea to try to stretch the one-day-event season and the media coverage. The Rose Parade does this by parking the floats together in a display area for several days, so that visitors and media can view them up close for photographs and selfies.

Making One-time Visitors into Regulars

The media will cover tourism attractions that have new stories to tell. The stories motivate return visitors: opening day; a seasonal celebration; a new attraction or one that has been re-themed; a special show for a limited time only; a new theme; or an anniversary that shines a fresh light on something visitors have loved for a long time.

Creating traditions

Another reason for repeat visits is to participate in a tradition: shared screams at Knott's Scary Farm; Christmas at Disneyland; or summer vacation at the cottage on Lake Michigan. Traditions can be personal or they can be communal. Many locals in Southern California make a tradition of viewing the Rose Parade on television, and then viewing and admiring the parked floats up close and personal.

Relationship Marketing

Relationship marketing means recognizing one's best customers by offering rewards, personal touches, and hassle-free services to those who return frequently. Sometimes called **loyalty programs** or **frequent buyer programs**, these special efforts are widespread with travel, destination, and restaurant businesses. Examples include airline frequent flyer programs and frequent-stay programs for hotel chains. Both of these are particularly effective with travelers who rack up points for business travel at a chain's mid-level hotels, but are able to redeem the points for free weekends and family vacations at the chain's top resort hotels. Others include casino players club cards and frequent buyer cards.

The Disney Season Pass is a more complex example of a loyalty program, because it involves an expensive, upfront purchase and a number of return visits before entry into the park is free. Free membership in **D23**, the official Disney fan club, allows one to receive numerous communications and special offers. To attend special events, however, requires an upgraded $79.99 membership. Entry to the D23 expo is an additional cost. From the Disney example, it is clear that repeat customers who have become fans are willing to pay for special access that both demonstrates their loyalty and deepens it.

Two-way communication with tourism customers

Digital media are making two-way conversations easier to achieve. Review sites such as Yelp and TripAdvisor have, however, upped the ante for travel and tourism destinations. Because a customer's dissatisfaction is on display permanently on these sites, many hotels, for example, respond to all postings on TripAdvisor, whether positive or negative. Usually the hotel representative thanks the client for both kinds of comments. With negative reviews, a typical response will be an apology and a statement that the problem has been remedied, or that the problem was due to a one-time set of circumstances and will not recur. The transparency of responding on the public site demonstrates the company's willingness to listen to its customers.

On the other hand, on the theory that a customer may only complain once—that he just wants to get it out of his system—many hotels take the offensive. They email a follow-up satisfaction survey instantly upon checkout, so that the customer will vent any complaint privately and then forget about it.

Conclusion

There are dozens of different kinds of businesses in the travel and tourism industry that have little in common on the surface. In fact, developing a unique destination identity is important in order to be differentiated from the competition. The unique identity allows client communications to sell the dream of a special visit by creating expectations in the imaginations of future visitors.

However unique the destination, looking at the specific client from a public relations perspective will nevertheless reveal a PR cycle. In tourism and travel, the cycle is a series of repeated focal points for gaining media attention and creating audience awareness based on one or another kind of seasonality. Types of seasonality and possible media pitches during the PR cycle include:

- Open all year, but with a high season and a low season; media pitches can focus on celebrations of one or more of nature's four seasons
- Open all year, but extending the high season through special events and holiday celebrations; media pitches focus on the buildup to and the opening of each special event
- Open all year, but developing a split personality during the low season or slow time of the week; media pitches can take advantage of events such as trade expos that are part of each separate PR cycle

- Open for high season and completely closed until next year; as in sports, media pitches can focus on what is going on behind the scenes in the off-season, and on the build-up to opening day
- And open for a single event or a few days once a year, and closed the rest of the time; pitches can focus on the stages of development, production, and the build-up to the big day(s)

Each pattern of seasonality suggests a pattern of public relations activity—a PR cycle—and even a pattern of specific story pitches.

Understanding which PR cycle most closely fits a tourism client allows the practitioner to pitch stories to local media when their audience will be interested, because soon they will be able to experience it themselves (opening day) or because they've loved the experience in the past and want to recapture the fun (a **customer tradition**). Understanding the PR cycle also allows the PR practitioner to pitch targeted national travel media with enough lead time when a story and client capacity are big enough to warrant the attention, and to handle the capacity.

Key Terms—In bold in the text

Sample two-sentence definition and example

Anniversary Celebrations: Anniversary Celebrations are opportunities for a year or a day's media attention to an ongoing business such as a tourist attraction, which may result in increased repeat visits by local residents. For example, Disneyland increased attendance over an 18-month period by scheduling its 50th Anniversary Celebration to include two summer high seasons.

Blowback
C-Suite
Chief Communications Officer (CCO)
Chief Executive Officer (CEO)
Chief Financial Officer (CFO)
Chief Operations Officer (COO)
Closed Season
Customer Tradition
D23
Delivering the Dream

Destination Identity
Extending the High Season
Frequent Buyer Program
Grand Opening
High Season
Iconic Image
Low Season
Loyalty Program
Nature's Four Seasons
Pitch
Relationship Marketing
Seasonality
Selling Moment
Selling the Dream
Special Exhibit
Staycation
Updating the Dream

Suggested reading and resources

Boroshok, J. (2005). A hospitality and leisure public relations primer. *Journal of Hospitality & Leisure Marketing, 12*(1–2). doi: 10.1300/J150v12n01_11
Stein, A. (2015). *Attracting attention: Promotion and marketing for tourism attractions.* New York, NY: Peter Lang.

REFERENCES

@Disney. (2016, February 3). Disney Twitter account. Retrieved from https://twitter.com/Disney

Aberford. (2015). Aberford: A video game of zombies and 50's housewives by Sketchy Panda Games. [Kickstarter project]. Retrieved from https://www.kickstarter.com/projects/910316779/aberford-a-game-of-zombies-and-50s-housewives?ref=nav_search

Abramowitz, R., Horn, J., & Welkos, R. W. (2005, February 26). A blockbuster campaign can be as good as gold. *Los Angeles Times*, pp. A1, A24.

Academy of Motion Picture Arts & Sciences. (n.d.). Education & Outreach. [Web page]. Retrieved from http://www.oscars.org/education-outreach/index.html

Air Force Public Affairs Agency Emerging Technology Division. (n.d.). Air Force blog assessment. Retrieved from http://www.prwatch.org/node/8104

Ames, C. (2012). Entertainment public relations: Engagement with celebrity, film, and TV brands through online and social media. In S. C. Duhé (Ed.), *New media and public relations* (2nd ed.), (pp. 96–104). New York, NY: Peter Lang.

Ames, C. (2016). The ethics of public relations. In P. Perebinossoff, *Real-world media ethics: Inside the broadcast and entertainment industries* (2nd ed.). Boston, MA: Focal Press.

Andreeva, N. (2012a, May 30). Tim Daly to depart ABC's "Private Practice." Retrieved from http://www.deadline.com/2012/05/tim-daly-to-depart-abcs-private-practice/

Andreeva, N. (2012b, October 29). Anderson Cooper's daytime syndicated talk show cancelled after two seasons. Retrieved from http://deadline.com/2012/10/anderson-coopers-daytime-syndicated-talk-show-cancelled-after-two-seasons-361617/

Angels and Dodgers unveil joint billboard highlighting MVPs. (2015, February 17). [Press release]. Retrieved from http://m.mlb.com/news/article/109515592/angels-and-dodgers-unveil-joint-billboard-highlighting-mvps

Archive of American Television. (n.d.). Capturing television history one voice at a time. Retrieved from http://emmytvlegends.org/

Arellano, J. (2015). *Los Angeles Angels baseball public relations analysis and success.* Unpublished undergraduate paper, Comm465: Entertainment PR, California State University, Fullerton.

Aronson, M., Spetner, D., & Ames, C. (2007). *The public relations writer's handbook: The digital age* (2nd ed.). San Francisco, CA: Jossey-Bass.

Associated Press. (2015). *The Associated Press stylebook and briefing on media law.* New York, NY: Basic Books.

Axisa, M. (2015, July 15). Watch: HBO releases trailer for "Ferrell Takes the Field." Retrieved fromhttp://www.cbssports.com/mlb/eye-on-baseball/25241757/watch-hbo-releases-trailer-for-ferrell-takes-the-field

Bandcamp. (n.d.). Bandcamp for artists. [Web page]. Retrieved from http://bandcamp.com/artists

Barnes, B. (2013, May 6). Solving equation of a hit film script, with data. *The New York Times*, pp. A1, B3.

Barnes, B. (2014a, August 17). Lassie as salesdog: One more trip to the well. *The New York Times*, pp. A1, A23.

Barnes, B. (2014b, August 30). Movies have worst summer since 1997. *The New York Times*, pp. C1, C6.

Barnes B. (2015a, January 22). Small screen is a big player at Sundance. *The New York Times*, pp. A1, B2.

Barnes, B. (2015b, June 27). Too high a bar to the big screen. *The New York Times*, pp. B1, B2.

Barnes, B. (2015c, June 29). Eisner takes media savvy to local TV. *The New York Times*, p. B6.

Barnes, B., & Cieply, M. (2015, July 10). Fresh tack for Lionsgate at Comic-Con. *The New York Times*, pp. B1, B4.

Barnes, J. N. (2015). *The creative, unique, and well-organized public relations efforts of E! Entertainment's The Royals television series.* Unpublished undergraduate paper, Comm465: Entertainment PR, California State University, Fullerton.

Barron, J. (2014, January 25). Welcome or not, 4,000 football fans will be afloat at a Hudson River Pier. *The New York Times*, p. A13.

Baskerville, D., & Baskerville, T. (2013). *Music business handbook and career guide* (10th ed.). Thousand Oaks, CA: Sage.

Batcha, S. (2015, July 13). Comic-Con 2015: Top 10 moments from SDCC. Retrieved from http://www.dailynews.com/arts-and-entertainment/20150713/comic-con-2015-top-10-moments-from-sdcc

Batchelor, J. (2013, February 27). The new rules of video games marketing. Retrieved from http://www.mcvuk.com/news/read/the-new-rules-of-games-marketing/0111541

Bates, D. (2015, July). Research corner: What PR agencies require of new-hire junior AEs. *PR Update: The News Journal for the Public Relations Division of the Association for Education in Journalism and Mass Communication, 50*(3), 10.

Battaglio, S. (2015, July 17). TLC cancels "19 Kids." *Los Angeles Times*, p. E2.

Bennett, M. (2012, August 2). Grand Theft Auto V viral marketing campaign begins. Retrieved from http://www.egmnow.com/articles/news/grand-theft-auto-v-viral-marketing-cam-paign-begins/

Bernard, J. (2009, February 26). Five tips for getting iPhone reviews. [Guest blog entry]. Retrieved from http://whatsoniphone.com/blog/five-tips-for-getting-iphone-reviews/

Billboard Charts. (n.d.). Charts. Retrieved from http://www.billboard.com/charts

Billboard Staff. (2015, August 22). Taylor Swift's 1989 tour: See all of her special Guests! Retrieved from http://www.billboard.com/photos/6634335/taylor-swift-1989-tour-guests/1

Billings, A. C., Butterworth, M. L., & Turman, P. D. (2012). *Communication and sport: Surveying the field.* Thousand Oaks, CA: Sage.

Bilton, N. (2013, June 10). Blurred line in plugs by celebrities. *International Herald Tribune*, p. 15.

Blair, I. (2015, February, No. 3). There's no business like show business. *Variety*, 88.

Block, A. B. (2011, September 20). "Big Bang Theory" starts off strong in syndication ratings. *The Hollywood Reporter.* Retrieved from http://www.hollywoodreporter.com/live-feed/big-bang-theory-starts-strong-237839

Boehm, M. (2015, October 7). Delay for Oscars museum. *Los Angeles Times*, p. E4.

Bolduc, E. Y. (2014). *1,989 reasons to buy 1989.* Unpublished undergraduate paper, Comm465: Entertainment PR, California State University, Fullerton.

Boroshok, J. (2005). A hospitality and leisure public relations primer. *Journal of Hospitality & Leisure Marketing, 12*(1–2). doi:10.1300/J150v12n01_11

BostonHerald.com. (2012). Comment guidelines. Retrieved from http://news.bostonherald.com/news/regional/view.bg?articleid=1061127350&format=comments&cnum=6

Bowen, S. A. (2010). An examination of applied ethics and stakeholder management on top corporate websites. *Public Relations Journal, 4*(1). Retrieved from http://www.prsa.org/SearchResults/download/6D-040101/1012/An_Examination_of_Applied_Ethics_and_Stakeholder_M?

Boxofficemojo.com. (2015, July 5). All time box office: Worldwide grosses #1–100. Retrieved from http://www.boxofficemojo.com/alltime/world/

Boxofficemojo.com. (n.d.). Film box office listings by title. Retrieved from http://www.boxofficemojo.com

Braff, Z. (Producer), & Snead, J. (Director). (2014). *Video games: The movie* [Motion Picture]. USA: Mediajuice Studios. (Available for streaming on Netflix).

Bryce, I. (Producer), & Berg, P. (Director). (2008). *Hancock* [Motion Picture]. USA: Sony Pictures Entertainment.

Burchett, R. (2014). *X marks the charts for Chris Brown.* Unpublished undergraduate paper, Comm465: Entertainment PR, California State University, Fullerton.

Buckley, C. (2014, Sept. 12). Journalists in China describe extortion. *The New York Times*, p. B2.

Busch, A. (2014, August 9). B grade for "Turtles": What CinemaScores mean and why exit polling matters. Retrieved from http://deadline.com/2014/08/b-grade-for-turtles-what-cinemascores-mean-and-why-exit-polling-matters-816538/

Carr, D. (2012, February 13). Twitter is all in good fun, until it isn't. *The New York Times*, pp. B1, B7.

Catsoulis, J. (2014, July 17). A long and winding history of gaming: "Video Games: The Movie," produced by Zach Braff. Retrieved from http://www.nytimes.com/2014/07/18/movies/video-games-the-movie-produced-by-zach-braff.html?_r=0

Chang, A., & Pierson, D. (2015, October 29). Nintendo finally pulls the trigger on first mobile. *Los Angeles Times*, pp. A1, A10.

Chang, A., & Rodriguez, S. (2014, August 26). Amazon gains a valuable gaming asset with Twitch. *Los Angeles Times*, pp. B1, B5.

Chen, C. Y., & Lin, Y. H. (2006). A new market research approach in sport—Data mining. *The Sport Journal*, 9(3). Retrieved from http://www.thesportjournal.org/2006Journal/Vol9-No3/Chen.asp

Chmielewski, D. C. (2007, October 28). Dispatch from China: Monumental. *Los Angeles Times*, p. P3.

Chmielewski, D. C. (2012, June 12). TV broadcasters launch app that syncs with shows. *Los Angeles Times*, p. B3.

Cieply, M. (2015, June 15). Engaging movie fans, from teaser to premiere. *The New York Times*, pp. B1, B6.

Cision. (2011, May 19). Top 10 video game magazines. Retrieved from http://www.cision.com/us/2011/05/top-10-video-game-magazines/

Conn, B. (2006, March 23). Public relations? Chris Cameron is Sea Dogs' guy. Retrieved from http://www.timesrecord.com/website/main.nsf/news.nsf/0//1513021CD23E8D2E0525713A/

Considine, A. (2012, April 26). Celebrity spats thrive on Twitter. *The New York Times*, p. E6.

Cross, H. (2015). Holiday windows at New York City department stores. Retrieved from http://gonyc.about.com/od/christmassights/tp/holiday_windows.htm

Daly, T. (2012, May 29). Wonderful fans of PPP [Twitter post]. Retrieved from https://twitter.com/#!/timmydaly

Dave, P. (2015a, September 11). Putting game players on stage: Audiences can watch competitors do battle at the new 15,000-square-foot eSports Arena in Santa Ana. *Los Angeles Times*, pp. C1, C4.

Dave, P. (2015b, September 26). Twitch to allow video uploads *Los Angeles Times*, p. C2.

Dave, P. (2015c, October 16). YouTube seeks game-fan fees. *Los Angeles Times*, pp. C1, C4.

Dave, P. (2015d, October 24). An eSports chance: ESL becomes the world's biggest video-game events company. *Los Angeles Times*, pp. C1, C3.

Dawn, R. (2011, November 10). Fests can start the buzz and carry it through. *Los Angeles Times*. Retrieved from http://articles.latimes.com/2011/nov/10/news/la-en-festivals-20111110

Day, P. (2015, April 23). TV viewers go on a binge. *Los Angeles Times*, p. E2.

De Castro, M. (2014). *Christina Perri on tour with Demi Lavato*. Unpublished undergraduate paper, Comm465: Entertainment PR, California State University, Fullerton.

Disney Parks Blog. (2016). Comment policy [Official blog]. Retrieved from http://disneyparks.disney.go.com/blog/

Disneyland Resort Twitter. (2016, February 3). @Disneyland [Twitter handle]. Retrieved from https://twitter.com/Disneyland

Duhé, S. C. (2012). A thematic analysis of 30 years of public relations literature addressing the potential and pitfalls of new media. In S. C. Duhe (Ed.), *New media and public relations* (2nd ed.), (pp. xiv–xxvi). New York, NY: Peter Lang.

Entertainment Software Association (ESA). (2015, April). Essential facts about the computer and video game industry. Retrieved from http://www.theesa.com/wp-content/uploads/2015/04/ESA-Essential-Facts-2015.pdf

Entertainment Software Rating Board (ESRB). (n.d.). About ESRB ratings. Retrieved from http://esrb.org/ratings/

Entertainment Software Rating Board (ESRB). (n.d.). Principles and guidelines for responsible advertising practices. Retrieved from http://esrb.org/ratings/principles_guidelines.aspx

ESPN Sports Business. (2013, January 14). Stadium naming rights. Retrieved from http://espn.go.com/sportsbusiness/s/stadiumnames.html

Falls PR doesn't go with the flow. (2007, October 29). Retrieved from http://articles.latimes.com/2007/oct/29/nation/na-falls29

Favorito, J. (2013). *Sports publicity: A practical approach*. New York, NY: Routledge.

Federal Communications Commission (FCC). (n.d.). Broadcasting contests, lotteries, and solicitation of funds. Retrieved from https://www.fcc.gov/guides/broadcasting-contests-lotteries-and-solicitation-funds

Federal Trade Commission (FTC). (2009). 16 CFR Part 255, Guides concerning the use of endorsements and testimonials in advertising. *Federal Register, 74*(198), 15 October, 53124–53143.

Fendi—Great Wall of China fashion show 2007. (2007, October 19). [YouTube video]. Retrieved from https://www.youtube.com/watch?v=fQ3eeWi-4vA

Ferrell takes the field: Trailer (HBO). (2015, July 27). [YouTube video]. Retrieved from https://www.youtube.com/watch?v=2zthfWPzsM4

Foggia, L., & Neal, K. (2007, November). Breaking through the clutter at film festivals. *Film Arts Magazine*. Retrieved from http://www.filminflorida.com/wh/news/NewsletterArchive/1-4-08.pdf

Follows, S. (2015, January 12). How much does a Hollywood Oscar campaign cost? [Blog post]. Retrieved from http://stephenfollows.com/how-much-does-a-hollywood-oscar-campaign-cost/

Free, G., & Domingue, C. (2007). *Publicity and marketing: A producer's handbook*. Ontario, Canada: Queen's Printer.

Frere-Jones, S. (2010, August 16 & 23). The dotted line: What do record labels do now? *The New Yorker*, 92–93.

Friedman, J. (2007, March 19). The movie dating game. *Los Angeles Times*, pp. C1, C5.

Friend, T. (2009, January 19). The cobra: Inside a movie marketer's playbook. Retrieved from http://www.newyorker.com/magazine/2009/01/19/the-cobra

Friend, T. (2016, January 11). The mogul of the middle: As the movie business founders, Adam Fogelson tries to reinvent the system. *The New Yorker*, 36–49.

Frost, J. (2010, May 17). Twitter takes Disney handle away from user [Blog post]. Retrieved from http://thedisneyblog.com/2010/05/17/twitter-takes-disney-handle-away-from-user/

Futter, M. (2015, October 9). 2015 video game release schedule. Retrieved from http://www.gameinformer.com/b/news/archive/2015/10/09/2015-video-game-release-schedule.aspx

Galaviz, X. (2015, August 25). History of Knott's Scary Farm [Blog post]. Retrieved from https://www.knotts.com/blog-article/online-fun/History-of-Knotts-Scary-Farm

Galloway, S. (2015, February 20). Oscar's final moves: Every card on the table. *The Hollywood Reporter*, 48.

Girl Scout Traditions. (2015). [Web page]. Retrieved from http://www.girlscouts.org/program/basics/traditions/

Glavas, A., & Piderit, S. K. (2009). How does doing good matter? Effects of corporate citizenship on employees. *Journal of Corporate Citizenship*, 36(4), 51–70.

Glusac, E. (2015, October 4). New "Star Wars" attractions for Disney parks. *The New York Times*, p. TR3.

Godley, C. (2012, March 21). THR's social media poll: How Facebook and Twitter impact the entertainment industry. Retrieved from http://www.hollywoodreporter.com/gallery/facebook-twitter-social-media-study-302273

Goel, V. (2015, March 9). Study of TV viewers backs Twitter's claims to be barometer of public mood. *The New York Times*, p. B5.

Goff, B. (2013, August 20). The $70 billion fantasy football market. *Forbes*. Retrieved from http://www.forbes.com/sites/briangoff/2013/08/20/the-70-billion-fantasy-football-market/

Goldstein, G. (2015, February, No. 1). No stars? No problem: Indie producers craft ways to finance riskier projects despite lack of name talent and directors. *Variety*, 51–52.

Gompertz, R. (1992). The Rolf Gompertz instant 3-step copy-test system. From *Publicity writing for TV & film*. North Hollywood, CA: Word Doctor.

Goodman, G. (2012, December). Be quick when working the entertainment beat. *O'Dwyer's*, p. 14.

Goodnough, A. (2012, April 27). Hockey loss sets off slurs, and Boston asks, "Again?" *The New York Times*, p. A11.

Gose, B. (2015, August 28). "Nightmare" naming-rights problems. *The Hollywood Reporter*, 65.

Graft, K. (2014, November 3). Grassroots marketing for your indie game. Retrieved from http://gamasutra.com/view/news/229330/Grassroots_marketing_for_your_indie_fame.php

Gray, T. (2015a, January Extra). Oscars are good for the ego and wallet. *Variety*, 8, 12.

Gray, T. (2015b, February Extra). Survival tips for first-time awards season candidates: Our awards expert offers his advice. *Variety*, 14.

Griffith, C. (2015, April 24). "Hey, why wasn't I invited?" (Psst: If you have to ask, you're not on the party A-list). *The Hollywood Reporter*, 64, 66.

Grunig, J. E. (2001). Two-way symmetrical public relations: Past, present, and future. In R. L. Heath (Ed.), *Handbook of public relations* (pp. 11–30). Thousand Oaks, CA: Sage.

Hamedy, S. (2014, October 4). Google helps Paramount market film. *Los Angeles Times*, p. B3.

Hamedy, S. (2015, June 3). Shows cope with off-screen drama: "19 Kids and Counting" is latest series to face scandal. *Los Angeles Times*, p. C3.

Hede, A., & Kellett, P. (2011). Marketing communications for special events. *European Journal of Marketing, 45*(6), 987–1004.

Heurta, J. (2015). *A path to the draft: The 2015 NFL draft.* Unpublished undergraduate paper, Comm465: Entertainment PR, California State University, Fullerton.

Higgins, B. (2012, October 18). Barbara Davis talks hosting the 26th Carousel of Hope Ball and honoring George Clooney. Retrieved from http://www.hollywoodreporter.com/news/barbara-davis-carousel-ball-charity-380173

Higgins, M. (2011, January 29). At X Games, battle for sponsors is also fierce. *The New York Times,* pp. B9, B10.

Hill, J. (2014, October 15). Netflix acquires streaming rights to Friends complete series. Retrieved from http://fansided.com/2014/10/15/netflix-streaming-friends-complete-series-2015/

History of the Rose Parade. (2015). [Web page]. Retrieved from http://www.tournamentofroses.com/history/rose-parade

Hollywood Foreign Press Association. (n.d.). Members [Web page]. Retrieved from http://www.hfpa.org/members/

Hyatt, A. (n.d.). 9 critical things you should know about music publicity before you make your first move. Retrieved from http://www.hypebot.com/hypebot/2011/10/9-critical-things-you-should-know-about-music-publicity-before-you-make-your-first-move-.html

IMDb.com. (n.d.). Film and television show listings by title. [Wiki].

Independent Games Festival. (2015). About the IGF [Web page]. Retrieved from http://www.igf.com/01about.html

International Federation of the Phonographic Industry (IFPI). (n.d.). Global statistics. Retrieved from http://ifpi.org/global-statistics.php

IPhone Development 101. (2015). Promoting your app. Retrieved from http://www.idev101.com/code/Marketing/promotion.html

James, M. (2016, January 22). The cost of Oscar furor? *The New York Times,* pp. C1, C5.

Jarvey, N. (2015, June 12). The most tweeted TV this season. *The Hollywood Reporter,* 14.

Judd, L. R. (1995). An approach to ethics in the information age. *Public Relations Review, 21*(1), 35–44.

Keath, J. (2011, May 2). Top corporate blogs, finalists announced. Retrieved from http://social-fresh.com/top-corporate-blog/

Kenneally, T. (2014, November 25). Ratings: Canceled "Queen Latifah Show" hit a season high right before the ax fell. Retrieved from http://www.thewrap.com/ratings-canceled-queen-latifah-show-hit-a-season-high-right-before-the-ax-fell/

Kiladis, G. (2014, December 17). Mobile game marketing in 2015. Retrieved from http://www.gamesindustry.biz/articles/2014-12-16-mobile-game-marketing-in-2015

Klepek, P. (2014, November 20). Steam updates early access rules, guidelines for developers. Retrieved from http://www.giantbomb.com/articles/steam-updates-early-access-rules-guidelines-for-de/1100-5101/

Knab, C. (2011, June). Words of wisdom from a music publicity pro: 25 music publicity tips from the mind of a publicity genius … Howard Bloom. Retrieved from http://www.music-bizacademy.com/knab/articles/musicpublicity.htm

Krantz, M. (2015, October 27). "Halo" mania invades video-game wars. Retrieved from http://www.usatoday.com/story/money/markets/2015/10/26/halo-microsoft-launch-game-xbox/74664968/

Kritsch, A. (2013). Six top athletes using social media to dominate [Blog post]. Retrieved from http://blog.hootsuite.com/top-athletes-social-media/

Kurutz, S. (2015, August 16). A brief history of the tough star profile. *The New York Times*, pp. 8–9.

Lang, B. (2014a, August 24). "If I Stay," "Sin City 2" and the trouble with tracking. Retrieved from http://variety.com/2014/film/news/if-i-stay-sin-city-2-tracking-box-office-1201289315/

Lang, B. (2014b, August, No. 4). Summer box office swings and misses. *Variety*, 36–37.

Laporte, N. (2013, November 26). Why "Ironman 3" squashed "Ironman 2," according to Hollywood's data-whispering script consultant. Retrieved from http://www.fastcocreate.com/1682939/why-iron-man-3-squashed-iron-man-2-according-to-hollywoods-data-whispering-script-consultant

Lee, C. (2015, January 30/February 6). How to win an Oscar in 34 days. *Entertainment Weekly*, 15–17.

Levine, R. (2008, May 5). An alternative approach to marketing rock bands. *The New York Times*, p. C8.

Levy, T. W. (2015). The Engagement Project: Connecting with your consumer in the participation age. *Think with Google*. Retrieved from https://www.thinkwithgoogle.com/articles/engagement-project-new-normal.html

Lieberman, A., & Esgate, P. (2014). *The definitive guide to entertainment marketing: Bringing the moguls, the media, and the magic to the world* (2nd ed.). Upper Saddle River, NJ: Pearson.

Littleton, C. (2015a, January, No. 3). TCA takeaways: New stars, trends, tchotchkes. *Variety*, 19.

Littleton, C. (2015b, February 11). TV's new math: Networks crunch their own ratings to track multiplatform viewing. Retrieved from http://variety.com/2015/tv/features/broad-cast-nets-move-closer-to-developing-ratings-that-consider-auds-delayed-viewing-hab-its-1201430321/

Longwell, T. (2015, February, No. 3). PR pros fighting blizzard of tech wizardry: Unit publicists chase miscreant merchants peddling storms of nicked images. *Variety*, 85–86.

Lowenstein, S. (2002). *My first movie: 20 celebrated directors talk about their first film*. New York, NY: Penguin.

Lowry, B. (2014, February 20). Emmy rules change restores movie and miniseries split. Retrieved from http://variety.com/2014/tv/news/emmy-rules-change-restores-movie-and-miniseries-split-1201114252/

Lowry, B. (2015, February, No. 1). What every Hollywood crisis manager could learn from NFL. *Variety*, 26.

Luistro, K. (2015). *The unbreakable PR efforts of an online original series*. Unpublished undergraduate paper, Comm465: Entertainment PR, California State University, Fullerton.

Macy, S. G. (2015, January 28). Here are the sales numbers for Wii U. Retrieved from http://www.ign.com/articles/2015/01/28/here-are-the-sales-numbers-for-wii-u

Maglio, T. (2014, February 19). The most and least liked morning TV hosts—From Robin Roberts to Kathie Lee Gifford. Retrieved from http://www.thewrap.com/q-scores/

Manjoo, F. (2015, October 5). The dawn of social TV. *The New York Times*, p. F3.

Marich, R. (2013). Chapter 11: Indies. In *Marketing to moviegoers: A lively handbook explaining cinema marketing* (3rd ed.). Carbondale: Southern Illinois University Press. Retrieved from http://marketingmovies.net/chapters/chapter-11-indies/

Martens, T. (2014, September 6). Ugly side of gaming comes to light. *Los Angeles Times*, pp. D1, D7.

Martens, T. (2015a, October 28). SXSW action sparks outcry. *Los Angeles Times*, pp. E1, E6.

Martens, T. (2015b, October 31). SXSW talks harassment. *Los Angeles Times*, p. E2.

Martens, T. (2015c, November 14). The magic empire: Disneyland goes big on "Star Wars," offering a glimpse of the future. *Los Angeles Times*, pp. E1, E4.

Martin, H. (2010, May 2). After dark, the dirty work at Disneyland begins. *Los Angeles Times*. Retrieved from http://articles.latimes.com/print/2010/may/02/business/la-fi-cover-disney-20100502

Maxon, S. (2013, December 10). Do Americans spend more on video games or movies? Retrieved from http://www.npr.org/sections/money/2013/12/10/247521444/do-americans-spend-more-on-video-games-or-movies

McCann, J. E., & Selsky, J. (1984). Hyperturbulence and the emergence of Type 5 environments. *The Academy of Management Review*, 9(3), 460–470.

McClintock, P. (2012, April 9). Ben Affleck's "Argo" release moves into heart of awards season. Retrieved from http://www.hollywoodreporter.com/news/ben-affleck-argo-release-date-awards-season-309723

McFarlane, B. (2015). *The Hunger Games: Mockingjay—Part 1, The Rebellion Begins*. Unpublished undergraduate paper, Comm465: Entertainment PR, California State University, Fullerton.

McGrath, B. (2014, November 24). Good game: The rise of the professional cyber athlete. *The New Yorker*, 86–97.

McNamara, M. (2015, February 2). A powerful message. *Los Angeles Times*, pp. A1, A2.

Metz, E. (2015, March 28). Why Singapore banned chewing gum. Retrieved from http://www.bbc.com/news/magazine-32090420

Michael Jordan: Adidas's biggest mistake! (2009, March 10). [YouTube interview with Darren Rovell]. Retrieved from https://www.youtube.com/watch?v=nWi_VZlIhP0

Miller, D. (2015, September 11). Disney to launch new lands in 2016. *Los Angeles Times*, p. C4.

Morris, C. (2015, July 23). The top 10 selling video games of 2015 (so far). Retrieved from http://fortune.com/2015/07/23/top-10-selling-video-games-2015-so-far/

Music Outfitters. (n.d.). Music journals, music magazines, music newspapers and music periodicals. Retrieved from http://www.musicoutfitters.com/musicpublications.htm

The national entertainment state: 10th anniversary. (2006). *The Nation*. Retrieved from http://www.thenation.com/wp-content/uploads/2015/03/2006_entertainment5.pdf

NBA: BOBCATS: Behind the scenes: Public relations. (n.d.). Retrieved from http//:www.noticias.info/asp/PrintingVersionNot.asp?NOT=153270

Nededog, J. (2012, March 29). The Voice's Christina Milian to host live-streaming after show. Retrieved from http://www.hollywoodreporter.com/live-feed/the-voice-nbc-christina-milian-after-show-305989

Need for Speed: Shift. (2015). True driver's experience. Retrieved from http://www.needfor-speed.com/shift

"New Music Fridays" go live as albums and singles switch over to global release date. (2015, July 9). [Media release]. Retrieved from http://ifpi.org/New-Music-Fridays-go-live

New "Star Trek" television series coming in 2017! (2015, November 2). [Media release]. Retrieved from http://www.prnewswire.com/news-releases/new-star-trek-television-series-coming-in-2017-300170230.html

Newman, A. A. (2014, November 4). Emotional response to team's name change. *The New York Times*, p. B5.

Ng, D. (2015, October 29). Pushes buttons in video debate: Gamergate advocate Milo Yian-nopoulos says feminism is trying to ban discussions. *Los Angeles Times*, pp. E1, E6.

Norris, K. (2015). *Mad Men: The proper goodbye*. Unpublished undergraduate paper, Comm465: Entertainment PR, California State University, Fullerton.

Nunez, J. (2013, September 12). Kanye West rants at album launch party [Blog post]. Retrieved from http://blog.sfgate.com/dailydish/2013/09/12/kanye-west-rants-at-album-launch-party/#15867101=0

Oates, G. (2015, November 4). Visit Phoenix CEO on how conventions drive down-town development. Retrieved from http://skift.com/2015/11/04/visit-phoenix-ceo-on-how-conventions-drive-downtown-development/

Peele, A. (2015, August 5). Miles Teller is young, talented, and doesn't give a rat's ass what you think. Retrieved from http://www.esquire.com/entertainment/movies/interviews/a36894/miles-teller-interview-0915/

Perebinossoff, P. (2016). *Real-world media ethics: Inside the broadcast and entertainment industries* (2nd ed.). Boston, MA: Focal Press.

Pettigrew, J. E., & Reber, B. H. (2010). The new dynamic in corporate media relations: How Fortune 500 companies are using virtual press rooms to engage the press. *Journal of Public Relations Research, 22*(4), 404–428.

Pierson, D. (2015, November 12). "Call of Duty: Black Ops III" racks up weekend sales. *Los Angeles Times*, p. C2.

Pierson, D., & Villarreal, W. (2015, June 17). Fans are new to the game: E3 morphs into a pub-licity extravaganza by letting in up to 5,000 hardcore gamers for the first time. *Los Angeles Times*, pp. C1, C4.

Public Relations Society of America (PRSA). (2009–2015). PRSA Member code of ethics. Retrieved from http://www.prsa.org/AboutPRSA/Ethics/documents/Code%20of%20Eth-ics.pdf

Public Relations Society of America (PRSA). (2012, March 2). Public relations defined. Retrieved from https://www.prsa.org/AboutPRSA/PublicRelationsDefined/index.html#.VjmXrqS8A-8

Queen drops f-bomb during Christmas speech. (2014, December 25). [Video]. Retrieved from https://www.youtube.com/watch?v=H9Kq6tKtzAI

Raczkowski, F. (2012). "And what do you play?": A few considerations concerning a genre theory of games. In J. Fromme & A. Unger (Eds.), *Computer games and new media cultures: A handbook of digital games studies* (pp. 61–74). Heidelberg, Germany: Springer.

Rancilio, A. (2014, December 13). Show-runners on rise as TV Twitter celebrities. *Desert Sun*, p. E1.

The Recording Academy. (n.d.). Music in the schools [Web page]. Retrieved from http://www.grammy.org/grammy-foundation/grammy-in-the-schools

The Recording Academy Today. (n.d.). [Online brochure]. Retrieved from https://www.grammy.org/files/grammys_org_brochure_resized.pdf

Rhoden, W. C. (2014, August 29). N.F.L. rights a wrong, but only after further (and further) review. *The New York Times*, p. B11.

Roberts, R. (2014, December 6). Music-industrial complex flexes its muscle once again. *Los Angeles Times*, pp. D1, D10.

Rose, L. (2014, February 5). "Elementary's" syndication sale nets CBS a whopping $3 million an episode. Retrieved from http://www.hollywoodreporter.com/news/elementarys-syndication-sale-nets-cbs-676893

Rosen, C. (2015, February 1). The "Furious 7" Super Bowl trailer is better than the Super Bowl. Retrieved from http://www.huffingtonpost.com/2015/02/01/furious-7-super-bowl-trailer_n_6581612.html

Rothberg, J., & Brown, E. (2014, August 15). Widow says Williams had Parkinson's. *Los Angeles Times*, pp. AA1, AA4.

Rubenstein, H. J. (2014, August 20). The power of a stunt [Letter to the editor]. *The New York Times*, p. A18.

Saad, N. (2014, September 23). Taylor Swift fans treated to "1989" listening party at singer's home. Retrieved from http://www.latimes.com/entertainment/gossip/la-et-mg-taylor-swift-1989-fan-listening-party-secret-sessions-20140923-story.html

Salcido, M. (2015). *Showtime with the Lakers*. Unpublished undergraduate paper, Comm465: Entertainment PR, California State University, Fullerton.

Sarkeesian, A. (2014, October 29). Game over for the "Gamers" [OpEd piece]. *The New York Times*, p. A23.

Sayre, S. (2008). *Entertainment marketing and communication: Selling branded performance, people, and places*. Upper Saddle River, NJ: Pearson.

Sayre, S. (2010). *Entertainment promotion and communication: The industry and integrated campaigns*. Dubuque, IA: Kendall Hunt.

Scott, A. O. (2014, August 29). Film festivals scramble for first dibs. *The New York Times*, pp. C1, C6.

Scott, D. M. (2011). *The new rules of marketing & PR*. Hoboken, NJ: John Wiley & Sons.

Scott, D. M. (2012). *Real-time marketing & PR*. Hoboken, NJ: John Wiley & Sons.

Shankman, P. (2007). *Can we do that?! Outrageous PR stunts that work—And why your company needs them*. Hoboken, NJ: John Wiley & Sons.

Sisario, B. (2012, May 7). Out to shake up music, often with sharp words. *The New York Times*, pp. B1, B8.

Sisario, B. (2014a, July 24). No joke! He's topping the charts. *The New York Times*, pp. C1, C4.

Sisario, B. (2014b, August 18). Taylor Swift maximizes use of social media in release of new album. Retrieved from http://www.nytimes.com/2014/08/19/business/media/taylor-swift-maximizes-use-of-social-media-in-release-of-new-album.html?_r=0

Sisario, B. (2015a, August 16). "Cheerleader"? "See You Again"? Looking for the next summer song. *The New York Times*, pp. 26–27.

Sisario, B. (2015b, September 15). Streaming fuels rise to top of album chart. *The New York Times*, p. C3.

Sisario, B. (2015c, October 5). Managers say Ticketmaster hinders bands' fan services. *The New York Times*, p. B4.

Smith, T. (2011, August 23). Disney Parks Mobile Magic app is now free. Retrieved from http://disneyparks.disney.go.com/blog/2011/08/disney-parks-mobile-magic-app-is-now-free/

Spangler, T. (2015, July, No. 3). Why movie marketers snuck in on VidCon's turf. *Variety*, 12.

Spector, J. (2015, March 24). Five bold predictions for the 2015 Chicago Cubs. Retrieved from http://www.sportingnews.com/mlb/story/2015-03-24/cubs-2015-preview-lineup-predic-tions-fantasy-world-series-joe-maddon-kris-bryant-jorge-soler

Sperling, N., & Littleton, C. (2005, April 28). The art of creating awareness for Hollywood product has always been crucial to the industry. *The Hollywood Reporter*, S1–S3, S8.

Spin Lists. (n.d.). Best new artists. Retrieved from http://www.spin.com/lists/

Stadiums of Pro Football. (2015). [Web page]. Retrieved from http://www.stadiumsofprofoot-ball.com/afc/NRGStadium.htm

Steel, E. (2015a, January 19). ComScore to tally viewers across their many devices. *The New York Times*, p. B2.

Steel, E. (2015b, January 29). Pepsi's Super Bowl ad blitz starts a conversation early. *The New York Times*, p. B3.

Steel, E. (2015c, September 30). Merger deal for comScore and Rentrak. *The New York Times*, p. B5.

Stein, A. (2011). *Why we love Disney: The power of the Disney brand*. New York, NY: Peter Lang.

Stein, A. (2015). *Attracting attention: Promotion and marketing for tourism attractions*. New York, NY: Peter Lang.

Stein, A., & Evans, B. B. (2009). *An introduction to the entertainment industry*. New York, NY: Peter Lang.

Steinberg, S. (2011, May 9). Video game marketing: The new bible part 1. Retrieved from http://www.gamesindustry.biz/articles/2011-05-09-video-game-marketing-the-new-bible-article

Stoldt, G. C., Dittmore, S. W., & Branvold, S. E. (2012). *Sport public relations: Managing stakeholder communications*. Champaign, IL: Human Kinetics.

Suellentrop, C. (2014, October 26). Can video games survive? *The New York Times*, pp. SR1, SR7.

Surowiecki, J. (2015, February 23 & March 2). The financial page: Rethinking the seasonal strategy. *The New Yorker*, 76.

Sweetser, K. D. (2010). A losing strategy: The impact of nondisclosure in social media on relationships. *Journal of Public Relations Research*, 22(3), 288–312.

Take-Two Interactive. (2013, September 20). Grand Theft Auto V worldwide sales surpass $1 billion in first three days: Fastest entertainment property in history to reach significant milestone [Press release]. Retrieved from http://ir.take2games.com/phoenix.zhtml?c=86428&p=irol-newsArticle_print&ID=1856686

Telekinetic coffee shop surprise. (2013, October 7). [*Carrie* YouTube video]. Retrieved from https://www.youtube.com/watch?v=VlOxlSOr3_M

Thomsen, M. (2009, August 11). Public relations in games: The science of secrets. Retrieved from http://www.gamasutra.com/view/feature/132492/public_relations_in_games_the_.php

Thunderclap. (2015). Thunderclap amplifies your message with the power of the crowd [Website video]. Retrieved from https://www.thunderclap.it

TMZ.com. (2012, May 30). Kim Kardashian: Luggage thieves jacked priceless sunglasses: Exclusive. Retrieved from http://www.tmz.com/2012/05/30/kim-kardashian-luggage-stolen-british-airways/

Trade Publications List: Industry: Sports (n.d.). [Web page]. Retrieved from http://www.webwire.com/TradePublications.asp?ind=SPT&curpage=1

TuneCore. (n.d.). What is TuneCore? [Web page]. Retrieved from http://www.tunecore.com/index/what_is_tunecore

Twittercounter. (2016, January 31). Top 100 most followers. Retrieved from http://twittercounter.com/pages/100

Unbreakable Kimmy Schmidt. (2015, February 6). @The Kimmy Schmidt "Who has a tape player?" [Tweet]. Retrieved from https://mobile.twitter.com/TheKimmySchmidt/status/563791495472631809

Vail Cascade Resort & Spa. (2015). Experience everything summer Vail has to offer [Web page]. Retrieved from http://www.vailcascade.com/vail-summer-vacations.php

Vodnala, S. (2015, June 24). Now playing in movie theaters: Video games. *Los Angeles Times*, p. C3.

Wachter, P. (2009, February 1). You just can't keep the girls from jamming. *The New York Times Magazine*, 18–21.

Wagmeister, E. (2015, January 15). "The Royals" renewed for Season 2 before series debut on E! Retrieved from http://variety.com/2015/tv/news/the-royals-e-scripted-series-season-2-renewal-1201404541/

The Walt Disney Company. (2012). Disney newsroom: Social media index. Retrieved from http://thewaltdisneycompany.com/disney-news

Wasteland 2. (2012). Wasteland 2 by inXile Entertainment [Kickstarter project]. Retrieved from https://www.kickstarter.com/projects/inxile/wasteland-2?ref=nav_search

Waters, R. D., Tindall, N. T. J., & Morton, T. S. (2010). Media catching and the journalist-public relations practitioner relationship: How social media are changing the practice of media relations. *Journal of Public Relations Research, 22*(3), 241–264.

Wedge, D. (2012, April 26). Bruins "disappointed" by fans' racist Twitter comments. Retrieved from http://news.bostonherald.com/news/regional/view.bg?articleid=1061127350

Weiner, J. (2015a, June 18). Comedy Central in the post-TV era: The network is in the middle of a creative renaissance—and a business-model crisis. Retrieved from http://myti.ms/1GuiWM9

Weiner, J. (2015b, June 21). The laugh factory: Comedy Central in the post-TV era. *The New York Times Magazine*, 38–45, 52–55.

Weisman, A. (2012, October 4). Meet the 20 most powerful publicists in Hollywood (ranked). *Business Insider*. Retrieved from http://www.businessinsider.com/20-most-powerful-publicists-in-hollywood-2012-10?op=1

Welc, D. (2015). Gone Girl *public relations examination: How meta can we get?* Unpublished undergraduate paper, Comm465: Entertainment PR, California State University, Fullerton.

Welcome: Portraits of America. (2007). [Video]. Retrieved from https://www.youtube.com/watch?v=2NpHwYrlXWY

Wharton, D. (2015, November 13). Cricket gets turn at bat at Chavez Ravine. *Los Angeles Times*, p. D10.

Wicks, F. (2015). *Public relations: The Cinderella movie's fairy godmother*. Unpublished undergraduate paper, Comm465: Entertainment PR, California State University, Fullerton.

Williamson, P. (2015, September 5). The difference between a successful band, and YOUR band. Retrieved from http://www.musicthinktank.com/blog/the-difference-between-a-successful-band-and-your-band.html

Wingfield, N. (2014, August 26). What's Twitch? Gamers know and Amazon spent $1 billion on it. *The New York Times*, pp. A1, B4.

Wingfield, N. (2015a, October 27). SXSW event calls off game panels after threats. *The New York Times*, p. B3.

Wingfield, N. (2015b, November 9). Game makers will again have their night. *The New York Times*, p. B6.

Wood, M. (2014, August 19). Swift pops open "1989." *Los Angeles Times*, p. D2.

Word of Mouth Marketing Association (WOMMA). (2009). WOMMA ethics code. Retrieved from http://womma.org/ethics

Worldwide Motion Picture Group. (n.d.). [LinkedIn company profile]. Retrieved from https://www.linkedin.com/company/worldwide-motion-picture-group

Yoshimo, K. (2007, November 14). A ride to the great beyond at Disneyland: Secret scattering of remains at parks, golf courses and other sites may be growing. Retrieved from http://articles.latimes.com/2007/nov/14/business/fi-disney14

Zal, D. (2015). *The media and public relations attributions of* Furious 7. Unpublished undergraduate paper, Comm465: Entertainment PR, California State University, Fullerton.

Zecher, A. (2014, September 1). Open letter to the gaming community. Retrieved from https://medium.com/@andreaszecher/open-letter-to-the-gaming-community-df4511032e8a#.xgar3j9hj

INDEX

A

ACDC, 221

A&E, 119

A&R, 207–08, 213
  music development, 208

AAA title. *See* Blockbuster video game

ABC network, 44, 49, 56, 74–75, 77, 83, 89, 104, 116, 126, 219–20

About/Boilerplate. *See* Boilerplate/About

Above-the-line, 133–34, 141

Academy Awards (Oscars), 62, 71–73, 82, 84, 162, 272
  See also Oscar public relations cycle
  announcement, 184–85
  campaigns, 182–83
  eligibility, 182
  fundraising objective, 74
  Governors Ball, 71
  nominations, 73, 184
  public relations cycle (*see* Oscar public relations cycle)
  publicity value, 72–73, 184–85
  television broadcast, 74

Academy of Interactive Arts & Sciences, 238

Academy of Motion Picture Arts and Sciences (Motion Picture Academy), 11, 73–74, 84, 180–83
  Margaret Herrick Library, 74
  Museum of Motion Pictures, 74
  nonprofit initiatives, 74
  president (*see* Isaacs, Cheryl Boone)
  producing Oscars, 72–73

Academy of Television Arts and Sciences (Television Academy), 74–76
  Archive of American Television, 75
  Emmys (*see* Emmy Awards)

Access Hollywood, 15, 50, 79, 97, 111, 157, 160, 174

Accredited investor, 168, 186

Activision Blizzard, 231–32, 248

Adidas, 199–200

Advertising (ad), 12, 25–26, 46, 111, 233, 245

See also Controlled PR
advertorial, 46
agency, 11–12, 82, 154, 194
banners, 190, 268
billboards, 91, 104, 137, 154, 159, 195
bus/bus stop, 91, 104
online, 244
outdoor, 91, 104, 134
paid content, 46, 233
print, 12, 46, 83, 91, 32,
vs. public relations, 91, 104
radio, 114
television commercials, 12, 80, 132
Advertising Dept., 91
Advertising Review Council (ARC),
    232–33
Advertising Sales Dept., 90
Affiliate Relations Dept., 92
Affleck, Ben, 141, 182
Agency. *See* Public relations agency;
    Advertising: agency
Air Force, 54
Airbnb, 254
ALA Ass., 178
Album launch parties, 80
Alert line, 65
A-list, 44, 68–69
Alpha testing, 229
AMAs, 219–20
Amazon, 107, 126–27, 129, 189, 249
AMC, 119–20
American Music Awards. *See* AMAs
America's Got Talent, 56
Ames, Carol, 3, 36, 118, 155, 231, 260
Anderson Live, 115
Android smartphone, 231
Angles for stories, 13, 16, 26–27, 31, 77,
    123, 140–41, 149, 153–54, 162, 170,
    189, 198, 210, 216–17, 222, 255–56,
    267–68, 270, 272
    local angle, 23, 173, 210–11
    negative angle, 26
Anniversary event, 8, 66, 101, 267–68,
    273–75

Annual report, 33, 46
AP. *See* Associated Press
AP style. *See* Associated Press/AP
Apatow, Judd, 56
App public relations cycle, 227, 229, 232,
    244–45, 255
Apple, 92, 245
    Apple Music, 210, 212
    developer publicity, 245
    iOS, 231
    iPhone, 49, 245
Apps, 3, 49, 54, 99
Approval process, 31–32, 48, 156
ARC. *See* Advertising Review Council
Argo, 182, 183
Armstrong, Lance, 203
Aronson, Merry. *See* MerryMedia
Artist, The, 167
Artists and Repertoire. *See* A&R
Associated Press (AP)
    style, 27
    Stylebook, 27
Atlanta Journal-Constitution, 16
Athlete endorsement. *See* Celebrity
    endorsement
*Attracting Attention: Promotion and Marketing
    for Tourism Attractions*, 254
Audience expectations. *See* Customer
    expectations
Audience questionnaire, 145, 148
Audience segmentation, 21–24, 29
    film, 23, 144–45, 169
    niche audience, 119, 129, 145, 148, 169
    public relations plan, 135
    television, for, 23
    urban vs. rural (TV), 23, 93, 95
    video games, 228
Audience share, 23
Avatar, 144
Award event, 62, 64–65
Award PR cycle. *See* Emmy or Oscar public
    relations cycles
Awareness objective, 51–52, 64, 66–67,
    102–103

B

Back-end deal, 171
Background, 26, 32, 98
   backgrounder, 157
   less important information, 30, 32
   media alert, 66
   media releases, 28, 30–32
   public relations plan, 132, 135–37, 142,
     145, 161–62, 169, 234–37, 256, 258
Backpacker, 198
Balanced story. *See* Ethics: journalistic
Bandcamp, 213
Bankable elements, 141–42, 147, 151–53,
   166–67
Baseball, 14, 64, 154, 190, 192–94, 203,
   248, 263, 266, 271
   See also Sports public relations cycle
Basketball, 125, 192–94, 197–98, 248,
   271–72
   See also Sports public relations cycle
Basic cable, 110, 115–16, 118–19,
   212, 129
   channels (*see specific listings*)
Basic cable public relations cycle, 118–21,
   125–26, 28
Bateman, Jason, 7, 125
Batman v Superman, 158
Battlefield franchise, 232
Beckham, David, 48
Behind-the-scenes, 75, 120, 132, 141, 174,
   265, 275
   photography, 157, 174
   video, 51, 157, 174
Beijing Olympics, 72
Bellagio Hotel, 265
Below-the-line personnel, 133–34
Best Buy, 229
Beta testing, 229–30
Better Call Saul, 120
Beyoncé, 214, 217, 221
Bicycle Retailer and Industry News, 198
Bieber, Justin, 212–13
Big Bang Theory, 109–11

Big Boy's Neighborhood, 16
Billboard, 14, 82, 209–10, 216, 224
   Charts, 210
Birdman, 184
Bjork, 222
Binge viewing public relations cycle,
   126–28
Blockbuster motion pictures, 131–62
Blockbuster motion picture public relations
   cycle, 132, 151–62
   bankable elements, 141–42, 147, 151–53,
     166–67
   development, 133, 135, 146–47,
     151–554
   green lighting, 146–47, 151–56
   post-production, 146, 148, 158–59
   premiere, 79–80, 134, 138, 140,
     142–44, 146, 149, 151–52, 155–60,
     162
   pre-production, 147, 153–54, 156
   pre-release, 149–51, 154–55,
     159–60
   production, 141–42, 146–48, 151,
     156–57, 158
   second week of release, 141, 144, 151,
     160–61
Blockbuster video game, 227–29
Blockbuster video game public relations
   cycle, 230, 233–43
   background and situation analysis,
     234–35
   communications opportunity/problem,
     238–39
   content marketing, 241–42
   buyer personas, 239–40
   development, 229, 233–34
   downloadable content, 229, 232, 242
   goal, 239
   post-release, 242–43
   pre-release, 230
   production, 229–30, 233–35,
     241–42
   release, 229–34, 240–42
   SWOT, 237–38

Blogs, 3, 17, 41–42, 44, 46–49, 53–55, 57–58, 99, 216, 241–43, 263
   official, 55, 156
   unofficial, 4, 49, 54–55
Blood Simple, 168
Bloomberg News, 15
Blowback, 258
Bluefin Labs, 51
Body of media releases, 30
Boilerplate/About, 28, 32–33
   media alert, 66
   media releases, 28, 32–33
Bornstein, Steve, 248
Boroshok, Jon, 255
Boston Globe, 255
Boston Herald.com, 53
Boston Red Sox, 291
Box-office gross, 5, 29, 72–73, 132, 135, 142–44, 150, 182, 184
Box-office potential, 142, 147
Box-office split, 143
B-roll, 139–40
Bravo, 50, 119, 121–22, 128–29
Breaking Bad, 120
Breaking the rules, 214
Bright, Torah, 196
British Airways, 56
Broadcast Dept., 91
Broadcast Standards & Practices Dept. (BS&P), 44, 90–91
Brochure, 9, 12, 33, 46
Brown, Chris, 215
Bryant, Kobe, 125, 199
BS&P. *See* Broadcast Standards & Practices Dept.
Bud Light, 194
Budget. *See also* Above-the-line talent; Below-the-line personnel
   advertising, 12, 134, 182
   blockbuster motion picture, 18, 29, 132–34, 142, 144, 152
   event, 67
   independent film, 166–67, 170–71, 174, 182, 184

   marketing budget, 132, 134, 145, 166, 170, 184, 221, 244
   music, 221
   public relations plan, 2, 4–5, 46, 59, 67, 83, 134, 145, 169–70, 179, 211, 214, 256
   television, 118
   30–50 percent rule of thumb, 132
   tourism, 256
   video game, 237, 243–44, 250
Business, The. See KCRW
Business Affairs & Legal Dept., 90
Business media, 13–15, 18–19, 153
Buyer personas, 24–25, 29, 145, 170, 239–40, 257
Buzz, 6, 24–25, 68, 78–79, 98, 117, 119, 120, 141, 147, 150, 162, 167, 177, 180, 182–85, 225
BWR, 10

C

Cable channels. *See* Basic cable; Premium cable
Caesar's Palace, 265
Call of Duty, franchise, 227, 241
Cameron, James, 144
Carousel of Hope Ball, 70
Carrie PR stunt, 179
Casting Dept., 90
Casual game public relations cycle, 244–45
CBS network, 3, 75, 77–78, 89, 101, 110, 126, 220–22, 226
CCO. *See* Chief communications officer
Celebrity crisis PR image-repair cycle, 7–8, 122–26
   disappear, 124
   Hancock, 7–8, 19, 124–25
   misbehavior, 122, 125
   statement (*see* Press statement: celebrity)
   reappear, 125
Celebrity endorsement, 42, 44, 51–52, 179, 187, 199–200

CEO. *See* Chief executive officer
CES. *See* Consumer Electronics Show
CFO. *See* Chief financial officer
Chamber of Commerce, 258
Charlotte Hornets, 197–98
Charter Cable, 11
Chicago Cubs, 191
    Wrigley Field, 191
Chicago Tribune, 16
Chief communications officer (CCO), 8,
    266
Chief executive officer (CEO), 266
Chief financial officer (CFO), 266
Chief operating officer (COO), 266
China, 46, 72, 125, 155
    Great Wall of, 72
Christmas
    film release, 82, 138
    music, 217, 219–20
    season (tourism), 264, 265, 266, 271, 273
    television, 102, 182–84
Cinderella, 135, 142
CinemaCon, 81–82
CinemaScore, 146, 150
Cirque du Soleil, 71
Cision, 16, 17
Clearances, 112–13
Cleveland Cavaliers, 198
Clips
    film clips, 22, 79, 156, 159, 161, 172
    press clips, 109, 172–74, 209–10, 226
    television clips, 77–78, 90, 98, 192
Clooney, George, 68
Closed season. *See under* Tourism public
    relations cycle
CMAs. *See* Country Music Association
    Award
CNBC, 15, 18, 179
CNN, 3, 48, 115
Code of ethics, 41–43, 44–45, 48
Coen brothers, 168
Collaborative filtering, 189, 204
College sports, 188–89, 191, 203
    Big Ten, 263
    Rose Bowl, 261, 272

Comcast, 3, 44, 119
Comedy Central, 119, 145
Comic-Con International, 157–58
Comments policy, 53
Commercial speech, 41
Communications opportunity, 5–6, 18, 75,
    77, 81, 92, 113–14, 141, 169, 185, 215,
    238–39, 242–43, 266, 268
Communications problem, 5–8, 18, 39, 92,
    124–25, 141–42, 169, 202, 238–39,
    258, 269, 274
Community Relations Dept. *See*
    Government & Community
    Relations Dept.
ComScore/Rentrak, 94
Conan O'Brien Show, The, 110
Conglomerates, 3, 41
ConnecTV, 51
ConstantContact.com, 211
Consumer Electronics Show (CES), 230–31
Consumer media, 13, 15, 77, 158, 198, 210,
    218
Consumer publicity, 153–54, 217
Content marketing, 120, 241–42, 246
Contests (legal), 17, 49, 99, 103, 111, 159,
    194
    definition, 114–15
Contracts, 46, 90, 110, 113, 115, 195, 208
    music, 207–08
    publicity clauses, 68, 69, 121, 159
    union, 108, 133–34, 152, 168, 197
Controlled PR, 44–45, 46, 57–58. *See also*
    annual report
    brochure
    email marketing
    newsletter
    Twitter
Controversy, 13, 73, 92, 94, 123, 141, 183,
    190, 195, 202–203, 219, 228, 232,
    235–37, 247, 249. *See also* Public
    relations crisis cycle
COO. *See* Chief operating officer
Cooper, Anderson, 115
Corbet, Philip B., 48
Corporate communications, 6, 8–9, 254

Corporate social responsibility (CSR), 6, 188, 195, 198, 200–202

Corporate standards of ethics, 47–48

Cosmopolitan, 15

Cost per install (CPI), 244

Costa Concordia, 8–9

Country Music Association Awards (CMAs), 220

Cowboys and Aliens, 154

CPI. *See* Cost per install

Craigslist.com, 11

Crisis management. *See* Public relations crisis cycle

Crisis PR cycle. *See* Public relations crisis cycle

CRM. *See* Customer relationship management

Cross-brand tie-in, 121, 153–56, 170, 199, 257

CSI: Los Angeles, 22

CSR. *See* Corporate social responsibility

C-Suite, 265–66

Current Programming Dept., 90, 91

Customer comments online, 2, 25, 39, 43, 47, 49, 52–54, 56, 58, 78, 101, 124, 194, 199, 238, 274

official blogs, 55

responding to, 53–55

unofficial sites, 54–55

Customer expectations, 25

beating, 143–44, 160

disappointing, 25, 160–62

events, 68

marketing creates, 25

sports, 191, 195

television ratings, 95

travel, 257–58, 259, 261, 262, 263, 274

video games, 234

Customer perceptions, 258–59

Customer relationship management (CRM), 211–12

Customer tradition, 266, 273

CW network, The, 80, 89, 101

Cyrus, Miley, 219

D

D23, 273

Daly, Tim, 56–57

Dateline in media releases, 28, 30

Davis, Barbara, 70

DeadlineHollywood.com (deadline.com), 15, 50, 56–57, 98, 152

Deadpool, 158

Debt financing, 158

DeGeneres, Ellen, 111, 213, 218, 222

Delivering the dream, 261–63

Demographics, 13, 22–24, 29, 204

definition, 22

film, 144–45, 159 (*see also* Quadrants)

television, 93, 95, 102, 104, 109, 114 (*see also* Nielsen ratings)

tourism, 257

video games, 228–29, 237

Destination identity, 256

Development Dept., 90

Development publicity. *See under a specific public relations cycle*

DGA, 134, 182

DGA Awards, 182

D.I.C.E. video game awards, 238

Digital strategies, 38–39, 46–47, 98–99, 120–22, 211–15, 274

Directors Guild of America. *See* DGA

DirecTV, 119

Disasters, 138–39. *See also* Crisis public relations cycle

Disclosure required, 42

affiliation, 42

material connections (payments), 42

origin, 38, 42, 47

Disney, 3, 49, 133, 135

fan club, 273

merchandise, 135, 155–56

Shanghai store, photo, 156

"Star Wars" attraction, 266–67

Disney/ABC. *See* ABC network

Disney Parks Blog, 44, 53, 55

Disneyland, 54, 264

Halloween Party, 265

Jungle (Jingle) Cruise, 264
 season pass, 273
Distribution deal, 179–80
DLC. *See* Downloadable content
Doritos, 194
Doughty, Rob, 269
Downloadable content (DLC), 229, 232,
 242, 250
Dr. Phil, 115
Dream (tourism PR), 261–63
 delivering, 261
 destroying, 262
 selling of, 259–63
 updating, 262–63
Drive-time. *See* Radio: drive–time
Drone racing, 204. *See also* Sports public
 relations cycle
Drunk Wedding, 166
Duck Dynasty, 121
DVR, 23, 94–95. *See also* Time shifting; VOD

E

E! Entertainment Television, 15, 50, 77, 80,
 97, 119–20, 129
E3. *See* Electronic Entertainment Expo
Early access, video games, 245–47, 250
Electronic Arts, 231–34, 238–39, 247
Electronic Entertainment Expo (E3), 238,
 241, 247
Electronic press kit for film (EPK), 157,
 172–76
Elementary, 110
Elevator pitch, 175
Ellen DeGeneres Show, The, 111, 218
Email marketing, 211–12
Embargo, 28. *See also* For immediate release
Eminem, 221
Emmy Awards, 74–78, 83–84
 as headline stimulants, 34
 PR cycle (*See* Emmy public relations cycle)
 producer, 74–75
 red carpet, 77–78, 96, 114, 117, 128
 statuette photo, 76

Emmy pubic relations cycle, 75–78,
 102–104, 117–18, 128
Emmys. *See* Emmy Awards
Empire, 100
Employment. *See* Jobs; Jobs in
 entertainment PR
Endorsement. *See* Celebrity endorsement
Engle, Mary K., 44
Entertainment beat, 12, 15–16, 33. *See also*
 Journalists
Entertainment industry, 3–6, 38, 49,
 50–51, 58. *See also under* Event
 strategy
 management structure, 89–92
Entertainment Publicists Professional
 Society (EPPS), 4, 11
Entertainment Research and Marketing,
 LLC, 148
Entertainment Software Association (ESA),
 228, 232
Entertainment Software Ratings Board
 (ESRB), 232–33
Entertainment Tonight, 15, 50, 79, 97, 157
Entertainment Weekly, 15
EPK. *See* Electronic press kit
Equity investment. *See* Equity partners
Equity partners, 168
ESA. *See* Entertainment Software
 Association
ESPN, 49, 119, 196, 203, 248
eSports, 248–49. *See also* Sports public
 relations cycle
eSports Arena, Anaheim, Calif., 249
Esquire, 157
ESRB. *See* Entertainment Software Ratings
 Board
ESRB ratings, 232–22
 rules for advertisers, 232–33
 rules for PR, 233
Ethics, 39–44, 58–59
 codes of ethics, 41–43, 44–45
 corporate standards, 47–48
 journalistic, 39–40, 123–24
  balanced story, 40–41
  multiple sources, 40

online, 48–52
public relations, 40
Event public relations cycle, 68–84
Event strategy, 61–84
   attendance, 64, 67
   awareness objective, 64–65, 66–67
   budget, 67
   charity, 8, 64, 70–71, 92, 103, 170, 188,
      201, 222, 266
   elements of (*see below* WOW factors)
   entertainment industry events, 62, 64,
      67, 68–84
   media coverage objective, 62, 64–67,
      70–72, 79, 83
   memorable impression, 62–63, 70–71,
      79, 83
   objectives, 64–67, 71
   party elements (*see below* WOW factors)
   security, 69, 79
   sponsorships, 71, 80
   types of (*see listings for types of events*)
   vendors (*see* Vendors)
   WOW factors, 62–63, 67–72
      #1: guest list/invitations, 62, 68–69
      #2: venue/décor/date, 63, 69–70
      #3: food (and drinks), 63, 70–71
      #4: entertainment, 63, 71
      #5: souvenir gift bag, 63, 71
Executive producer
   independent film, 167–70
   television, 100
Expectations. *See* Customer expectations
Extending high season, 264–65
Extra, 79

F

Facebook, 44–47, 98–99, 156
   character pages, 99–100
   company pages, 48, 49
   controlled PR, 46
   customer feedback on, 47
   endorsements, 44
   ethics, 44, 48

likes, 12, 47, 101, 150
links to, 50–51, 172, 202
measurement (*see* Social media
   measurement)
ownership of content, 55
public relations uses, 29–30, 150, 192,
   196, 199, 213, 216
publishing on, 34
timelines, 179
two-way conversations, 46, 47, 99, 101
uncontrolled PR, 46–47
viral posts, 30, 120
word of mouth, 25, 51–52, 245
Fact sheets, 27, 157, 174
Fan community, 2, 17, 99, 101, 140,
   158–59, 189, 230, 250
Fan sites, 4, 46, 49, 54–55, 58
Fandango, 150
Fans, 2–4, 6–7, 55, 57–58, 101
   film, 23, 29, 140–42, 152, 155, 158–60
   music, 208, 211–16, 223–26
   sports, 52, 188–203, 263
   television, 78, 99, 101–02, 109, 120, 122,
      124
   tourism, 267, 273
   video games, 232–34, 237–38, 241–43,
      247–49
   word of mouth, 158–60
Fantasy sports, 203. *See also* Sports public
   relations cycle
Fashion Police, 222
Fast and Furious franchise, 148. *See also*
   Furious 7
Fast ratings. *See* Overnights
FBI, 235
FCC. *See* Federal Communications
   Commission
Fearless Records, 213
Federal Communications Commission
   (FCC), 41, 44, 58, 88, 89, 90, 114
Federal Trade Commission (FTC), 38,
   41–42, 44, 46, 58
Fendi, 71
Ferrell, Will, 191–92
Festival participation press release, 176–77

5ᵗʰ *Wave, The*, 155
Fight Club, 149
Film distribution, 5–6, 165–69, 171–72,
    177, 180–85
  planting the flag, 151
  platform release, 183–84
Film festivals, 166–69, 171, 174–78,
    182–85. *See also listings of festivals*
Film franchise. *See under* Franchise
Film premiere 79–80. *See also under*
    Blockbuster motion picture public
    relations cycle
Film research, 145–50. *See also*
    CinemaScore; Focus group; Q Score;
    Test screening; Tracking survey
Film website, 156, 158–59, 170, 172–74,
    176
Firing offense, 32
First Amendment, 13
First-run syndication, 111
  NATPE, 113
  sales/clearances, 112–13
First-run syndication public relations cycle,
    111–15
  cancelation, 115
  daily PR, 114
  development, 112
  premiere
  pre-release, 114
  production, 113–14
  snowball strategy, 111, 112–13
  timeline, 111
5 W's, 25, 30, 34, 65–66
  media alert, in, 65–66
  media releases, in, 25, 39–40
Flixster, 150
Flop. *See* Hit vs. flop
Flynn, Gillian, 141
Focus group, 91, 100, 145, 146, 147–48,
    240, 259
Fogelson, Adam, 147
Football, 188, 190, 191, 192, 193, 194–96,
    197, 203, 260, 271–72.
    See also Sports public relations cycle;
    Super Bowl

For immediate release, 28, 65
  media alert, 65
  media releases, 28
For your consideration, 75, 182
Forbes, 14, 203
Fortune, 232
40 percent rule of thumb. *See under*
    Hit vs. flop
Four-quadrant film, 144
Four seasons, 263, 266, 274
Fox network, 16, 75, 77, 80, 82, 89, 100,
    109
Franchise, 179
  film, 18, 31, 69, 79, 133, 135, 137, 142,
    144, 155, 159, 161
  sports, 195–96, 200
  television, 101, 122, 125, 129
  video game, 229, 231–33, 237, 241–43,
    250
Free samples, 156
Freelance publicist, 10–11
Friend, Tad, 133–34, 157, 159
Friends, 127
Frequent buyer program, 273
Fresh Air, 15
Front page above the fold, 31
Front page story, 172, 179, 249
FTC. *See* Federal Trade Commission
Fueled by Ramen record label, 216
Fundraising objective, 64, 67, 74
Furious 7, 140–41 159
Further reading. *See lists at end of chapters*

G

Game Awards, 238
Game Developers Conference (GDC),
    243
Game devices, 229–30
Game Informer, 240
Game testing, 229–30
GamePro, 240
GamerGate, 235–37
GameStop, 229

Gaming community, 247. *See also* Fans;
    Fan community
Garbo, Greta, 68
GDC. *See* Game Developers Conference
Gehry, Frank, 267
Gem Creative, 240
Geographics, 13, 22–24, 29, 93, 211, 257
Gibson, Mel, 147
Girl Scout Motto, 138
Glamour, 15
Goal. *See* Public relations goal
Goal statement, 95–96, 239
Goff, Brian, 203
Gold standard of two-way, symmetrical
    conversation, 2, 4, 17, 39, 59, 99, 197
Golden Globe Awards, 73–74, 81, 182
Gompertz, Rolf, 28–29
Gompertz's news stimulants, 28–30, 65, 73,
    77, 141, 147, 158
Gone Girl, 141–42
Good Day Chicago, 109
Good Day LA, 16
Good Morning America (GMA), 15, 76, 108,
    218
Goodman, Gayle, 255
Google, 55, 100, 159, 263. *See also* Social
    media measurement
Government & Community Relations, 8,
    50, 89, 173, 197, 201
GPS, 159
GQ, 15
Grammy Awards (Grammys), 78, 220–22
Grand opening, 266–67
Grand Theft Auto franchise, 228, 233, 241
Gravity, 183
Gray, Tim, 175–76
Green-lighting, 153, 68–69
    blockbuster motion picture, 153
    independent film, 168–69
Grey's Anatomy, 101
Griffith, Kathy, 68
Gross, Terry, 15
Groundhog Day, 173
Grunig, J. E., 2, 39, 282

Guerilla marketing, 27, 132, 170, 178–79,
    191, 214
Guggenheim Museum (Bilbao, Spain), 267
Guilds, 4, 108, 121, 133–34, 154, 182

H

Halloween, 69, 264–66
Halo franchise, 230, 242
Hancock, 19, 124–25
Hanks, Tom, 147
HARO, 17
Hashtags (#), 49, 120, 128, 192, 195, 215,
    236
HBO, 68, 116–20, 126, 127–29, 191–92
Headline/Sub-head, 29, 65
    media alert, 65
    media releases, 29
    news stimulants (*see* News stimulants)
    uses, 29
Help-A-Reporter-Out. *See* HARO
Here Comes Honey Boo Boo, 122, 125
HGTV, 119
High-concept film. *See* Blockbuster motion
    picture
High season, 263–65, 266, 270
Hit vs. flop, 160–61
    40 percent rule of thumb, 160
Hockey, 52, 201. *See also* Sports public
    relations cycle
Hollywood as a concept. *See* Entertainment
    industry
Hollywood Blvd., 262
Hollywood, Calif., 261–62
Hollywood, FL, 82
Hollywood Foreign Press Association, 73,
    81
    Golden Globes (*see* Golden Globe
        Awards)
Hollywood Forever Cemetery, 69
Hollywood Reporter, 14, 38, 49, 65, 72, 75,
    82, 98, 152, 177, 182
HomeAway, 254

Homophobia, 48
Hook, 30, 166, 175, 217
Hootsuite, 199
Hopeless Records, 213
House of Cards, 127, 128
Households, 23, 93, 116
Households using television (HUTs), 23
Houston Texans, 197
   NRG Stadium, 197
How I Met Your Mother, 115
How to Get Away with Murder, 100
Howe, Peter, 255
HuffingtonPost.com, 16
Hughes, Howard, 262
Hulu/Hulu Plus, 89, 94, 110, 126–27
Hundreds, 244
Hunger Games franchise, 140, 158–59
Hurley, Elizabeth, 120
HUTs. *See* Households using television
Hyatt, A., 209, 223
Hype, 25, 29, 257, 259
Hyperturbulence, 123–24. *See also* Public
   relations crisis

I

IATSE, 4, 134
Ice bucket challenge, 178–79
Iconic buildings, images, monuments,
   scenery, 155, 192, 257
ICP Publicists of Local 600, IATSE. *See*
   Publicists Guild
Image URLs, 28, 30, 33
Images, 28, 30, 139, 148, 182, 258–59, 261,
   263
IMDb.com (Internet Movie Database
   website), 8, 12, 150, 156, 167, 184
Implied third-party endorsement, 25, 40, 45
In Style, 16
Independent film public relations cycle,
   169–85
   Academy Awards (*see* Oscar public rela-
     tions cycle)
   definition, 165–7

   development, 167–68
   distribution deal, 179–80
   film festival participation, 176–79, 183
     (*see also various film festivals*)
   green-lighting, 168–69
   media kit (*see* Media kit for film)
   platform release pattern, 183–84
   PR goal, 172
   pre-release, 180, 182
   production, 165–69, 173–74, 176–77,
     185
   start of production release, 156–57, 173
   website, 172
Independent films, 165–86
Independent Spirit Awards, 185
Independent television stations, 116
Independent video games, 243–44
Independent video games public relations
   cycle, 243–44, 246–47
   early access, 245, 246–47
   Kickstarter (*see* Kickstarter)
   reviews, 244
   Steam, 246–47, 250
   Thunderclap, 247
Indie games. *See* Independent video games
Info. *See* Information
Information/Why (Info.), 28, 66
Inside Edition, 15
Insider, The, 50
Instagram, 50, 172, 174, 192, 213, 215–17,
   245
Intellectual property (IP), 34, 154
International Alliance of Theatrical Stage
   Employees. *See* IASTE
International Cinematographers Guild,
   4, 134
Internet Movie Database website. *See*
   IMDb.com
Internet radio, 98
Internships, 74, 75, 189
Internsteller, 159
Inverted pyramid story format, 28, 30,
   32, 40
Invitation to press. *See* Media alert
IP. *See* Intellectual property

iPhone, 49, 245
Ironman franchise, 137
Isaacs, Cheryl Boone, 11, 181
   photo, 181
Ismail, Rami, 242

J

Jagger, Mick, 224
James Bond franchise, 154
James, LeBron, 198
Jimmy Kimmel Live, 15
Jobs, 9–11, 161, 171–72, 180, 188–89,
   203–204
   advice, 171
   cautions, 171–72
   entrepreneurial opportunities, 203–204
   entry level, 11, 190
   experience needed, 171, 180
   expertise, 43, 70, 180, 255
   internships (*see* Internships)
   networking, 10–11, 180
   professional advancement, 10–11
   promotion, 10–11
   qualifications, 10, 161, 188–89
   PR agency, 9–10
   referrals, 10
   sources, 11
   staff jobs, 9
Jobs in entertainment PR. *See also*
   Corporate communications; Freelance
   publicist; Government and community
   relations; Motion picture publicist;
   Network publicist; Personal publicist;
   Product publicity; Production publicist
   (Unit); Public relations agency
   publicist; Unit publicist (the Unit)
Johansson, Scarlett, 137
John, Elton, 231
Jonas, Nick, 224
Jordan, Michael, 199–200
   Nike Air Jordans, 199–200
Journalists
   beats, 12–13, 15, 16, 33

   deadlines, 3, 11, 49–50, 190, 198
   ethics (*see* Ethics: journalistic)
   pitching to (*see* Pitches)
   servicing of, 13–17, 50, 177, 189
July 4th weekend, 150
Junket. *See* Press junket
Juno, 183
Jurassic World, 227

K

Kardashian franchise, 121–22, 129
Kardashian West, Kim, 56, 122
KCRW, 14
   Business with Kim Masters, The, 14
   Treatment with Elvis Mitchell, The, 14
Kellogg, 201
Kernel, 155
Kershaw, Clayton, 195
Key publics, 196. *See also* Audience
   segmentation; Buyer personas;
   Stakeholders; Target audience
Key terms. *See boldface terms; lists at end of*
   chapters
Kickstarter, 245–46
King, Marlene, 100
King World, 112
King's Speech, The, 167, 184
Knott's Berry Farm, 258–59
Knott's Scary Farm. 264–65, 273. *See also*
   Extending high season
Kutcher, Ashton, 3

L

LA Live, 78
Lady Gaga, 213, 219
Las Vegas
   seasonal strategy, 265
   slogan (*see* What happens in Vegas), 256
   Strip (LV Blvd.), 265
   Trade shows, 82, 92, 230–31
Lassie franchise, 179

Late Night with Seth Meyers, 15, 50, 77, 218, 224
Late Show with Stephen Colbert, 15
Lavigne, Avril, 224
Lawrence, Jennifer, 29
Lead
   media release, 28, 30
   summary lead, 30, 34
Lead-ins (television), 110
League of Legends franchise (LOL), 248
Lede. *See* Lead
Legs, or having legs, 143
Less important information, 30, 32
Licensing agreement
   intellectual property (IP) (*see* Intellectual property)
   merchandise, 154–54
   programming, 74–75, 88, 90
Lieberman, Carole, 55–56
Linear viewing ratings, 94
LinkedIn, 32, 172
Lionsgate, 82, 140, 158, 167
Little Miss Sunshine, 167
Live + 3 ratings, 23, 94
Live + 7 ratings, 23, 94
Live viewing, 99
LL Cool J, 222
Local media coverage, 14–16, 22–23, 51, 57, 64–65, 79–80, 109, 111, 115, 153, 157, 160, 173, 178, 191–92, 197–98, 209–12, 223–24, 226, 275
Lohan, Lindsay, 124
LOL. *See League of Legends*
Long-lead magazine, 15, 157, 218
Lopez, Jennifer, 222
Lorde, 140
Los Angeles Angels of Anaheim, 192, 195
Los Angeles Clippers, 192, 200
Los Angeles Dodgers, 195
Los Angeles Lakers, 192
Los Angeles Times, 14–15
   award advertising, 77
   Business section, 14, 248–49
   Calendar section, 14, 49, 72, 221, 225
   stories in, 51, 177, 215, 258, 269

Lottery (illegal)
   avoiding (*see* Contest/legal)
   definition of, 114–15
Lovato, Demi, 224–25
Love, Courtney, 50
Low season, 263–65, 270
Lowry, Brian, 118
Loyalty program, 273
Lucy, 137

M

MacDowell, Andie, 173
Mad Men, 119–120
Madison Square Garden, 248
Madonna, 219
Magic Mountain, 258–59
Major League Baseball (MLB), 191–92
Making news. *See* News Making strategies
Marich, Robert, 170
Marketing Dept., 8
   film studio, 146
   syndicated television, 108–09
   television network, 91
Marketing research. *See* Film research
Marketplace (public radio), 15
Marvel, 49
Masters, Kim, 14
Media, definition of, 11–12. *See also* Business media; Consumer media; Online media; Opinion-maker media; Social media; Trade media; Traditional media
Media advisory. *See* Media alert
Media alert, 65–66.
   alert line, 65
   background, 66
   boilerplate/about, 66
   5 W's, 65–66
   for immediate release, 65
   headline/sub-head, 65
   info./Why, 66
   media RSVP, 66
   PR contact, 66

Media buy, 134, 141, 146, 149–50, 160. *See also* Advertising
Media coverage objective, 64–65
Media kit/press kit, 27, 33
    film, 157–58, 170, 172–74, 176, 180
    music, 209, 210, 218
    online availability, 51, 52
    television, 91, 97
Media list, 12–16, 18, 24, 29, 32, 255
Media relations, 11–12, 17–18, 25
    music, 208–11
    strategy, 22, 25
    tactics, 26
    television, 95, 104
    tools, 26–27
    unpaid media messages, 12, 209, 26
Media releases, 27–34
    approval (*see* Approval process)
    drafting, 31
    elements of, 29–33
        background/less important information, 26, 31–32
        body, 30
        boilerplate/about, 28, 32–33
        dateline, 28, 30
        embargo, 28 (*see also* For immediate release)
        headline/sub-head, 29
        image URLs, 30
        inverse pyramid story format, 30
        news stimulants, 28–29
        PR contact, 33
        quotation, 30–31
        related links, 33
        repurposing as online content, 33–34
        social media links, 29–30
        stimulants (*see* News stimulants)
        summary lead, 30, 24
        template for, 28
    types
        festival participation press release, 176–77
        start of production media release, 156–57, 173–74, 177–78, 185

Media RSVP, 66
Media tip sheet. *See* Media alert
Media training, 175–76, 190
Memes, 238
Memorial Day weekend, 150
Merchandise, 154–56
    Disney films, 135, 155–56
    licensing (*see* Licensing agreement)
MerryMedia, 115
Millennials, 254
Minecraft franchise, 232
Mitchell, Elvis, 14
MLB. *See* Major League Baseball
MMO or MMOG, 229
Mobile applications. *See* Apps
Modern Family, 115
Money equivalents. *See under* Public relations goals
Moretz, Chloë, 155
Mortal Kombat franchise, 232
Motion Picture Academy. *See* Academy of Motion Picture Arts and Sciences
Motion picture marketing, 8, 146, 157–62
Motion Picture Pioneers, 70
Movie premiere. *See* Film premiere
Movie website. *See* Film website
MTV, 50, 212
MTV Video Music Awards (VMAs), 125, 219
Multi-media presentations, 98, 103
Multiple sources. *See under* Ethics: journalistic
Murray, Bill, 173
Museums, 69, 74, 78, 254, 256, 267
Music artists. *See listings for specific artists*
Music festivals, 224–25
Music Outfitters, 210
Music public relations cycle, 208–226
    album, 215
    awards, 219 (*see also specific awards*)
    development, 215–16
    distribution, 208, 212, 225
    Grammys (see Grammy Awards)
    launch party, 80
    local media coverage, 210–11

music festivals, 224–25
post-production, 217
post-release, 223–25
pre-release
production, 216–17
release, 218–19
single, 208, 216–19, 223–25
tour, 223–25
Music videos, 212
My Life on the D–List, 68
Myspace, 212

N

Nadal, Rafael, 199
Naming rights, 196–97, 200
National Ass. of Television Programming
     Executives. *See* NATPE
National Ass. of Theatre Owners (NATO),
     82
National Basketball Ass. (NBA), 193,
     197–98, 199, 200
National Football League (NFL), 193, 202,
     248, 272
     NFL Pay 60 PSA, 201
National Public Radio (NPR), 15
     All Things Considered, 15
Nationals/weekly ratings, 95
NATPE, 113
Natural disasters. *See* Disasters
Nature's four seasons, 263, 266, 274
NBA finals, 193. *See also* Sports public
     relations cycle
NBC network, 3, 44, 50, 75, 77–78, 89,
     116, 126
     CNBC, 15, 18, 179
     nbc.com, 50
     NBC Peacock Panel, 50
NBC Saturday Night at the Movies, 46
NBC/Universal, 3
Need for Speed franchise, 239
Neighborhood residents, 197–98
Nelly, 217
Netflix, 8, 89, 94, 126–29

Network affiliate, 82–83, 88–92, 104, 110
Network O&Os, 88
Network owned & operated stations, 88
Network publicist, 91–92, 104
Network television, 87–103
Network television public relations cycle,
     102–103
     development, 89–92, 101
     Emmys (*see* Emmy public relation cycle)
     hiatus, 102
     premiere, 95, 100, 102–103
     production, 89–90, 92, 102
     ratings (*see also* Nielsen ratings)
     upfronts, 82–83, 102–104
New Music Fridays, 216
New York City, 138
     Big Apple, 256
New York Times, 9, 14–15, 48, 56, 72, 77,
     81, 97, 137, 150, 176–77, 179, 194,
     213, 215, 217, 229, 236, 238, 249
     "Arts," 45, 49
     "Arts, briefly," 14
     Business, 14
     Sunday Magazine, 12, 15–16, 25
News, 13, 21–22
News catching, 17
News making strategies, 122, 264
News Corp., 3
News Division, 89
News release. *See* Media releases
News stimulants, 28–30, 65, 73, 77, 141,
     147, 158
News story, 41. *See also* Media releases
     PR sources of, 41
Niagara Falls, 257–58
Niche audience, 119, 129, 145, 148, 169
Newsworthy quotation. *See* News stimulants
Nickelodeon, 118, 119
Nielsen NRG film research, 148
Nielsen ratings, 92–95. *See also* Audience
     segmentation: television
     demographics, 93, 95, 102, 104, 109, 114
     households using television (HUTs), 23
     linear viewing, 94
     live + 3 days, 23, 94

live + 7 days, 23, 94
live viewing, 99
money equivalent, 92–94
nationals/weekly ratings, 95
out-of-home viewing, 93–94
overnights/fast ratings, 94–95
share, audience, 23
sweeps periods, 93, 96, 102–103, 115
total viewers, 23
urban vs. rural, 93–95, 104
Nike, 199–200
Night at the Museum, 69
19 Kids and Counting, 125
Nintendo, 230, 244
Nonprofit initiatives, 74
Non-union, 171
Nostalgia, 120, 127

O

O&Os, 88
Obama, President Barack, 213
Objective statement, 24, 51, 88, 95–96, 239
Off-cycle premiere strategy, 119–20
Off-network syndication, 107–111
Off-network syndication public relations cycle, 108–111
    clearances, 112–113
    NATPE, 113
    PR strategy, 109, 110–11
    price per episode, 109–10
    promos, 46, 111
    sales process, 109–110
    selling into syndication, 90, 108
    station tags, 109
Ogilvy PR Worldwide, 10
Olympics, 72
On-Air Promotion Dept., 83, 91, 111
Once-a-year season, 272–73
One-Sheet (music), 209, 218
Online media, 23, 211, 222, 240. *See also* Digital strategies; Social media; names of companies

OpEd, 236
Open vs. closed seasons, 270–71
Opening the picture, 160
Opening weekend, 3, 5, 24–25, 132, 143–44, 150–51, 184, 227–28, 272
Opening wide. *See* Film distribution
Opinion-maker, 13, 24–25
Orange County, Calif., slogan, 256
Orange Is the New Black, 127
Oriental Pearl Radio and TV Tower photo, 155
Oscar eligibility. *See under* Academy Awards
Oscar public relations cycle, 180–85
    campaigns, 182–83
    fundraising objective, 74
    nominations, 73, 182, 184
    post-Oscar publicity, 185
    pre-Oscar events, 185
    producing entity, 72–73
    publicity value, 72–73, 184–85
    red-carpet, 84
    value to network, 183
    value to winners, 182–83
Oscars. *See* Academy Awards
OTT, 94
OTX Research, 148
Out-of-home viewing, 93–94
Outdoor advertising. *See* Advertising: outdoor
Overnights/fast ratings, 94–95
Over-the-top viewing. *See* OTT
Owned and operated stations, 88

P

Paid content. *See under* Advertising
Pandora, 212
Panic at the Disco, 216
Paparazzi, 69, 79–80, 124
Parade, 15
Paramount Pictures, 39, 69, 82, 101, 112, 153, 159, 166, 181
Party elements #1, #2, #3, #4, #5. *See* Events: WOW factors

Pasadena Tournament of Roses Parade.
    See Rose Parade
PBS network, 89, 93, 116
Peele, Anna, 176
People, 15
Pepsi Half-time Show, 195
Perebinossoff, Philippe, 45, 56
PerezHilton.com, 16, 50, 123
Perri, Christina, 223–24
Perry, Katy, 213
Perry, Tyler, 145
Personal publicist, 7–9, 124–25
Philadelphia Phillies Citizen Bank Park,
    photo, 193
Phoenix Convention Center, 254
Photos, 79, 157, 174, 176, 260
    media releases, 28
    photo URLs (*see* Image URLs)
    releases, 174
    social media, 120, 158, 176, 199, 217
    websites, on, 49, 120, 156
Photographers. *See* Paparazzi
Pinterest, 50, 240
Piracy, 13, 208, 216
Pirates of the Caribbean franchise, 144
Pitches, 9–10, 12–13, 16–17, 22, 24, 27, 41,
    59, 77, 97, 113–14, 117, 123, 140, 149,
    152–53, 160, 170, 173, 175, 191, 196,
    199, 204, 209–210, 218, 233, 240–241,
    244–46, 255–56, 263–65, 268, 270,
    217, 271–72, 274–75
Pitt, Brad, 147
Planet Money, 228
Planting the flag, 151
Platform release, 183–84
Playbook, 119, 127, 136–37, 143
PlayStation. *See* Sony PlayStation
Podcasts, 17, 98–99
Post-production, 6, 90, 132, 146, 148–49, 158
Post-production publicity, 158–59. *See also*
    listings for specific PR cycles
Powell, Sandy, 137
PR contact, 33, 66
    media alert, 66
    media releases, 33

PR Newswire, 17, 28–30
PR stunt. *See* Guerilla marketing
Premium cable, 115–16
    history, 116–17
Premium cable public relations cycle,
    · 117–18
Pre-production publicity, 153–55
Pre-release publicity. *See listings for specific*
    PR cycles
Presentation, 112
Pre-sold element/title, 109, 111, 140–42,
    166, 184, 250
Press junket, 27, 81, 97–98, 134
Press kit. *See* Media kit
Press queries, 150, 268–69
Press release. *See* Media releases
Press room/tab, 34, 49, 156
Press statement, 7–8, 31, 52–53, 56,
    122–24, 129, 139, 150, 203, 235–37,
    269
Pretty Little Liars, 100
Prime time, 9, 34, 77, 82–83, 88–89, 93, 95,
    97–98, 108, 110, 128, 192, 222
Print advertising. *See* Advertising: print
Private Practice, 56
Product placement, 44, 58, 153–54
Product publicity, 6, 8, 92
Production. *See also under specific public*
    relations cycles
    film, 8, 19, 132–33, 140–42,
        146–48, 151–53, 156–58,
        161–62, 165–67, 168–69, 171,
        174, 176–77, 185
    television, 9, 89, 92, 108–109, 118
Production company, 9, 90, 108–109,
    112–13, 115, 154
Production publicist. *See* Unit publicist
Production publicity. *See listings for specific*
    PR cycles
ProfNew, 17
Programming Dept., 89–90
    current programming, 90
    development, 90
Project Runway, 121
Prometheus Global Entertainment, 82

Promotions 2, 8, 21–22, 32, 53–56, 78, 88, 108–109, 114–15, 153, 189, 195, 204, 222, 225, 233, 245, 258. *See also* Cross-brand tie-in; On-air promotion; Radio: promotions

PRSA. *See* Public Relations Society of America

PSA. *See* Public service announcement

Psychographics, 13, 22–23, 29, 145, 257

Public Broadcasting System. *See* PBS

Public radio, 15, 228

Public relations, 2–6. *See also* Gold standard of two-way communication
contact 33, 66
definitions, 2–5, 12
unpaid media mentions, 209, 244, 260

Public relations agency, 8, 10–11, 32, 66, 88, 91, 114. *See also names of agencies*
publicist, 10, 11

Public relations crisis, 8–9, 10, 38, 58, 138, 203, 235–37

Public relations crisis cycle, 7–8, 202–206
celebrity crisis, 7–8, 122–26
crisis management, 138–40, 203
hyperturbulence, 123–24
press statement (*see* Press statement)

Public relations cycle, 6–8, 18, 88. *See also individual cycles for the following:*
basic cable
binge viewing
blockbuster motion picture
blockbuster video game
casual game
celebrity crisis
crisis
Emmy
eSports
event
first-run syndication
game devices
independent film
independent video game
music
network television
off-network syndication
Oscar

premium cable
reality TV
sports
streaming service
tourism

Public relations ethics. *See* Ethics: public relations

Public relations goals, 5–6, 18, 92–93, 142–44, 239, 258
awareness (*see* Awareness objective)
money equivalents
album sales, 210, 212
box-office totals, 142–44
digital downloads, 92, 219, 239
Nielsen ratings for television, 92–93
song streams, 210
ticket sales, 2, 5, 64, 67, 143, 188, 192, 195, 196, 222–24, 226
total sales/revenue, 188, 239, 259
total viewers, 23
visitor spending, 258–59

Public relations objectives, 6, 24–26, 62–67, 71–72, 102–103, 240–41
awareness objective, 51–52, 64, 66–67, 102–103
fundraising objective, 64, 67, 74
media coverage objective, 64–65
objective statement, 24, 51, 88, 239

Public relations opportunity, 141–42, 215

Public relations plan, 5–6, 9, 21–27, 29, 58, 169–70, 233–35, 237–41

Public relations plan elements. *See listings for the following:*
background
buyer personas
communications opportunity
communications problem
goal
goal statement
objective statements
objectives (*see* Public relations objectives)
research
situation analysis
SWOT

Public relations plan for
  blockbuster film, 132, 134–38, 141–47,
    152–53, 159, 161–62, 179
  crisis, 138–40, 203
  events, 62–67, 83–84
  independent film, 168–69, 170–71,
    177, 179
  music, 209–15, 218–19, 223, 225
  network television, 88, 91–92, 95–96,
    99–101, 104
  off-network syndication, 109, 111, 113,
    128
  sports, 188, 202–203
  tourism destinations, 254–56, 258–59,
    262–63, 268
  video games, 233–42, 246, 250
Public relations practitioner. See Publicist
Public relations problem, 141–42
Public Relations Society of America
    (PRSA), 2
  definition of public relations, 2
  ethics code, 38, 41, 42–43, 60, 287
Public relations stunt. See Guerilla
    marketing
Public service announcement (PSA),
    201–202
  role in CSR, 201–202
Publicist, 4–18
  industry status, 4–5
Publicists Guild, 4
Publicity Dept., 91–92, 156, 158
Publics, 2, 5, 38, 196, 250. See also Audience
    segmentation; Buyer Personas;
    Stakeholders; Target audience
Pusha T, 80

Q

Q Score, 146–47, 168
Q&As, 97–98, 99, 101
Quadrants, 23, 132, 144, 145, 147–48, 169,
    171, 185
Quads. See Quadrants
Qualitative research, 146

Quantitative research, 146
Queen Latifah Show, The, 115
Quotations, 17, 30–32, 41, 180
  approval (see also Approval process)
  media releases, in, 30–31
  newsworthiness of (see News stimulants)
  press statement (see under Press
    statement)
  use by journalists, 31, 40–41, 81, 98, 123,
    139

R

Rachel Ray Show, The, 115
Racism, 53, 182
Radio
  drive-time, 16, 159, 217–218
  formats, 114–15
  promotions, 111, 114–15, 170
Ramis, Harold, 173
Ratings. See Nielsen ratings
Rawlings, Katie, 240
Readings and resources. See end of chapters
Real Housewives franchise, 121, 125, 129
Real Madrid, 199
Real–World Media Ethics, 44
Reality TV, 121–22
Reality TV public relations cycle, 121–22
Record company publicity, 2, 9, 208, 212,
    214, 221, 223
Recording Academy, The, 78
  Grammy Museum, 78
  Grammys (see Grammy Awards)
  Music in the Schools, 78
  MusiCares, 78
Redbook, 16
Red-carpet events, 61–83. See also specific
    events
Related links. See Social media links
Relationship events, 82–83
  network affiliate, 83
Relationship marketing, 273
Release publicity. See listings for specific PR
    cycles

Renaldo, Cristiano, 199
Rentrak, 94
Repurposing as online content, 33–34
Reputation management, 7, 52–53,
    235–37
Request for proposal/RFP. *See* Public
    relations plan
Reporters. *See* Journalists
Reruns. *See* Off-network syndication;
    Television scheduling
Research, 10–11, 23–25, 30, 38–40, 43, 66,
    74–75, 146
  film (see Film research)
  PR plan, 133–37
  sports, 189, 198, 200, 202
  television, 91–92, 123
  tourism, 255–56, 258–59, 269
  video games, 228, 233–34, 238, 240, 250
Research Dept., 91
Residual payments, 108
Responding to online comments, 53–55
  Air Force flow chart, 54
  Disney, 53–55
Retargeting ads online, 244–45
Reviews
  apps, 244–45
  film, 176, 183, 184, 185
  music, 209–11, 218–19, 226
  online, 39, 42, 274
  television, 117, 125–28
  video games, 244
RFP/Request for proposal. *See* Public
    relations plan
Rhimes, Shonda, 100
Rice, Ray, 202
Rihanna, 213, 217
Riot Games, 248
Rise Records, 213
Roberts, Randall, 221, 225
Rockefeller Center tree lighting, 264
Rogers & Cowan, 9
Roller derby, women's, 204
Rolling Stone, 210
Rose Bowl, 261, 262
  flea market, 272

Rose Parade, 259–262
  history, 259–60
  photo, 260
  tourism marketing, 259–262
Round-robin interviews, 81, 97, 98
Rovall, Darren, 199–200
Roxy clothing, 195
Royals, The, 120
RSVP, media alert, 66
Rubenstein, Howard J. 179

S

SAG. *See* Screen Actors Guild
Salesforce, 211
Saltsman, Adam, 244
Saturday Night Live (SNL), 218
Samsung, 92
Saxophone Journal, 210
Sayles, Matt, 96
Scandal, 100
Schachter, Tammy, 238–39
Scheduling Dept., 91
Schneider, Susan, 124
School-year pattern. *See under* Television
    scheduling
Scott, David Meerman, 47, 255
Screen Actors Guild (SAG), 134
  SAG Awards, 182
Script consultant, 146
Seacrest, Ryan, 15, 69, 217–18
Search engine optimization (SEO), 50, 172
Seasonal celebrations, 69, 264–66
Seasonal public relations cycles, 254–75
Seasonality. *See* Tourism seasonality
Second weekend box-office gross. *See*
    Hit vs. flop
Seinfeld, 34, 110
Selling moment, 259–60
Selling the dream (tourism), 259–63
SEO. *See* Search engine optimization
Shankman, Peter, 17
Show runner, 98, 100
ShowEast, 82

Showtime, 116–17, 119, 129

Silver Linings Playbook, 167

Singapore, 262

SiriusXM radio, 203

Situation analysis, 132, 135–38, 142, 161–62, 169, 234–35, 256, 258

Slogans, 117, 147, 256, 262–63

Smartphones, 229, 231, 234, 244, 250

Smith, Will, 7, 125

Snapchat, 99

Social media, 10, 17, 25, 28–30, 38–39, 41, 41, 45–51, 53–54, 56–59, 78, 88, 91, 87, 98–100, 103–104, 112, 121–23, 129, 132, 140, 145, 158, 170, 172, 174, 178–79, 192–95, 197–200, 212–15, 222–25, 228, 235–36, 244–47, 250, 261, 265

Social media analytics/metrics. *See also* Social media measurement

Social media companies. *See listings for*
Facebook
Instagram
Pinterest
Snapchat
Tumblr
Twitter
YouTube

Social media engagement, 100–02, 216, 221–22, 239, 241, 244–45

Social media links, 28, 29–30, 33, 49, 50, 51–53, 55, 120, 156, 172, 174, 176, 196, 202

Social media measurement/analytics/ metrics, 25, 67, 100–102, 146, 150, 204, 239

followers, 3, 51, 55–56, 100, 101, 120, 121–22, 179, 213, 215

likes, 47, 51–52, 101, 150, 204

page views, 67

Social media as megaphones, 56–57

Social media metrics. *See* Social media measurement

Social media monitoring, 42, 53, 89

Social networking sites (SNSs). *See company listings*; Social media

Socialfresh, 55

Sony Pictures, 39, 69, 82, 155, 169

Sony PlayStation, 230

Sound bite, 98, 175

Soundcloud, 213, 219

Spears, Britney, 125

Spec script, 152

Special exhibit, 267

Spin/spin.com, 14, 210

Spin-offs, 101

Split-personality tourist destinations, 270

Sponsored content. *See* Advertising: paid content

Sponsorships
events, 71, 80
sports, 196

Sports. *See listings for specific leagues, teams, and sports*

Sports crisis/scandal, 52–53

Sports Illustrated, 198

Sports information. *See* Sports public relations cycle

Sports marketing. *See* Sports public relations cycle

Sports public relations cycle, 188–204. *See also* Super Bowl
audience development, 190
big games, 192
charitable giving, 201
crises, 202–203
draft, 195–96
fantasy sports (*See* Fantasy sports)
finals, 191, 193–94
freeway series, 195
goal, 188
key publics, 196
media targets, 198–99
off-season, 188, 195
online, 190
opening day, 192
playoffs, 191, 193
PR jobs, 188–90
pre-season, 188, 191–92
social media, 199
sponsorships (*see* Sponsorships)

Spotify, 210
Spruce Goose, 262
Stakeholders, 2, 38, 52, 200, 202
Staples Center, 78, 192, 248
Star Trek franchise, 101, 230
    Convention, 4, 101
Star Wars franchise, 158. *See also* Disneyland
Start of production media release, 156–57,
    173–74, 177–78, 185
State fair, 272
Staycation, 254, 263
Steam, 246–47
Stein, Andi, 193, 254
Steinberg, Scott, 239–40
Sterling, Donald, 200
Stern, Howard, 56
Stimulants. *See* News stimulants
Story angles. *See* Angles for stories
Story pitches. *See* Pitches
Strategic communications, 2, 4, 10
Strategy. *See under* specific public relations
    cycles
Streaming services, 89, 108, 126–28. *See
    also listings for* Amazon Prime, Hulu,
    Netflix
Streaming services public relations cycle,
    126–28
Streep, Meryl, 29
Strip syndication, 111
Studio films. *See* Blockbuster motion picture
STX Entertainment, 147
Subculture. *See* Niche audience
Sub-head. *See* Headline/Sub-head; News
    stimulants
Suicide Squad, 158
Suits, 119
Summary lead, 30, 34
Summer reruns. *See under* Television
    scheduling
Sundance Film Festival, 167, 176–79, 243
Super Bowl, 48, 73, 141, 188, 192–95, 222,
    254
Super League Gaming, 248
Swayze, Patrick, 124
Sweeps periods, 93, 96, 102–103, 115

Sweepstakes. *See* Contests/legal; Lottery
Swift, Taylor, 213–15, 217–19, 221,
    224–25
SWOT analysis, 132, 137–38, 141, 169–70
    blockbuster motion pictures, 137–38,
        140–42, 147
    independent films, 169
    tourism, 256, 257
    video games, 234–38
SXSW Interactive, 235–37
Syndication *See* First-run syndication;
    Off-network syndication; Television
    scheduling

T

Take Two Interactive, 228, 231–32
Talent. *See* Above-the-line talent
Target audience, 6, 13, 17, 24, 45, 50, 96,
    145, 152–53, 169–70, 239–40, 257.
    See also Audience segmentation; Buyer
    personas; Key publics
TBS, 110
TCA. *See* Television Critics Association
Television Academy. *See* Academy of
    Television Arts and Sciences
Television Critics Association press tour
    (TCA), 81, 97–98, 104
Television network, 88, 89–92. *See also
    listings for* ABC, CBS, CW, Fox,
    NBC, CW
    departments, (*see specific depts.*)
    News Division, 89
    O&Os, 88
Television scheduling, 91
    lead-ins, 110
    network programming, 108
    off-cycle premiere strategy, 119–20
    school-year pattern, 104
    strip syndication, 111
    summer reruns, 75, 103
Television upfronts. *See* Upfronts
Teller, Miles, 176
Telluride Film Festival, 183, 184

Tennis, 196, 199. *See also* Sports public relations cycle

Tent-pole film. *See* Blockbuster motion picture

Test screening, 146, 148–49, 158

Thanksgiving, 138, 151, 184, 195, 266

Theme parks, 9, 155, 197, 256, 258–59, 270–71. *See also specific company names*

There Will Be Blood, 167, 168

Third-party endorsement, 12, 25, 40, 51–52, 210

Thunderclap, 247–48

Ticketmaster/Live Nation, 212

Timberlake, Justin, 213

Time shifting, 94, 100, 221. *See also* DVR; VOD

Time Warner, 3

Timing and context, 57–58

Titanic, 144

TMZ, 16, 50, 56, 123, 175

Today Show, The, 15, 76, 218, 223–24

Tonight Show Starring Jimmy Fallon, The, 15, 80, 218

Toronto Film Festival, 176, 183, 184

Total viewers, 23

Tour. *See under* Music public relations cycle

Tourism public relations cycles, 253–75
customer expectations, 257–58
development, 254, 264, 270, 272, 274, 275
extending season, 271–72
goal, 258
opening, 266–67
pre-opening, 271, 272

Tourism seasonality, 263–68, 270–72. *See also listings for*
anniversary event
customer tradition
extending high season
four seasons
grand opening
high season
low season
once-a-year season
open vs. closed seasons

seasonal celebration
special exhibits

Tourism bureau, 254, 258, 262–63

Tourist wants, 256–57

Tracking survey, 149–50

Trade event, 6, 81–82, 230, 250, 270, 274
NATPE, 113
network affiliate meeting, 83, 92, 104

Trade media/trade press, 6, 13, 29, 31, 40–41, 49, 75–77, 98, 111, 112–13, 118, 152–53, 157, 182, 198–99, 209–210, 216, 218, 225, 233

Trade publicity, 152–53

Trade show. *See* Trade event

Traditional media, 46, 95, 97–98, 99, 102, 104, 123, 140, 179, 192, 196, 209, 215
magazines, 13, 15, 22, 24, 31, 75, 79, 91, 113, 140, 157, 198, 222, 240, 243, 244, 260
newspapers, 13, 16, 46, 49, 77, 79, 81, 91, 111, 113, 145, 173, 196, 218, 232, 235, 260
radio, 15–16, 41, 91, 103, 114–15, 140, 145, 150, 159, 170, 189, 191, 196, 202, 203, 208, 212–13, 217–18, 221, 225, 228, 260
television appearances, 22, 45, 77–78, 80, 91, 97, 128, 132, 159, 160, 162, 175, 182, 218, 219–20, 223–24

Trailers, 12, 39, 46, 49, 120, 134, 158, 170, 184, 217, 234

Trans-media storytelling, 158–59

Travel. *See* Tourism public relations cycles

Treatment, The, 14

TripAdvisor.com, 257, 274

Troll, 199

Trout, Mike, 195

Tumblr, 50

TuneCore, 212–13

Turner, Tina, 221

12 Years a Slave, 183

21st Century Fox, 82, 158

24/7, 49–50, 99, 108

Twitch, 229, 248, 249, 250

TwitchCon, 249

Twitter, 3, 17, 25, 30, 34, 42, 44, 46, 48–52,
    54–55, 56–57, 99, 100, 120, 122, 128,
    150, 172, 174, 179, 196, 199, 202,
    213–16, 221, 241, 245
   re-tweet, 78, 199
   spats, 55–56
   tweet, 99
   twittercounter, 122, 213
Two and a Half Men, 100
Two-way, symmetrical communication, 4,
    101–102, 122, 245
   avoiding as a strategy, 57
   comments, 2, 25, 39, 43, 47, 49, 52–54,
    56, 58, 78, 101, 124, 194, 199, 238,
    274
   community relations, 197
   digital media, 39
   Facebook, 245
   fan engagement, 101
   gold standard of (*see also* Gold standard
    of …)
   sites, on, 274
   social media on, 46, 59, 101–102
   sports, for, 197
   TripAdvisor on, 274
   Twitter on, 99, 122, 245
   versus control, 59
   websites, on, 46, 99
   Yelp on, 274
Tyler, Steven, 224

U

UCLA, 200
Unbreakable Kimmy Schmitt, 128
Uncontrolled public relations, 44–47,
    50–55, 57–58, 233, 244
Union Bank Rose Parade float photo, 260
Union contracts, 108, 133–34, 168. *See also*
    Non-union
Unions. *See* Guilds
Unit, the. *See* Unit publicist
Unit publicist, 8, 156–58, 171, 173–74
Unit publicist responsibilities

EPK (*see* Electronic press kit)
   media kit (*see* Media kit)
Universal Pictures, 3, 39, 82, 137, 140
Universal Studios theme park, 258–59, 261
Unpaid media mentions. *See under* Public
    relations
Updating the dream, 262–63
Upfronts, 82–83, 102–104
Urban vs. rural, 93, 94, 95, 104
US Weekly, 15
USA cable channel, 119, 159
USA Today, 15

V

Vanity Fair, 16
Variety/variety.com, 14, 49–50, 65, 72, 75,
    98, 118, 152, 168, 175–77, 182
Vendors, 43, 272
Venice Film Festival (Italy), 183
Venues, 5, 8–9, 63–64, 66–67, 69–71,
    79–81, 83, 198, 208, 218, 223, 225,
    230, 263, 267, 270–71
Vergara, Sofia, photo, 96
Vevo, 213
Viacom, 3
Vibe, 210
VidCon, 157–58
Video game competitions. *See* eSports
Video game devices/platforms, 229–31. *See*
    also specific devices
Video game distribution, 229, 240, 243
Video game public relations cycle, 227–50.
    See also
   Blockbuster video game public relations
    cycle;
   Casual game public relations cycle;
   Independent video game public relations
    cycle
Video games, 231–32. *See also specific games*
   demographics, 228
Video Games: The Movie, 228
Video on demand. *See* VOD
Vine video, 99

Vlogs/vlogers, 158
VMAs. *See* MTV Video Music Awards
VOD, 94–95
Vogue, 16
Voice, The, 50

W

Walker, Paul, 140, 141
Walking Dead, The, 125
Wall Street Journal, 15
Walt Disney Company. *See* Disney
Warner Bros., 8, 18, 82, 101, 109–112, 158, 182, 232
Washington, Kerry, photo, 96
Wasteland franchise, 246
Watch What Happens Live, 121
Website, 170, 172–73, 213
    analytics (*see* Social media measurement)
    content, 33–34, 44, 50, 55, 99, 120, 156
    front page, 172
    landing page, 34, 51–52
    media links (*see* Social media links)
    press room/tab, 34, 49, 156
    publicity, as, 156
    search engine optimization (SEO), 50, 172–73
Weekly ratings/Nationals, 95
Weinstein Company, 167, 184
Weissmuller, Johnny, 161
Welcome: Portraits of America, 258
Wembly Stadium, 272
West, Kanye, 80, 219
WGA. *See* Writers Guild of America
WGN America, 110
What happens in Vegas, 256. *See also* Slogans
Wheel of Fortune, 111
White Collar, 119
Wide opening (Opening wide). *See* Film distribution
Wii, 230
Wikipedia, 156

Williams, Robin, 124
Window displays, New York City, 264
Winfrey, Oprah, 111
Winter's Bone, 167
Wolf, Annette, 124
WOMMA. *See* Word of Mouth Marketing Ass.
Woods, Tiger, 123, 200
Woodstock, IL, 173
Word of Mouth Marketing Ass. (WOMMA), 38, 41–42
World Series, 191, 193, 263
WOW factors #1, #2, #3, #4, #5. *See* Event: WOW factors
WPP Communications, 10
Writers Guild of America (WGA), 134
    minimum, 121

X

X Games, 196
Xbox, 230, 244

Y

Yahoo, 203
Yankovic, Weird Al, 214
Yelp, 25, 257, 274
Yiannopoulous, Milo, 236
YouTube, 4, 12, 33, 46, 49–50, 98, 101, 120, 126, 145, 158, 179, 192, 202, 208, 212, 213–14, 258
    video game content on, 229, 246, 248–49

Z

Zecher, Andreas, 235–36